CAMPAIGNS OF T

THE BOER WAR
A MILITARY HISTORY
JOHN P. WISSER

THE ILLUSTRATED EDITION
EDITED BY J.B. GARDINER

This book is published in Great Britain in 2012 by
Parchment Publishing Ltd

www.parchmentpublishing.co.uk

Copyright © 2012 Parchment Publishing Ltd

All rights reserved. No part of this publication may be reproduced or transmitted in any form or by any means, electronic or mechanical, including photocopy, recording, or any information storage and retrieval system, without the prior permission in writing from the publisher.

This book was first published by Hudson-Kimberly Publishing Company, Kansas City, Missouri, in 1901 as
"The Second Boer War 1899-1900"
by John P. Wisser

Please note all original spellings have been preserved. The Editor.

CONTENTS

PREFACE 5
PART I. 8
   Introduction 8
   The Theatre of War 11
   The Forces Engaged 13
   The English Troops 13
   The Boer Troops 15
   The Strategic Position 15
   The Operations 16
PART II. 30
   The Campaign in Natal 30
   Events in the Southern and Western Theatres. 33
   General Situation. 38
   Events South of the Orange River. 40
   The Campaign in the West 45
   The Campaign in Natal 51
   Comments 55
PART III. 62
   The Campaign in Natal 68
   The Third Attempt to Relieve Ladysmith 76
   The Campaign in the South and West 80
   Lord Roberts' Campaign 82
   The Southern Theatre of War 90
   The Situation in Natal 91
   Comments 94

PART IV. 104
General Roberts' Campaign 107
Events in the Southern Theatre 110
Events in the Western Theatre 112
Events in Natal 112
Lord Roberts' Campaign 114
The General Situation 119
Lord Roberts' Campaign 124
Events in the South 127
Events in Natal 128
Events in the Extreme West 128
Lord Roberts' Campaign 130
Events in the South 133
Events in the Extreme West 133
Events in Natal 133
Comments 134

PART V. 143
Events in the Orange River Colony 143
Events in Natal 145
Events in the Transvaal 147
Events in the Orange River Colony 149
Campaign of Middelburg 154
The Situation in the Orange River Colony 159
The Third Campaign against Louis Botha 160
General Situation 164
Comments 167
Tactical Deductions from the War 172

APPENDIX 180

MORE FROM PARCHMENT PUBLISHING 224

PREFACE

The account here given was derived from a careful study of the following exchanges of the Journal U.S. Artillery (to which were added from time to time such original thoughts on organization, tactics and strategy as suggested themselves), viz.:
- Internationale Revue,
- United Service Gazette,
- Revue du Cercle Militaire,
- Milittär-Wochenblatt,
- Army and Navy Gazette,
- Deutsche Heeres-Zeitung,
- Schweizerisohe Militarische Blatter,
- Allgemeine Schweizerisdie Militärzeitung,
- Armée et Marine,
- Mittheilungen über Gegenstände des Artillerie und Genie-Wesens-,
- Umschau,
- New York Sun,
- The Engineer (London),
- Engineering (London),
- Kriegstechnische Zeitschrift,
- Proceedings Royal Artillery Institution,
- Jahrbucher für die Deutsche Armee und Marine.

The author also desires to express his obligations to the following works, which appeared during the progress of the war, and which were freely used by him:
- Briton and Boer, James Bryce and others,
- Boer War, Lieut.-Col. H. M. E. Brunker,
- Der Buernkrieg in Sudafrika, Maj. L. von Estorff, Gen. Staff,
- La Guerre au Transvaal: L'offensive des Boers, Lieut.-Col. Frocard and Capt. Painvin,
- Der Krieg in Transvaal, von Tiedemann, Oberstleutnant,
- The Siege of Ladysmith (64 Photographs), H. St. J. Tugman,
- Four Months Besieged, The "Daily News,"
- Der Krieg in Südafrika, Kunowaki and Fetzdorff.

The best current accounts of the war were undoubtedly those of the German and French military periodicals, especially those of the Militär-Wochenblatt and the Revue du Cercle Militaire, but the prejudice against the English in nearly all of our exchanges (other than British) was so evident that the author had great difficulty in arriving at a fair and unprejudiced view, and in presenting an unbiased account of the events—his particular aim in writing this history. Other difficulties presented themselves: in the early part of the war the British official despatches were very meagre, and the available maps very unsatisfactory, so that little information could be gleaned from them; moreover, few British writers took up the subject in its early stages, and the only material at hand was the warped accounts in both British and foreign journals. It was not until Lord Roberts opened his brilliant campaign that the foreign journals began to change their tone and the British journals and official despatches began to assume an authoritative air and to offer reliable and really useful information.

Little original material will be found in this work, but it is believed that no other single account thus far published presents the subject in a fairer light. This history has been carefully compared with the recently published British, French and German works above mentioned, and every effort has been made to insure accuracy. One great difficulty in the way is the lack of all reliable information from the side of the Boers, especially as regards losses in battle.

The lessons to be learned are brought out in the comments, and while the thoughts expressed, are those of the author, the ideas at the foundation of these thoughts were generally derived from the authorities consulted.

JOHN P. WISSER,
Captain 7th Artillery.
Fort Monroe, Va., October 9, 1900

South Africa at the time of the Boer War

PART I

INTRODUCTION

The history of the South African Republic (formerly called the Transvaal Republic) and the Orange Free State begins with that of Cape Colony.

The Dutch East India Company, recognizing the importance of the Cape of Good Hope as a station where their vessels might take in water and provisions, formed a colony there in 1652. The colonists gradually drove the natives back, reduced them to slavery and introduced Malays and negroes as slaves. The Dutch government harassed the farmers, demanding a large part of their produce, and thus inspired the colonists with their dislike to interference by the home government, and a love of independence. In 1795 they attempted to throw off the yoke of the Dutch, when the British sent a fleet to support the authority of the Prince of Orange, and took possession of Cape Colony in his name; but as Holland was not able to hold it, the British ruled there until 1802, when, at the peace of Amiens, it was again restored to Holland. In 1806 it was again taken by the British, and was finally ceded to them in 1815.

The Boers ill-treated the natives to such an extent that they were often in danger of extermination, and Great Britain had to protect them.

By a succession of wars with the natives, or Kaffirs, the boundary was gradually extended. The first of these wars took place in 1811-12, the second in 1819. In 1820 British emigrants laid the foundation of the settlements around Port Elizabeth, and in 1834 the slave-emancipation measure took effect in Cape Colony, and this gave great offense to the Dutch Boers, who were large slave-owners. In 1835 the third Kaffir war took place, and not long after that the Boers resolved to free themselves from the British government (which began to enforce measures to protect the natives against Boer injustice) and removed beyond the Orange River, a portion also crossing the Drakensberg Mountains into Natal establishing in both places republican governments, which they maintained till 1842, when the

British extended their authority into Natal, and the Boer colony there passed again under British rule. The Boers had so incensed the natives that the peace of the whole country was menaced, and interference became necessary. The fourth Kaffir war occurred in 1846-8.

The Boers beyond the Orange River maintained their independence till 1848, when, at the solicitation of the Boer authorities (in consequence of the lawless state of the country), the British annexed the country under the name of the Orange River Sovereignty. Not long after, the Boers of Natal crossed the mountains, joined some of the disaffected Orange Boers and raised the standard of rebellion. A detachment of British troops met and defeated them, and a number retreated over the Vaal River and established a government of their own, first called Trans-Vaal, which was afterwards recognized by the British in 1852, and then called the South African Republic.

The fifth Kaffir war was conducted between 1850 and 1853, and by it British Kaffraria was formed into a separate colony. In 1853-4 the Orange Free State was formed, with the consent of England.

The discovery of diamonds in the districts north of the Orange River in 1867 led in 1874 to the annexation by the British of Griqualand West, in 1881 of Basutoland, and in 1885 of Bechuanaland. Later, Cecil Rhodes, manager of the South African Chartered Company, succeeded in adding Mashonaland, Matebeleland, and finally Barotseland.

In 1877, in consequence of Boer trouble with the natives, an empty treasury, and general discouragement due to repeated reverses in the contests with the natives, England intervened and annexed the Transvaal. In 1879 England fought the Zulu war to protect the Transvaal and the Boers.

In 1881, after the revolt of the disaffected Boers and the defeat of the English at Majuba Hill in 1880, the republic was restored under the suzerainty of England, but this was so far modified in 1884 as to render the South African Republic practically independent.

The discovery of rich gold deposits in 1886 led to a great influx of British subjects, and difficulties arose from the attempts of the Boer government to enforce military service on them, though they were debarred from franchise. The tension grew stronger as the number of foreign gold-seekers (Uitlanders) increased, and the latter began to ally themselves with Cecil Rhodes, with Chamberlain, the Colonial minister, and with other influential Englishmen. This finally led, in 1890, to an attack by Dr. Jameson and 500 men of the Chartered Company on Mafeking, with the intention of moving on Johannesburg, but he was met at Krugersdorp and repulsed by the Boers, under Cronje, who killed a number of his force and sent the rest for trial to England.

In 1897 the Uitlanders amounted to 180,000, and possessed 63 per cent of the landed, and 90 per cent of the personal property of the country.

In April, 1899, a petition signed by 11,000 Englishmen living in Johannesburg was transmitted to Greene, the British agent at Pretoria, to Sir Alfred Milner, Governor of Cape Colony, and by him forwarded to the Queen. The petition set forth the fact that they were debarred from franchise, and complained of the dynamite monopoly. Krüger promised reforms in the franchise, and fixed upon 9 years as the term of residence required to obtain the right to vote, instead of 14, previously established. The discontent, however, continued. Steyn (the President of the Orange Free State) then proposed the Bloemfontein conference. Milner demanded 5 years as the term for naturalization, but Krüger would only compromise, and proposed 7, but without any retroactive effect. Milner then broke off the conference. The Orange Free State then intervened and persuaded the Volksraad in Pretoria to grant also the retroactive effect of the 7-year naturalization law, and to give four new seats in the lower house to the Uitlanders.

Now, complaints about the police, the language taught in the schools, and organization laws began to be made, and Chamberlain began to make inquiries as to the suzerainty of England and to express a desire for a mixed Commission in Cape Colony, a proposal which was interpreted to aim at the independence of the Republic.

Upon this Krüger proposed to grant the 5-year naturalization law, with retroactive effect, and 10 seats in the lower house, provided England gave up all claim to suzerainty. The British government would not consider the last point at all, and on the 12th of September Chamberlain, through the British representative in Pretoria, Conyngham Greene, submitted as a fundamental condition for the proposed conference: 5 years naturalization, one-quarter of the seats for the Uitlanders, and equality of Boers and Englishmen in the Volksraad and in the election of President. On the 14th both

Volkraads decided on the 7-year naturalization law, and demanded as a basis for the conference the convention of 1884.

The situation was critical. Early in September England had ordered 5,000 troops in India and an equal number from European stations to hold themselves in readiness to proceed to Africa, and towards the end of September these troops actually sailed from Calcutta and Bombay for Natal. The two Boer States also began their war preparations, and by the end of September there were 13,000 armed men on the Natal frontier, 1,500 in Boshof near Kimberley, and 4,000 near Malmain, opposite Mafeking.

On the 9th of October, 1899, Mr. Conyngham Greene the diplomatic representative of Great Britain at Pretoria received the ultimatum of the Transvaal Republic. It stated that if in 48 hours the British troops did not retire from the border, war existed, and demanded also that the reinforcements already landed, as well as those on the way, be sent back. It reached the Colonial Office in London on the 10th, and on the 11th the British government replied that the conditions imposed by the Transvaal were such that the British government could no longer discuss the subject. On that day Mr. Conyngham Greene left Pretoria, and at 5 p.m.p.m. The Transvaal was declared in a state of war, and the offensive movements of the Boers began. The Orange Free State, bound by a treaty of alliance, joined the Transvaal.

THE THEATRE OF WAR.

South Africa is a wide plateau or table-land, which rises to an average height of about 5,000 feet, very gradually in the west, very rapidly in the east, from the sea towards the interior. In the south and southeast there are three well-marked terraces: the coast land, the karroos (between 3.000 and 4,000 feet elevation) and the plateau beyond the Orange River (about 5,000 feet). Between the last two are the Schneeberge on the south of the Orange Free State and the Drakensberge on the east.

In Natal the end of the coast land is marked by Pietermaritzburg (2,225 feet), after which the ground rises rapidly and the country becomes very difficult, Colenso having an elevation of 3,156 feet, Glencoe 4,300 feet and Laings Nek 5,400 feet. The Drakensberge rise to over 11,000 feet in the peaks, and from 5,500 to 7,500 feet in the passes.

In Cape Colony the karroo southwest of the Schneeberge is about 70 miles wide from north to south; southeast of the Schneeberge, about 50 miles. Water in these regions is very scarce.

Beyond the Schneeberge rises the Orange Free State plateau, with comparatively low ranges. North of the Schneeberge and west of the Drakensberge the country for some distance is not level, but rolling and mountainous, with ranges running parallel to the eastern border, till they are lost in the plains of the western Orange River. The Transvaal near the southern part is very hilly (from the foot-hills of the Drakensberge), and is intersected by several minor ranges as at Pretoria and a few other points. To the northwest the country slopes away gradually.

Aside from the few intersecting chains rising above the plateau, the broad, unbroken and treeless plains of the Boer States present only isolated tables, which often serve as landmarks for several days' march.

The principal stream of South Africa is the Orange River, with its main branch, the Vaal.

The climate of South Africa is sub-tropical, the rainy season, or summer, lasting from October to March, the dry season, or winter, from April to September. During the rainy season the nearly or quite dry streams suddenly become filled and converted into impassable mountain torrents, while the larger streams are all very high. In the dry season it is difficult to find water, for not only do the smaller streams and springs dry up entirely, but even the large streams are so low as to become everywhere passable, and the entire country is dry and parched.

The country is very poorly settled (about 3 inhabitants to the square mile); the roads are few and very poor, hard roads being extremely rare. Only the ox-wagons, 12 to 20 a team, can get over the country. In the rainy season the roads quickly become almost impassable. The railroads are consequently of more than ordinary importance, but, as these are generally- narrow-gauge, their carrying capacity is not over one-fifth that of a good wide-gauge road.

The South African Republic (Transvaal) has a population of about 288,750 whites, of whom 80,000 are Boers, capable of putting 30,000 men in the field. The Orange Free State has about 77,716 whites, of whom 75,443 are Boers, with 30,000 capable of bearing arms.

The Transvaal is divided into 31 districts, each of which is under the command of a commandant, or field cornet, who has an assistant field cornet. In time of war there is about one field cornet to every 200 men. The Orange Free State was similarly organized.

The principal strategic points in the Transvaal are the fortified capital, Pretoria, and the gold center, Johannesburg; in the Orange Free State, the capital, Bloemfontein; in Cape Colony, the sea-ports, Cape Town, Port Elizabeth and East London, and the seat of the diamond-fields, Kimberley; in Natal, the port, Durban, the capital, Pietermaritzburg, and the depot and supply station for northern Natal, Ladysmith.

Among the minor strategic points may be mentioned Sterkstrom and De Aar, important railroad centers, Colesberg, the point of assembly of the disaffected Cape Colony Boers, Mafeking, with a garrison threatening Pretoria directly, and the bridges at Orange River Station, Norvals Pont and Bethulie.

THE FORCES ENGAGED.

To understand the initial operations, it will first be necessary to obtain a clear conception of the positions and strengths of the respective armies at the opening of the campaign.

THE ENGLISH TROOPS.

The English forces for the Boer war are divided into three groups; viz.: the troops in Natal, the troops in Cape Colony and the newly mobilized army corps to be sent to South Africa from England.

The Natal Force.

The Natal force, commanded by Symons, comprised
- 10 battalions of infantry: 7650 men.
- 4 regiments of cavalry: 1650 men.
- 6 field batteries and one mountain battery (42 guns): 1218 men.
- 4 companies of pioneers: 600 men.
- 4 companies train: 300 men.
- Natal volunteers: 760 men.
- Natal Carabiniers: 120 men.
- Imperial Light Horse volunteers: 500 men.
- Durban volunteers: 750 men.
- Mounted Natal police (9 guns): 550 men.
- Total.: 51 guns, 14,098 men.

Reinforcements arriving (from India),
- 3 field batteries (18 guns): 530 men.
- Total for the first act of the drama: 69 guns, 14,628 men.

The Cape Colony Force.

The Cape Colony force, commanded by White, comprised
- 8 battalions of infantry: 4090 men.
- 2 companies heavy artillery: 200 men.
- 2 companies train: 150 men.
- Total: 4440 men.
- Reinforcements arriving (due October 29), 2 battalions infantry: 700 men.
- Total for the first act: 5140 men.

There was no cavalry or artillery with this force. The strength of the volunteer forces on the western border of the Boer States cannot be accurately determined, but they are estimated at about 4,000 men. Besides these troops, the English squadron had also landed a naval brigade of about 1,000 men, which was to be sent to the western border of the Boer States.

The Army Corps

The mobilized army corps, under General Sir Redvers Buller, was organized into 3 divisions (commanded respectively by Lord Methuen, Sir Clery and Sir Gatacre) and a cavalry division under French.

Its total strength was about 40,000 men, with 114 guns.

***

On the eleventh of October the British had in Glencoe camp (near Dundee) about 4,000 men, at Ladysmith about 9,000 men.

At Aliwal (on the southern border of Orange Free State) there was only a half-regiment and 100 mounted infantry; further south a small reserve. In Kimberley (on the western border of Orange Free State)
- 4 half-companies infantry: 700 men.
- Volunteers: 1500 men.
- Artillery: 20 guns.

Mafeking (on the western border of the Transvaal Republic) had only 600 volunteers under Colonel Baden-Powell. There were also 400 volunteers opposite Tuli (on the northern border) under Colonel Plumer.

THE BOER TROOPS.

The Boers had about 35,500 men under arms in the Transvaal (commanded by General Joubert), and about 14,000 regulars in the Orange Free State (under General Grobeler), posted as follows:

- At Sandspruit (main body), north of the wedge of Natal, under Joubert: 12,000 men.
- West of Majuba Hill, right column under Kock: 3,000 men.
- At Wakkerstroom, left column under Erasmus: 2,000 men.
- Between Utrecht and Vryheid, under Schalk Burger: 4,500 men.
- Outposts on the Buffalo River opposite Vryheid, under Lukas Meyer.
- On the road to Dundee, under Viljoen: 1,000 men.
- In Zoutpansberg district (northern border): 2,000 men.
- At Komatipoort (opposite Delagoa Bay): 2,000 men.
- Opposite Mafeking (on the western border), under Piet Cronje: 6,000 men.
- Reserve, in the interior: 3,000 men.
- At Albertina Station and Van Reenens Pass (west of Ladysmith), under Andries Cronje: 8,000 men.
- From Botha Pass to Bezuidenhouts (to watch the passes west of Ladysmith): 3,000 men.
- Opposite Kimberley (on the western border), under Prinsloo: 3,000 men.

THE STRATEGIC POSITION.

The wedge of Natal, projecting as it does into the Boer country, would be advantageous were it properly occupied by a sufficient force, because it would give the British the great advantage of always operating on interior lines, but the superior force of the Boers enabled them to overcome this strategic advantage, and turn the British positions. The weakness of the small British force on the- western border was an element of great danger, especially as it exposed the important railroad from Cape Town to Buluwayo.

In occupying their too advanced position at Glencoe the British were exposing their troops to disaster, for it is a maxim of war that when a commander endeavors to cover too much he covers nothing. It would have been better to have concentrated further back, as at

Ladysmith, and utilized the advantages of interior lines by falling upon the separate Boer columns in turn before they could unite.

THE OPERATIONS.

Preliminary Operations on the Western Border.

The object of these operations on the part of the Boers was to isolate the two important towns of Kimberley and Mafeking, and to prevent invasion of their territory; and on the part of the British to gather supplies preparatory to siege, and to check further advances of the Boers beyond the Orange River.

On the 12th of October the Transvaal Boers, under Cronje, advanced in two columns on Mafeking; one (4,000 strong) from the Lichtenburg district, crossing the border at Maritsani, south of Mafeking—500 men of this column attacked and captured, at the station of Kraaipan, an armored train which was repairing the telegraph line north of Vryburg and carrying ammunition to Mafeking; the other column from Zeerust and the Marico valley, threatening Mafeking from the north. On the 13th Cronje's troops destroyed the railroad and the railroad bridge over the Molopo River, 8£ miles north of Mafeking. On the 14th all rolling material and stores in the vicinity were sent to Kimberley. On the 14th the Boers occupied Ramathlabama, north of Mafeking. Soon after, the railroad and bridge at Modder River Station were destroyed by the Boers. On the 16th the Boers took possession of the railroad north and south of Kimberley and a Boer commando from Bethulie moved towards Norvals Pont and destroyed the railroad. On the same day another Boer force occupied Taungs. On the 17th the Boers destroyed the bridge over the Vaal at. Fourteen Streams station. On the same day the British destroyed the railroad bridge at Hopetown. On the 18th the Boers destroyed the railroad north and south of Kimberley. While these preparatory measures were being taken on the western border, the principal campaign was going on in the east, in Natal.

Operations in Natal.

On the night of October 11-12 the Boers advanced in several columns: one from Sandstruit, on the road to Laings Nek, occupying with artillery the defile of the railroad to Newcastle ;another from Wakkerstroom south through the Belebas Hills to the Buffalo River, occupying its bridges; a third marched from Utrecht on the

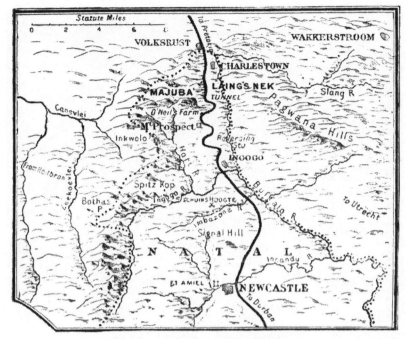

THE NATAL FRONTIER

road towards Glencoe; a fourth from Doornberg to Rorkes Drift, occupying the cross-roads leading to Glencoe and Ladysmith opposite Waschbank and Wessels Nek stations; a fifth marched to the right of Majuba Hill along the border to Botha Pass; a sixth from Vrede to the Muller Pass; and the Orange Boers (with ox train and 11 guns) from Albertina and Harrismith in three columns to Van Reenens Pass, Tintwa Pass and Bezuidenhout Pass.

By midnight of the 12th all the passes on the eastern, and western borders of Natal were in the hands of the Boers, and on the 13th the British abandoned this district to within six miles of Glencoe and Dundee.

At 3 a.m., October 13th, General White (then commanding at Ladysmith) advanced on the road toward Acton Homes to attack the Boers and prevent the junction of the columns from the passes; he struck the column from the Tintwa Pass (under Major Albrecht), and attacked it, but the attack was repulsed, and General Grobeler from Van Reenens Pass threatened to cut him off from Ladysmith. White was therefore compelled to retire. The Boers followed the retiring British and occupied positions commanding Ladysmith, along the

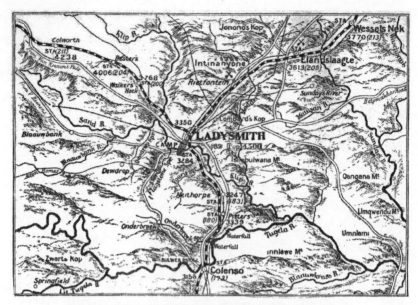

BIRD'S-EYE VIEW OF LADYSMITH AND ENVIRONS.

line Acton Homes—Blaauwbank—Bester's Station.

In the north the columns united at Ingagane, near Königsberg, and pushed outposts out to Glencoe on the evening of the 13th. They then set to work to intrench themselves, awaiting the advance of the left wing. The British ordered the garrisons of Pietermaritzburg and Durban to work night and day to put these points in a state of defense.

By October 15th the Boers had 1,500 men in Newcastle, with 10 light and 2 heavy guns; advance guard under Viljoen at Ingagane. On the 10th the main body of the Boers was at Ingagane, and on the 18th Joubert made his headquarters at Dannhauser. On the 19th the latter marched towards the Impati Hill, while Lukas Meyer, commanding the advance guard of the column from Utrecht (1,000), was ordered to attack from the east. During the night the latter succeeded in getting 1 guns on Dundee (or Talana) Hill, and at 5:30 a. in. opened the attack.

The advance of the Boers is open to the criticism that in subdividing into so many columns they exposed themselves to the danger of being separately attacked and destroyed before they could reunite, but in all probability the explanation of their action lies in the fact that this subdivision was forced upon them by the nature of the country and the character of the roads.

By October 20th the left wing of the Boers had arrived in position:

their strategical movements were completed, and the tactical operations began.

The Battle of Dundee or Glencoe.

The occupation of Dundee (or Talana) Hill (between the Glencoe—Newcastle railroad and the Glencoe—Dundee branch) by the Boers on the 20th led General Symons to attempt to dislodge them with portions of two regiments supported by 20 rapid-fire guns, but he only succeeded in causing the withdrawal of the Boer artillery (4 guns). General Symons tried again and again to strike the enemy in flank, but failed, and at 9 a.m. he received the report that Dundee was also threatened by a Boer column of 9,000 men and a battery, under Joubert in person, coming from the direction of Hatting Spruit to the east of Dundee Hill. The position in which Glencoe would be placed by the advance of this column, unless Dundee Hill were taken, decided General Symons to make another advance in force. In this attack General Symons fell, mortally wounded, and General Yule succeeded to the command. At 1 p.m. the position was taken and the Boers retired. The British lost 12 officers and 33 men killed, 21 officers and 163 men wounded. The Boer loss is not known, but is given at 300 killed and wounded; their field hospital and entire train was taken by the British. Such was the battle of Dundee. A squadron of the 18th Hussars, sent in pursuit of the Boers after the battle, lost 4 killed, 9 wounded and 86 captured.

While General Symons with all his force was thus struggling against the advance guard of the Boers, their main body was quietly advancing in the rear, cutting communication between Glencoe and Ladysmith, and completing the environment of both these places. General Schalk Burgher, with the column from Vryheid, closed in on Glencoe from the east, his left flanking column occupying Waschbank; while General Viljoen, passing Glencoe on the west, pushed his outposts to the Impati Hill; and Joubert's right column under Jan Kock occupied the Biggars Hill, his forces reaching around to the right towards the Orange Boers, who were advancing towards the Pietermaritzburg railroad.

This situation forced the British to act, but it was a question whether to strike in a northerly direction to prevent the union of the column near Dundee with the main column farther west, or in a southerly direction to prevent that of the columns from east and west, now approaching each other at Elandslaagte.

On the 21st Yule made a demonstration against the Boers north of Glencoe and pushed them back, and in the -night began his retreat through Dundee on Beith. Dundee and Glencoe were abandoned, and a position nearer Ladysmith taken up.

Battle of Elandslaagte.

At the same time General White decided to reopen communication with Glencoe by attacking the Boers at Elandslaagte. General French was sent out by rail with the advance guard at 4 a.m., but the main body under White did not arrive till 3:30 p.m., when the battle opened.

The British forces were about 3,400 strong, comprising
- 1st Battalion Devonshire Regiment,
- ½ 2d Battalion Gordon Highlanders,
- ½ 2d Battalion Manchester Regiment,
- 5th Lancers,
- 5th Dragoons, 1 squadron,
- Natal Carabiniers,
- Imperial Light Horse,
- 2 field batteries,
- Natal field battery.

The Boers (the advance guard of Kock's column) occupied two kopjes, or heights, their principal camp being between these kopjes in the saddle, the artillery (2 guns) being intrenched on the lower of the two heights. They were about 1,400 strong. At about 4 p.m. the British artillery opened from a position 4,400 yards from the Boers and prepared the attack for the infantry. This artillery preparation was deemed sufficient in about half an hour, and General French decided to make the infantry attack, the artillery moving up to its second position at 2,250 yards from the Boers, finally supporting the advance at 1,950 yards.

The Devonshire regiment attacked in front, advancing over perfectly open ground. Three companies were deployed in first line on a front of 380 to 500 yards, furnishing their own supports. The other four companies remained in reserve in single-file columns at 50 paces interval, the latter being increased when the Boer artillery opened on them.

When the regiment arrived at about 1,200 yards from the enemy's position, Major Park, commanding the first line, halted it and opened

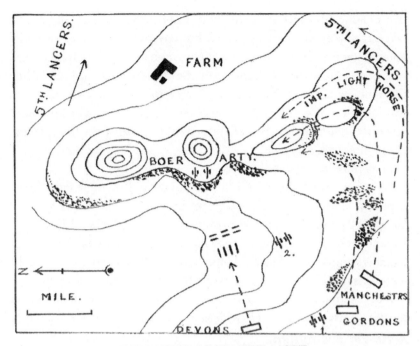

THE BATTLE OF ELANDSLAAGTE.

fire, the only protection for the men being low ant-hills. The advance was continued, and, after a few volleys executed at a halt, the line was reinforced by the supports, and again advanced. In spite of the hail of bullets, the line moved on without a break, unhesitatingly, to within 750 yards of the enemy, and there remained lying down for a full half-hour, exposed to artillery and infantry fire, awaiting the signal for the final assault. Their khaki uniforms and the approaching darkness probably saved them from destruction.

Meanwhile a flank movement was executed by the Manchester regiment, which, after passing the guns, was joined by a dismounted squadron of Imperial Light Horse, the Gordon Highlanders following in support. The movement was over the lowest of the chain of heights, turning the left flank of the Boers. On arriving at the foot of the hill a heavy storm broke forth, and when it was over, the Gordon Highlanders found themselves among the rocks covering the crest of the hill, and exposed to the enemy's fire. The supports then entered the line, filling up the interval between the columns. A small plateau was then crossed, next a depression between the hills, and finally a steep slope had to be scaled, but in spite of the difficulties and losses the line steadily advanced to within 600 yards of the enemy. The ground was entirely open as regards trees, but covered with stones and wire entanglements. The colonel, Dick Cunyngham, of the Highlanders, had been twice wounded, and half the officers were laid low, when Colonel Hamilton ordered a trumpeter to sound a charge, which was taken up by all the other trumpeters, and drum-major Lawrence jumped to the front and placed himself at the head of the line, playing the national air.

The entire line now advanced.

At 6:30 p.m. the Boers' position was taken, 2 of their guns being captured. The 5th Lancers were sent in pursuit. The Boers lost 100 killed, 108 wounded and 188 prisoners, including General Kock and Colonel Schiel (commanding the German volunteers); the British lost 6 officers and 49 men killed 29 officers and 178 men wounded, and 10 men missing. This is called the battle of Elandslaagte.

The communication with Yule was reestablished, and the latter on the 23d, started to join forces with White, concentrating at Ladysmith.

Action at Rietfontein.

On that day (23rd) Yule reached Beith by the Helpmakaar road, and at 9:30 a.m. on the 24th was at Waschbank Spruit; the column followed the valley of the Waschbank and on the morning of the 25th reached that of the Sundays, and on the 26th entered Ladysmith.

General White, knowing of Yule's approach, moved out to Rietfontein on the 24th to cover his flank from attack. He had heard that a force of Orange Boers from Bester's Station had taken up a strong position west of the road Glencoe—Ladysmith. His force consisted of about 4,500 men:

- 5th Lancers,
- Natal Volunteer Carabiniers,
- 19th Hussars,
- Border Mounted Rifles
- Imperial Light Horse,
- Natal Mounted Rifles,
- 1st Battalion Gloucestershire Regiment,
- 1st Battalion Liverpool Regiment,
- 1st Battalion Devonshire Regiment,
- 2nd Battalion King's Royal Rifles
- 42nd and 43rd field batteries,

- 10th mountain battery.

He met the Boers (about 1,500 men) at Rietfontein, the advance guard of cavalry under French coming upon them at 7 a.m., and held them in check until noon, when, learning that General Yule had passed through the defiles of the Biggarsberg, he retired to Ladysmith. British loss 116, Boers 230.

The Boers closed in on Ladysmith and cut the Ladysmith — Pietermaritzburg railroad at Colenso. Their concentric advance, in spite of the disadvantages they experienced after crossing the mountains in so many columns, succeeded. The Boers were forced to subdivide their forces by the difficult country they passed through, but the same excuse cannot, be applied to the British. The probable reasons for their dividing into two forces (Glencoe—Dundee and Ladysmith), instead of concentrating at some point as at Ladysmith, were the facts that Glencoe threatened a Boer advance on the main road over Newcastle, that Dundee possessed important coalfields, and that Ladysmith covered the very important line to Pietermaritzburg.

Meanwhile, another important movement took place. A Boer column started from Fort Evelin (the southernmost point of the Transvaal) and marched along the Ummula River over Melmoth to the coast, evidently with a view to influencing the Zulus to take an active part against the English.

Operations on Western and Southern Border.

In the west and south of the Boer Republics the strategic deployment and advance progressed more slowly. At the opening of the war there were about 2,000 Boers along the Bechuana railroad, and by October 14th Cronje had 6,000 men opposite Mafeking, which was garrisoned by about 600 colonial troops under Colonel Baden-Powell. At Kimberley there was a garrison of about 2,500 men, under Colonel Kekewich, half of which were British troops, with a considerable number of guns. A detachment of 3,000 Orange Boers under Prinsloo, had occupied Boshof, 36 miles northeast of Kimberley, and on October 15th moved against that place to besiege it.

On October 15th took place an action near Mafeking, in which the Boers were repulsed. The British lost two killed and 15 wounded; the Boers 53 killed and many wounded.

On October 24th a small but important engagement took place north of Kimberley, in which 500 British attacked and defeated 700

Boers. The British lost 3 killed and 21 wounded. A sharp skirmish also took place at Rhodes Drift, near Tuli. On the same day the Boers occupied Klipdam in Griqualand West., and on the 25th they occupied Vryburg and Barkly West. On the latter day the Boers made a determined attack on Mafeking, but were repulsed with considerable loss. Colonel Baden-Powell had a railroad track laid encircling the town and armored trains were placed in operation on it and could be taken quickly to any threatened point.

At the end of October the Boers drew from Mafeking to Kimberley considerable portions of the besieging troops. General Cronje himself went there, leaving Botha in command.

The Boers were masters of the situation on the western border, and the occupation of points like Taungs. 40 miles south of Vryburg, had enabled them to isolate the English at Mafeking and Kimberley. On the southern border they had occupied Norvals Pont, Bethulie, Rouxville, Aliwal North and the bridge over the Orange River, with outposts at Burghersdorp, threatening the railroad junction at De Aar.

They advanced southward in two columns: one over Norvals Pont on Colesberg and Arundel, the other crossing at Bethulie and advancing on Burghersdorp, and later on Stornberg. The weak British garrisons at Colesberg and Aliwal North had retired on Naauwpoort and Queenstown, respectively.

Summary and Review.

Let us review briefly the progress of events up to the end of October, which marks the end of the first act and the beginning of the second.

At midnight on October 11-12 General Joubert directed all the Transvaal and Orange Boers under his orders to break camp, and by noon the next day their concentric march on the British position, Dundee—Glencoe—Ladysmith, was well under way. The plan of campaign of the Boers was strategically sound, and its practical execution in detail was tactically correct in the main, all the circumstances being carefully considered. Among the tactical measures, to ensure the safety of the general movement, may be mentioned (1) the sending out beforehand the advance guard of the Sandspruit corps from Volksrust to Laings Nek and occupying this position and the railroad defile to Newcastle before daybreak; (2) the movement of the Wakkerstroom corps in the general direction of Newcastle, and occupying the bridges over the Buffalo River; (3) the

The British clambering on an armored train.

Dornberg corps taking up a position at Vants Drift opposite Rorkes Drift as early as the 11th, so as to be able to reach the cross-roads to Glencoe and Ladysmith opposite Waschbank and Wessels Nek on the 12th; (4) the advance on the same day of the Utrecht and Vryheid commands to De Jägers Drift on the Glencoe road.

The Orange Boers, in a similar manner, occupied the Botha, Muller, Bezuidenhouts and Tintwa passes before the evening of the 12th.

The danger of subdividing into many small columns we have already discussed. On the British side the Dundee—Glencoe—Ladysmith position was not well selected, and the coal-fields at Dundee are hardly a sufficient reason for a determined resistance at the Dundee—Glencoe line, and the excuse of political and moral reasons is too often advanced to cover military mistakes. A concentrated position north of Ladysmith, with a right flank column at Glencoe, appears to be the most reasonable solution; but such a Glencoe force should have considered itself part of the Ladysmith main body, and should not, therefore, have allowed itself to be surrounded, but should have retired slowly before superior forces toward Ladysmith or Colenso.

General White had but 3,000 men available, as it was, with which to attempt to prevent the union of the separate Boer columns, each of which was his superior in numbers, and the large and practically independent force at Glencoe tied him to Ladysmith. With the above arrangement he would have had at least 10,000 men available for the attack on the separate Boer columns, and nothing to look out for but his own communications. If, however, his attempts to prevent union failed, then his only course should have been to retire beyond the Tugela and occupy a strong position covering Pietermaritzburg and Durban.

The neglect of General Symons to occupy Dundee Hill, which commanded the British camp, cost him a hard fight. The battles of Glencoe, Dundee and Elandslaagte were really fought to redeem a bad position, made so by imperfect tactical dispositions. An energetic, combined struggle with one of the Boer columns from a good position north of Ladysmith would have been far better. As it was, the British frittered away their forces in advance guard and outpost affairs which had no effect on the advance of the Boer main columns.

General White's success at Elandslaagte was decisive, but it only reestablished a communication which had been unnecessarily lost, and it gave the Boer columns more time to complete their strategic plans and concentric march. Considered by itself, however, it was a well-planned and splendidly executed action. General Yule's night march from Glencoe, in presence of an enemy greatly superior in strength, was a remarkable achievement, and, taken in connection with General White's covering flank attack at Rietfontein, constitutes an excellent tactical study.

The bravery of the British officers commands the respect and admiration of the world. In these days of strong defensive lines and the great power of weapons in warfare, it is more difficult than ever to induce the soldier to come up to the enemy's lines, to come in contact with the enemy—by which alone the tide of battle can be turned; consequently the example set by the officer comes more than ever into play, is more than ever a necessity, and certainly the British officers left nothing to be desired in this respect. The British loss in officers at Glencoe was $14\frac{1}{2}$ per cent of the total losses: at Spicheren the Germans lost in officers $4\frac{1}{2}$ per cent of the total losses. Whether or not the officers exposed themselves unnecessarily is a very difficult question to decide: it is the officer's duty to get his men forward, to keep them under control, and to economize their offensive power until the crisis is over, and if he stops to consider his own safety he is liable to miss his main duty; on the other hand, a high percentage of officers killed or wounded is very demoralizing. Between these limits he must choose, and the best course of action left open to the officer appears to be to get his men forward as well as he can without too much exposing himself; but if it is necessary to advance farther, and there is danger of lagging if this method is kept up, then he must expose himself.

The campaign in South Africa, the first to fully illustrate the effect of the modern magazine rifle and of smokeless powder, furnishes no new principles of strategy or tactics, but substantiates the conclusions long ago reached by the best authorities from -a careful consideration of all the elements of modern warfare.

The reason that the results have impressed the world as unexpectedly great is that acts speak so much louder than treatises, even to professional men, and that the principles, heretofore known only to the initiated, now suddenly become the world's property.

The first great principle, long since established, which it emphasizes, is the power of the offensive, strategically and tactically, and the fact that this offensive alone, in spite of all the new power of defense, can furnish decisive results. In this early stage of the campaign the offensive is largely with the Boers, yet even here the limitations of their offensive power,—in failing to strike hard when they had the opportunity, and more especially in neglecting that other essential element of the offensive, pursuit,—is but too apparent.

Another important principle of the art of war is the correct estimation of the enemy's preparedness and strength. The one great cause of the early British disasters was their entire underrating of their enemy's offensive and defensive power. But many another nation has made this mistake—for example, France in 1870 and Russia in 1877; hence this is not so surprising, especially when we consider the great distance of the scene of action from the home country. Of course, this error of judgment falls upon the supreme heads of the army command and upon the diplomatic department, and does not concern the troops in the field.

Any other nation, under similar circumstances, might have made the same mistake, and yet history teaches us that wars against irregular troops, defending their country and their homes, are always to be rated among the most difficult undertakings. And when in addition the nation attacking has to do so over a long line of communications, extending across the ocean for thousands of miles, and against a nation well led, and fully armed and prepared, the difficulties increase a thousand-fold.

Another great principle of strategy that finds application of this campaign is the danger of holding on to what appear to be important points in the theatre of operations with large portions of the army of operations. The lesson of Metz, which caused France the loss not only of Bazaine's army, but also of MacMahon's at Sedan, was not taken to heart by the British authorities. White's decision to hold Ladysmith, and the announced intention to retain possession of Mafeking and Kimberley, tied the hands of the British leaders in the field, and increased the difficulties of the situation. The lesson to be drawn is that armies should never allow themselves to be shut up in fortifications, except when there is no other means left them to save themselves from destruction.

Still, simple as the principle is, it is so different in practice from what it appears to be in theory, that criticism must be passed with caution. If, as is stated, the fall of Ladysmith and Kimberley would have been the signal for a general uprising of the Dutch Boers in Cape Colony, the entire question at once assumes a different aspect, and cannot be answered on purely military grounds.

The principal tactical principle that has been corroborated by the battles in South Africa is that the purely frontal attack is no longer successful. It must be combined with flank attacks; but, since the latter will generally be met by counter-measures on the part of the enemy, converting them again into frontal attacks, these counter-attacks must be continued and extended into far outflanking movements, requiring much time for their execution, during which, between the two original fronts, a contest for position is taking place. These tedious maneuvers are rarely practiced in time of peace, because they take up so much time, but they should be, to make them second nature to the soldier. Moreover, many portions of the line, even of an army acting offensively, must stand temporarily on the defensive. Such portions should resort immediately to intrenchments; hence the necessity for practice in this important branch. In consequence of the growing importance of intrenching on the field, high authorities claim that the subject of temporary fortifications and field intrenchment should be embodied directly in the drill regulations.

In the way of organization the only striking feature in this campaign is the great use made of mounted infantry, which constitutes on the side of the Boers, indeed, the principal force, but is also much used by the British. The advantage of such a force is undoubted, especially for reconnoitering and holding points important for the deployment of the main body. This suggests that the cavalry be trained to regard its fire-arm not as its exceptional, but as its principal weapon, and that it be trained to fight on foot even more thoroughly than has been the custom in the past.

PART II.

THE CAMPAIGN IN NATAL.

After the battles of Dundee, Glencoe and Elandslaagte, the respective forces in Natal were probably about as follows:
- British: Infantry 7,800, cavalry 1,050, artillery 45 guns, volunteers (Natal Volunteers and Imperial Light Horse) 1,000.
- Boers: 30,000 men, 40 guns (including six 40-pounders).

The Boers under Meyer and Erasmus who pursued Yule's column came into position on Isimbulwana Hill; the Orange Boers (7,000) arrived at Matawans Hoek; while Joubert's main body closed in from the north, extending from Lombards Kop to the railroad to Harrismith.

The question naturally arises, why did not White retire toward Pietermaritzburg as soon as he found himself unable to longer hold his advanced position without danger of being cut off? The reasons probably are that he had orders to hold out (for political reasons and moral effect) as long as possible; moreover, the worn-out troops of Yule undoubtedly needed rest.

In case retreat had been attempted, there were three roads open to White. First, the road running east from Lady-smith and then branching to Weenen, or going on to Pomeroy and thence to Greytown; secondly, over the open ground between the Isimbulwana Hill and the Klip River; thirdly, the road south over Nelthorpe and Colenso. But the Boer guns on Lombards Kop and Isimbulwana Hill commanded the first and second, and the left bank of the Modder Spruit was occupied in force by two Boer commandoes (Meyer and Erasmus). It appears, however, that White had decided to hold Ladysmith.

The Battles of Farquhar's Farm and Nicholsons Nek.

On October 30 White decided to attack the Boer forces, but the difficulties were very great, for he had to start under artillery fire from the Isimbulwana Hill, and the Boer columns were now united.

Colonel Carleton with the Irish Fusiliers, the Gloucestershire battalion and a mountain battery, constituting his left wing, was sent to Nicholsons Nek to hold in check the Boers on Lombards Kop, and to cover the left and rear. The center or main column, under Hamilton, was composed of 4 batteries and 4 infantry battalions, and advanced along the railroad. The right, under Grimwood, composed of 2 batteries and 5 battalions, moved directly east, between Isimbulwana and Lombards Kop. The cavalry, 3 regiments and mounted infantry, under French, covered the extreme right. A naval brigade with two heavy guns, just arrived, also took part in the engagement.

The Boer outposts retired before the British center, and the latter in advancing lost touch with the right. This right soon found itself outflanked, was compelled to change front under Are, and had to call back the center to assist it. Nevertheless, the right thus reinforced was driven back completely routed, covered by the 23d battery. This is known as the battle of Farquhar's Farm.

Meanwhile, the left column moved on unmolested to Nicholsons Nek, except that as they arrived there two large boulders were roiled down from the heights by a Boer patrol, and at the same time there was a blast of artillery fire, and this so frightened the mules that they ran, and the entire mountain battery with all the wagons of reserve ammunition were lost. The infantry held the position, however, and intrenched. But the Boers having been reinforced, and the right and center having fallen back, this entire column was finally captured. This is called the battle of Nicholsons Nek.

The British lost in these two engagements several hundred killed and wounded, 5 guns, the entire train, the ammunition column, and 1,500 mules.

The losses in detail were: 6 officers, 57 men killed; 10 officers, 221 men wounded; 38 officers, 977 men missing.

It is probable that White, in first making this attack, had decided, if successful, to retire further south, but his failure determined him to hold on to Ladysmith rather than abandon the great supply of stores there.

The General Situation.

On the evening of the 30th there were 5 commandoes of Boers south of the city, between the Klip and the Flagstone, with a second line in rear occupying Nelthorpe and Pieter stations; another commando intrenched on the Lombard Kop; 2 commandoes (Meyer and Erasmus), 2,000 strong, east of the Bulwana Kopje; while on the north and northeast Joubert had seven camps in a semicircle from Lombards Kop to the road from Van Reenens Pass; and finally 2

Orange commandoes coming from Dewdrop Spruit, joining hands with Joubert west of the town.

On November 3 White once more attempted to push back the Boer lines between the Klip River and the Isimbulwana Hill. The point, 3,000 men, under General Murray, including a greater part of the cavalry and several batteries, managed to push through the Boer lines and escaped to Estcourt; the rest were forced back to Ladysmith.

Colonel Cooper, occupying Colenso with 600 volunteers, with a detachment of the Dublin Fusiliers at Fort Wylie, retired to Estcourt. The Boers occupied Colenso on the 3d.

General Joubert, after leaving the proper force to continue the siege of Ladysmith (the garrison of which was now reduced to 7,000), continued his strategic march in three columns: one to strengthen the corps at Colenso and advance west of the railroad, the second advancing over Weenen, the third over Greytown. The detachment which had penetrated into Zululand crossed the lower Tugela, and threatened the communication between Pietermaritzburg and Durban, from the vicinity of Stanger.

The further advance was thus to be a grand right wheel of the Boer army, to be followed by a concentric advance on Pietermaritzburg. But the arrival of the 2d Brigade, 1st Division, of British reinforcements under General Hildyard at Estcourt caused a temporary change. General Botha's Boer corps (7,000) from Colenso came to a stand, the corps originally at Colenso moving over Ulundi-Courton west of the railroad took the British in the left flank, that moving over Weenen took them on the right flank, while that sent over Greytown was to take position at Pietermaritzburg.

Heavy guns were gradually brought from Pretoria and Johannesburg to strengthen the Boer lines, which were drawn closer and closer around Ladysmith.

General Buller, who arrived at Cape Town on October 31, remained there until November 16, when he started north, and on the 26th was at Pietermaritzburg. Meanwhile 17 transports (with about 19,000 men) arrived at Cape Town, 10 being sent on to Durban, where the troops were landed to operate towards Ladysmith, the troops from the others being sent north by rail to Orange River Station, General Methuen in command.

The besieged cities of Ladysmith and Kimberley evidently

determined the British plan. Part of the reinforcements were sent to Sir Buller in Natal, another part from Cape Colony to Orange River Station under Lord Methuen, a third and fourth under Generals Gatacre and French; respectively, to threaten the Orange Free State. The reinforcements were too small to warrant such a subdivision into four widely separated columns. It would have been better to have concentrated the entire force in Natal against the main Boer army, or to have retained the Boer army there and invaded the Orange Free State with a strong column in the center or left.

In the composition of the units there are decided elements of weakness, for the force under Clery in Natal has parts of three different divisions, the others being in one or other of the other columns.

Action at Willow Grange.

General Clery assumed command of the forces south of Ladysmith on the 18th. A Boer column reached Nottingham road and moved over Ulundi to Highland Station(Mooi River) on the 21st, cutting off Estcourt. The British forces, 2,000 each, one under Hildyard at Estcourt, the other under Barton at Weston, were thus surrounded. The Boers had a splendid opportunity for a tactical offensive, which should have led to decisive results; but General Joubert, learning of the arrival of the British reinforcements in Pietermaritzburg, decided to retire and concentrate his forces in the strong position north of the Tugela. On the 21st General Hildyard attacked the Boers at Willow Grange and drove them back, restoring communication with Weston. Hildyard's force consisted of 700 mounted men, the 7th and 66th field batteries, and three battalions (East Surrey, West Surrey and West York). He lost 13 killed, 65 wounded, and 9 missing; the Boer loss is reported as 30 killed, 100 wounded. The troops from Estcourt and Weston then advanced to Frere, the Boers retiring to Colenso.

By the 22d of November, 33 troopships had arrived at the Cape, carrying 34,516 officers and men.

A fortified camp was established at Chieveley, where the reinforcements were concentrated.

EVENTS IN THE SOUTHERN AND WESTERN THEATRES.

On October 30th, a Boer attack on Mafeking was repulsed with loss: British lost 2 officers and 4 men killed, and 5 men wounded.

On November 1st, a Boer force crossed the bridge at Norvalfontein and occupied Colesburg, and another (3,000 under Commandant Dutoil) assembled at Bethulie bridge. On the 2d, a detachment (3,500) crossed the bridge at Bethulie, the British force at Stormberg Junction retiring to Queenstown. The Boers were operating at this time south of the Orange River in three columns: the right (2,000) against De Aar and the Cape railroad; the center (1,000) pushing out on the Colesberg road; the left (3,000) against Queenstown and Port Elizabeth; a reserve of 4,000 at Bethulie.

At Mafeking there was daily skirmishing. Colonel Plumer from Tuli was on the way to relieve this town.

Lord Methuen arrived at Orange River Station on November 9th. General French, who had escaped from Lady-smith on the last train out, November 2d, obtained command of the troops pushed out to Naauwpoort.

The troops actually placed under Lord Methuen's command were the following:
- 1st Brigade (Guards), 1st Division (Colville). *[see Appendix]*
- 9th Brigade (Featherstonehaugh, later Pole-Carew), comprising;
  1st Northumberland Fusiliers,
  2d Northamptonshire, 2d Yorkshire Light Infantry,
  ½ 1st Loyal North Lancashire.
- Mounted Infantry, 1 regiment.
- Naval Brigade and 4 navy guns.
- Cavalry, 9th Lancers and New South Wales Lancers.
- Artillery, 3 batteries.

Later there were added:
- 3d Brigade (Scotch Brigade), *[see Appendix]*
- 1st Battalion Gordon Highlanders.[1]

General Gatacre was placed in command of the troops of the Cape force already in position, receiving in addition the 5th Brigade. [see Appendix] General French (who had escaped from Ladysmith) was under his command.

On the 10th of November a British reconnoitering party, under Colonel Gough, composed of two squadrons of the 9th Lancers, 1½ companies mounted infantry and a field battery, struck a force of 700 Boers at a point about 3 miles west of Belmont and had a sharp

---

1 From the line of communications.

THE BRIDGE AT HOPETOWN.

skirmish with them.

On November 19th a Boer commando, 500 strong, attacked Kuruman, but was repulsed. On the 20th Cronje left Mafeking for the South, the commandoes of Snyman and Malan remaining to continue the siege.

Meanwhile, Lord Methuen developed his plan of operations in the West. After repairing the bridge at Orange River Station, he advanced with 6,000 men on the 21st of November against Belmont.

Action at Belmont.

The country is flat, with only low ridges, 100 to 200 feet high, crossing it, and two miles south of Belmont rises the Kaffirs Kop, which is much higher. On the 21st he reached Witteputs and on the 22d Devondale (about 5 miles south of Kaffirs Kop). The Boer forces around Kimberley were commanded by Cronje, the outposts at Belmont and Kaffirs Kop by Delarey. On the 23d the attack began against the first rise, which was quickly taken, followed by the storming the second rise, the cavalry acting on the left flank to turn the Boer right. The third rise was carried with more difficulty, but being most effectively supported by the artillery, the Boers retiring to the Kaffirs Kop. The cavalry was too much exhausted to pursue. This is known as the battle of Belmont.

The British lost 4 officers and 20 men killed 50 officers and 218 men wounded, and 2 missing. Among the wounded was General Featherstonehaugh, commanding the 9th brigade, who was succeeded by General Pole-Carew.

The Boer position on the Kaffirs Kop proved too strong, and Lord Methuen retired to Orange River Station.

Action at Graspan.

On the following night (24th and 25th) Lord Methuen again advanced. He moved over Schalk Farm, in order to go around the Kaffirs Kop and Belmont, and was approaching the railway station, Graspan, when the head of the column ran into 2,500 Boers concealed in a depression of the ground, near Enslin, while 500 Boers from the Kaffirs Kop attacked the rear guard. Lord Methuen engaged them in front with the naval brigade, and turned their flanks with the 9th brigade, while the cavalry threatened their rear. The Boers retired to the Modder River. The cavalry was too weak to pursue. This is called the battle of Graspan or Enslin.

The British force under Lord Methuen in this action comprised:
- 9th Lancers.
- Billington's Scouts.
- 2 field batteries.
- Guards Brigade (Colville).
- 9th Brigade (Featherstonehaugh).
- Naval Brigade (Captain Prothero, from the Doris).

The Boers under Cronje were about 3,000 strong, with 6 field guns and 2 machine guns.

The British lost 4 officers and 20 men killed, 5 officers and 161 men wounded, 7 missing.

The Battle of Modder River.

Lord Methuen, after resting for a day, and reconnoitering to the front, continued his advance in the night of the 20th. Nothing had been seen of the enemy. The column halted for the night at Klopfontein Farm. At 4 a.m. Methuen resumed his march, the 2d battalion Northamptonshire regiment as advance guard, the 2d battalion Yorkshire Light Infantry leading the main column. The total strength (including reinforcements joining on the battlefield) was about 8,500 men, with 22 guns (including 4 naval guns). The Boers numbered about 8,000, with 10 guns, and were under Delarey and Cronje, their artillery under Albrecht.

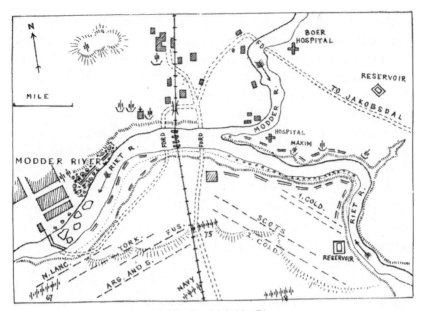

The Battle of Modder River.

The village called Modder River (see sketch) lies on the north bank of the Riet, just west of the junction of the Modder. The Boer position was in the shape of a crescent, its center opposite the bridge, its right flank resting on a group of houses north of the dam, its left flank at a farm beyond the Free State border. The Riet, although swollen at this time, was fordable at several points, and both banks are covered with trees and thick brush. The railroad bridge had been destroyed by the Boers, but a road bridge north of Sevenfontein remained for communication. The islands above the dam are covered with trees. The ground on the right bank rises gradually to the north and fully commands the south bank.

Although the principal Boer position was on the north side, their advanced line was on the south. Both were intrenched, the revetments covered with bags of sand and galvanized iron plates, and the approaches were obstructed with wire entanglements. Behind the advanced line the ground slopes down to the river, affording cover for horses and wagons, and communication over the river was effected by innumerable boats and rafts.

The artillery was all on the north side, 5 guns at the center, 2 on the right and 2 on the left flank; the Maxim gun near the junction of the rivers, and a Hotchkiss gun moved about as required.

Methuen, when at daybreak his patrols drew the enemy's fire, concluded it was merely an advance guard fight that confronted him. After the cavalry and mounted infantry came in contact with the advanced line of the Boers, the artillery, under Colonel Hall, at about 5:30 a.m., took position at 4,300 yards and bombarded the Boer left flank. The 9th Lancers and the mounted infantry protected the right flank of the artillery. The artillery duel lasted about two hours, then the infantry advanced in dispersed order, the naval brigade (1,000) and the artillery composing the center, the right formed of the Guard (3,500) under Colville, the left of the 9th brigade (4,000) under Pole-Carew. The latter was reinforced on the field by the first battalion of the Argyll and Sutherland Highlanders, coming from the Orange River. The line advanced to within 600 yards of the enemy's position, but could make no farther progress and lay there all day. On the right repeated attempts were made to turn the Boer position. On the left, however, a part of the 9th brigade succeeded in crossing at the dam, and in gaining a footing on the north bank. The artillery was active all day. At 3 p.m. the 62d battery arrived by rail. During the night the Boers evacuated their position. This is called the battle of Modder River.

The British lost in this battle 4 officers and 68 men killed, 19 officers and 377 men wounded, 7 missing.

The total losses of these British columns of invasion up to and including November 28th were about 3,000 killed and wounded. General Methuen remained at the Modder River, repairing the bridge there.

GENERAL SITUATION.

After the disaster of Glencoe and the siege of Ladysmith, England proceeded to raise another (the 5th) division, and to organize a siege train. The later disasters decided England to raise still another, (the 6th) division.

On the southern border of the Orange Free State the British (under General French) reoccupied Naauwpoort, November 19th, while the Boers from Aliwal North took possession of Jamestown, and moved on Dordrecht. Gatacre moved north from Queenstown and occupied Bushmans Hoek, November 27th, and the Boers destroyed the Steynsburg bridge, between Queenstown and Naauwpoort.

The general situation at the end of November may be summed up

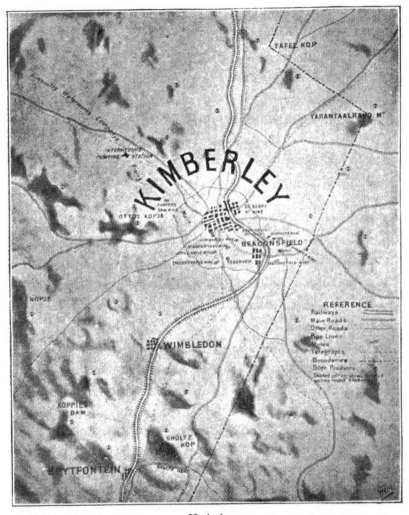

Kimberly

as follows:

In Natal the continuation of the siege of Ladysmith, and the holding in check of General Clery's relief force by the Boers on their strongly intrenched Tugela line. In the west the continuation of the siege of Mafeking and Kimberley, and the holding in check of the relief force under Lord Methuen on the Riet River. In the south the holding in check of Gatacre's division and French's brigade.

The strength of the. Boer forces in Natal was about 25,000 men, south of the Orange River about 10,000, and in the west about

12,000, with about 1,000 on the northern border, and about 2,000 in the interior, giving a total of about 50,000. They had about 45 field guns and 20 Maxims.

General Buller (after the arrival of the first reinforcements) had command of about 34,000 infantry, 6,800 cavalry, 200 field guns and 40 Maxims (after deducting garrisons, etc.). By the middle of December the second reinforcements brought his force up to 40,000 infantry, 7,650 cavalry, 206 field guns; and by the first of January (when the third reinforcements arrived) to 46,000 infantry, 7,650 cavalry, 226 field guns and howitzers, 50 Maxims.

EVENTS SOUTH OF THE ORANGE RIVER.

General Gatacre's troops were concentrated at Queenstown to act in concert with French, in order to throw back the invading Boer columns.

On the 18th of November he had the following troops:
- 2d battalion Royal Irish Rifles.
- 2d battalion Berkshire (part only).

These were reinforced later on by:
- 2d battalion Northumberland Fusiliers.
- 2d battalion Royal Scots Fusiliers.

And on December 5th by:
- 74th, 77th and 79th field batteries, and
- 12th company, field engineers.

He also had some Cape Police, Kaffrarian Rifles and Brabant's Horse, all volunteers and irregulars.

His total force amounted to 3,500 men.

On November 22d he established his camp at Putters Kraal, leaving about 1,000 men at Queenstown. He occupied Sterkstroom with about 300 men, and Bushmans Hoek with about 800, but early in December he combined the two advanced posts at Molteno.

General French, with a detachment comprising the 2d Berkshire Regiment, the 6th Guards Dragoon Regiment and mounted Cape Colony organizations, was directed to secure to line Port Elizabeth—Colesberg. He assembled his forces at Naauwpoort, reconnoitering to Arundel.

On December 8th the Boers were distributed as follows: 800 men at Dordrecht, 700 (with 6 guns) on the way to Dordrecht from

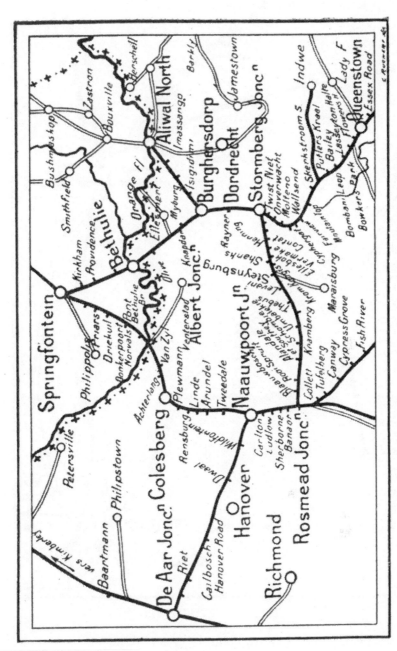

THEATRE OF OPERATIONS OF GENERALS FRENCH AND GATACRE.

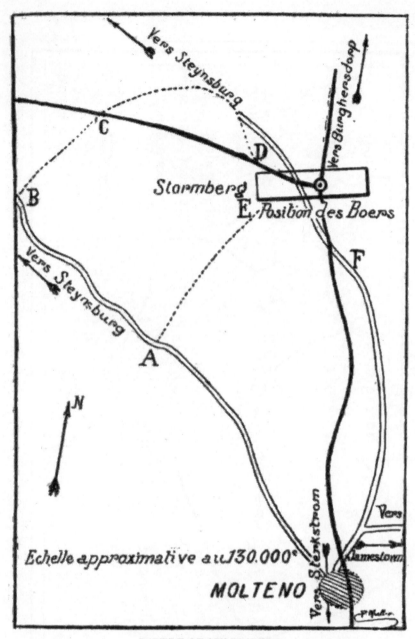

BATTLE OF STORMBERG

Jamestown, 1,500 at Stormberg, 400 near Molteno, and a small commando at Steynsburg. The Boers in the vicinity of Stormberg were commanded by Olivier.

The Battle of Stormberg.

At the beginning of December the Boers in the south were moving on Dordrecht, Molteno and Indwe. Meanwhile, Gatacre's troops remained inactive until the first week of December had passed. Then, to strengthen Lord Methuen's position, an offensive movement was decided upon.

This was begun by a reconnaissance of General French in the direction of Arundel. His efforts to get an insight into the enemy's position failed, and on the 10th he was compelled to retire.

To further prepare for his advance, General Gatacre, on the 8th, sent Colonel Dalgetty with all his available cavalry and a half-battery against Dordrecht, with a view to taking this town and threatening Stormberg (reported to be occupied by only 2,000 men) on the left flank.

General Gatacre himself, on the 9th, went by rail, with about 2,500 infantry, 200 cavalry and 2 batteries, to Molteno, and marched thence on the night of the 9th towards Stormberg (8½ miles), to surprise the Boer garrison. The column was to march along the Molteno—Steynsburg road for about 5 miles, then turn northeast directly towards Stormberg (at A, see sketch), but in the darkness the troops moved on too far (B, see sketch) and had to make a wide sweep (double the distance) to reach their objective, striking the latter on the northwest side, where it was practically unassailable. On arriving about three miles from Stormberg the head of column suddenly found itself under heavy fire in front and right flank. The Royal Dublins, composing the advance, broke and carried panic with them. A rally was effected behind a kopje, and a new position taken up to the rear, while the mounted infantry was sent against the right flank. Before the new position was occupied a Boer Maxim battery opened on the rear of the British, and they again retired in still greater disorder, and it was only behind the British artillery that order could be restored. The Boers never followed up the retirement of Gatacre, except with long-range artillery fire, and sniping at quite extravagant distances.

Gatacre continued his retreat to Molteno. The entire action lasted from 4 to 7 a.m. The reserves of the companies that assembled on the hills were many of them captured, but no prisoners were lost during the retreat. The British lost 60 killed and wounded, about 700 prisoners and 3 guns. This is the battle of Stormberg.

The 4.7 R.F. gun "Joe Chamberlain" during the barrage of Magersfontein.

The tactical mistakes in this advance are apparent. General French's movement could have for its object only one of two things—it was either a feigned attack, with a view to drawing away from Stormberg some of the forces there, or else it was a forced reconnaissance to get an insight into the situation at Arundel. In either case it was an error. In the first case it was absurd to hope to produce any effect on the garrison of Stormberg by a movement on a Boer force three days' march away. In the second case the object did not justify the use of such a large force: a few officers' patrols would have served the purpose.

Moreover, Gatacre's advance was not properly organized tactically, for there were no real flanking columns to insure against surprise, Colonel Dalgetty's raid not being such in a true tactical sense. Finally, the whole expedition was made by too great a force, over too great a distance, to give promise of surprise in a country friendly to the enemy.

This break in the center of the general British line endangered further advance by Methuen or Clery, and French was so weakened that he could hardly secure the railroad line to De Aar.

Dalgetty took and held Dordrecht; but French failed in his attempt to turn the Boer position at Arundel, and was compelled to return to Naauwpoort.

THE CAMPAIGN IN THE WEST

On the western theatre of operations, at about the same time, important events were transpiring. Lord Methuen was forced to inactivity after the battles on the Modder and Riet rivers, not only because his troops were exhausted, but also because the Boers under General Cronje held the strong position of Spytfontein—Magersfontein in his front, and threatened his right flank from their position (under Prinsloo) at Jacobsdal, and even his line of communications from the rear, Orange Boers under Delarey as early as December 2d, having turned up at Graspan, destroyed the railroad bridge there, and then worked round to the westward to cut off Lord Methuen. Efforts to dislodge these forces in rear proved unsuccessful; consequently Lord Methuen decided to proceed with his more immediate duty, the relief of Kimberley, and made his preparations to force the Boer lines in his front.

Immediately after the battle of the Modder River a bridge of boats was constructed over the Riet about 40 yards to the west of the railroad bridge, and an iron bridge was commenced to the east of the latter, which was completed by December 7, when the first train crossed.

Between the 3d and the 8th of December the following reinforcements reached Lord Methuen:

- 12th Lancers.
- Horse Battery G.
- Siege Howitzer Battery (4 pieces, 5-inch).

- The Highlander Brigade (Gen. Wauchope).
- A Balloon Section.
- The 4.7 R.F. gun "Joe Chamberlain," from the Doris.
- The Canadian and Australian contingents.

His entire command comprised 11½ battalions, 6 squadrons, 5 batteries, 1 battalion mounted infantry, 1 naval brigade, 1 naval battery of 5 guns, and about 1,100 volunteers, or, in all, about 13,000 men and 35 guns.

The Boer position was in the form of a semicircle, comprised of two ridges, Spytfontein in the western part, Magersfontein in the eastern, the railroad passing between them and dividing the position into two nearly equal sections, that on the east side being much more strongly occupied than that on the west. The position was well intrenched, and at Magersfontein the trenches were so arranged as to allow of fire at different elevations at the same time. Cronje had about 6,000 men and 13 guns.

The Boers were reinforced by a number of commandoes, one of which occupied Reads Drift, about seven miles west -of the Modder River, and another Jacobsdal to the east.

On the 10th of December, Lord Methuen, after leaving a flanking force to guard against a Boer advance from Jacobsdal, crossed the Modder River on the temporary bridge which he had constructed and advanced against the left (or stronger) flank of the Boer position.

The Battle at Magersfontein.

On the morning of the 9th of December the 12 cm. naval gun moved out about a mile beyond the camp and fired some 15 shots at the Magersfontein heights, ten of them lyddite shells; the cavalry had a light skirmish on the right, and the 9th brigade moved out in support. At 2 p.m. on the 10th, after leaving the 9th brigade to guard the train, Lord Methuen's command broke camp and began the advance, the artillery opening fire, from the position occupied on the preceding day by the naval gun, on the heights at Magersfontein. For two hours the firing continued, but the Boers made no reply. The artillery, the Highland Brigade and the 9th Lancers bivouacked on the field during the early part of the night of the 10th, about 2 miles from Modder River Station, and the Guards moved up in support. At 1 a.m., in a heavy rain, the advance was continued.

The station of Spytfontein is about 10 miles from Modder River.

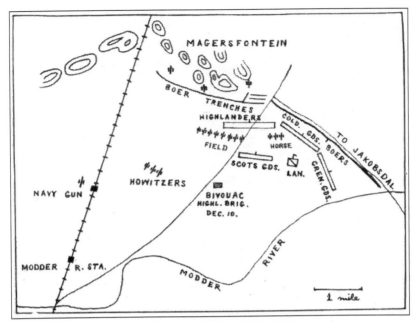

BATTLE OF MAGERSFONTEIN

The ground rises gradually to about 5 miles north of the Riet, then it begins to be cut up by kopjes. These lines of kopjes trend obliquely so that the open ground is like a wedge with Spytfontein at the apex, and Jacobsdal at one end of the base. The Magersfontein Kopjes constitute this portion of the Boer line. They rise to a height of 150 feet.

The Boer trenches ran along the foot of the heights they occupied, to the right of the British advance, then over the kopjes into the open country, so that a wide detour would have been necessary to turn them. But there was no thought of this, Lord Methuen's plan evidently being to surprise the position and attack in front only, nor was it known to the British that the Boer trenches lay along the foot of the hills; otherwise the artillery fire would not have been directed on the heights.

In the early dawn of December 11th the Highland Brigade, still in closed column, arrived within 500 yards of the enemy's trenches, having just passed a wire entanglement (at about 650 yards from the enemy) and reached a perfectly open terrain. Just as the order to deploy for attack was given, the enemy opened fire, and so murderously that the Highlanders broke and fell back in disorder with fearful loss.

47

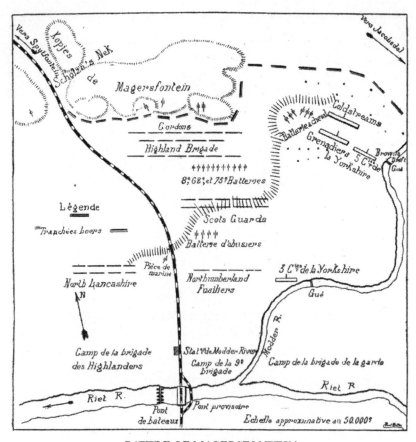

BATTLE OF MAGERSFONTEIN

General Wauchope fell among the first. The brigade was reassembled a few hundred yards to the rear, but its spirit was broken.

The Guard Brigade was then deployed, but could make no headway, and finally the whole of Lord Methuen's force was engaged—except a battalion of Gordon Highlanders left in reserve and to take charge of the train—the Guards on the right, Carew's brigade and the artillery in the center, the Highlander Brigade on the left. The howitzers on the left fired lyddite shell at about 3,800 yards range, while the three light batteries in the center advanced to within 1,700 yards of the Boer trenches, and the horse batteries moved to the right of the light batteries. The Boers occupied the road towards Jacobsdal as well as the trenches at the foot of the heights.

The Highlanders not being available for another attack, the reserve (Gordon Highlanders) was ordered up and arrived about 9 a.m., taking position in front of Wauchope's brigade, the two battalions of the Coldstream Guards strengthened the right wing, and the Grenadier Guards were detached to cover the extreme right flank. The howitzers advanced about 1,000 yards nearer. The field batteries were then about 1,200 yards, the howitzers 2,700 yards and the horse batteries about 1,600 yards from the enemy. But nothing availed. The Boers worked continually around towards the British right.

The Yorkshire Light Infantry had ascended the Modder during the night and occupied at daybreak a ford about 3 miles northeast of the bridge; after leaving 3 companies at this ford, the 5 others were sent to Browns Drift, further north. This force protected Methuen's exposed right flank during the entire day, and foiled Cronje's attempts to take the British lines in flank.

At about 2 p.m. the Highlanders were again demoralized and fell back in disorder, but were assembled, and, supported by the Scots Guards, took up their position again near the guns.

At about 5:30 p.m. the enemy's guns (which had remained silent up to this time) opened fire on the ammunition train and the cavalry. The Highlander Brigade again broke and fell back to the field hospital. Another attack was therefore not to be thought of. The British forces bivouacked on the field and in the morning began their retreat, falling back again to the Modder River.

During the day the balloon section made several ascents, remaining up each time about ten minutes.

General Methuen's advance was in reality a forced reconnaissance, for nothing was known of the enemy's strength or exact position. He made the great mistake of allowing an interval of several hours to elapse between his artillery combat and his infantry attack, and in the latter he brought his forces into action successively, consequently without definite result.

General Wauchope, commanding the Highland Brigade, was killed, and General Hector Macdonald succeeded him. Again we find that the British, in their anxiety to surprise the Boers, neglected all measures for security and information, and were themselves surprised. Lord Methuen lost about 1,000 men, or one-ninth of the forces actually engaged.

The British lost 21 officers and 139 men killed, 48 officers and 624 men wounded, 3 officers and 121 men missing, or a total of 956. The

Balloon Corps transport in Lord Roberts' army - the advance on Johannesberg.

Boers lost 219.

The Highlanders lost about 25.4 per cent of their entire force in ten minutes, and the brigade was placed hors de combat for the day. The Black Watch lost over 37 per cent. It has been stated by several authorities that in the battles of the future the losses of the army will probably not exceed 20 per cent, although, of course, particular units will be subjected to severer losses.

The battle was really lost in those ten minutes in which the Highlanders suffered their great losses, and it is clearly evident that nothing but imperfect reconnaissance is to blame for the British reverse in this case.

How General Methuen could decide to cross the Modder River and advance when he had left a Boer force on the south bank of the Riet, in his flank and rear, is inexplicable.

Before the close of the year but few further movements took place in the western and southern sections of the theatre of war, and none of any importance. On December 13th General French with the 6th Dragoon Guards, the 10th Hussars and 4 horse-artillery guns forced back a commando of Boers, about 1,800 strong, north of Naauwpoort; and again on the same day his mounted infantry drove back a column of Boers from Zoutpans Drift, 10 miles east of Orange River. On December 25th Dordrecht was occupied by Colonel Dalgetty, and on the 31st there was a small skirmish near this place.

THE CAMPAIGN IN NATAL.

The First Attempt to Relieve Ladysmith.
The Battle of Colenso.

General Buller remained inactive until the middle of December. The Boers under General Schalk Burgher (since Joubert's illness) had occupied with 12,000 men and strengthened the Tugela line at Colenso, sending out detachments to close the lines leading to Ladysmith, situated on their flanks: on the right flank the bridges over the Little Tugela at Springfield, and on the left flank the bridge over the Bush-mans River at Weenen, and the Tugela bridge in rear. In rear of Springfield they occupied a strong position on Zwarts Kop.

At Colenso the principal Boer position was north of the river, but they had also occupied the southern bank east of the railroad, resting their left flank on the Hlangwane Hill. From this last position they could take an enemy crossing at Colenso in rear, cut him off, and take him under crossfire. General Buller appears not to have been aware that this hill was occupied.

The country between Colenso, Frere and Springfield is without roads and very hilly, and that between Colenso, Weenen and Estcourt is also without roads and has the obstacle of the Blaauwkrass River besides. Moreover, to move on either of the flanks of the Boer position necessitated abandoning the railroad. Finally, such a movement in either direction would subject the British to flank attack from Colenso, and in addition the distance from Colenso to Springfield or to the Tugela bridge north of Weenen is shorter than the, distance from Frere to either of these objectives.

The railroad bridge just north of Colenso had been destroyed; the road bridge about 600 yards above remained, but was mined; there

BATTLE OF COLENSO.

was a ford between the two bridges, and one just above the road bridge. These were the only points where the river could be crossed without constructing a bridge, and they were, of course, strongly defended by the Boers. Moreover, just below Colenso, where the river makes a sharp turn to the north, the Boers had crossed to the south bank and occupied the Hlangwane Hill, commanding the Colenso—Weenen road, and threatening the river crossings from the eastward; and on the west they had continued their lines on the south bank, flanking the upper ford and the space between the bridges; finally, Colenso itself was occupied by the Boers.

General Buller had at Chieveley and Frere about 19,000 men and 52 guns. His plan was to have Barton's brigade with 2 field batteries and 6 12-pounder navy guns occupy the Hlangwane Berg, to support the advance of Hildyard and Lyttleton on Colenso in the center, while Hart's brigade on the left was to first force the Bridle Drift (upper ford), and. if successful, the troops crossed there would facilitate the passage of the other columns -at the iron bridge. If unsuccessful, the troops would hold the enemy in their immediate front while the right wing forced the passage of the iron bridge.

On the evening of December 14th and the morning of December 15th, General Buller prepared for his advance from Chieveley Camp by bombarding the supposed Boer positions by means of the naval guns and the howitzer batteries. On the 15th the advance was begun, Hildyard's brigade moving on the lower ford, Lyttleton's through Colenso on the road bridge, Hart's brigade on the upper ford. At 4:45 a.m. the navy 4.7-inch guns opened on Fort Wylie, and at 6 a.m. the 14th and 66th batteries advanced to the east of the railroad and came into position at 750 yards from the-Tugela (about 1,200 yards in front of the infantry). The battery of naval 12-pounders came up on the left and rear of the field guns. The Boers opened on the field guns not only with their artillery, but also with infantry fire from the trenches at short range, and the field batteries, under cross-fire from the front and from Hlangwane Hill, were soon destroyed and had to be abandoned.

Barton's brigade advanced against the western spurs of the Hlangwane Berg and reached the foot of the slope, when the Boers suddenly opened fire from front and flank, and forced back the right.

Meanwhile the infantry attack began.

Lyttleton's brigade and part of Hildyard's were held in check by

"Saving the guns at Colenso" - Lord Roberts' son Freddy died in this engagement and was awarded a posthumous Victoria Cross. Watercolour by Sidney Paget (1860-1908)

the garrison of Colenso, while Hart's advanced towards the upper ford. The troops of the latter were still in column when they found themselves under a cross-fire from the Boer trenches on the north and the south banks, as well as under artillery fire, and although they continued to advance and even succeeded in getting a few men to the other side, they lost heavily and were compelled to fall back, and joined the part of Hildyard's brigade, which had passed the eastern edge of Colenso and was advancing on the lower ford. But then they received the flank fire of the Boer trenches on the north bank, and the artillery fire from the Hlangwane Hill. Buller sent his entire cavalry and the mounted infantry against Hlangwane Hill, but the British artillery could take up no good position against the longer range Boer guns, and the cavalry and mounted infantry could make no progress. Finally, in consequence of the loss of the artillery, the troops fell back in disorder towards Frere.

This is known as the battle of Tugela River, or the battle of Colenso.

The British lost about 900 killed and wounded, and 11 guns: 9 officers, 137 men killed; 42 officers and 699 men wounded, 200 missing.

The Boers in the trenches in this locality were commanded by

Botha, and numbered only about 2,000 men.

The causes of these reverses on the Tugela are but too apparent.

While Buller was still at Frere Station, his advance guard was directed on December 12th to reconnoiter as far as Chieveley, and the presence of Boer forces south of the Tugela (between it and the Blaauwkrass River) was then established. Notwithstanding this, Buller advanced on the 15th to attack the Tugela line without making any attempt to determine the strength and position of these forces. It is not surprising, therefore, that he met with surprises, flank attacks and cross-fires. Moreover, it is an established principle that to cross a river in the face of a prepared enemy, it is necessary first of all to obtain full possession of the nearer bank, and Buller's neglect of this condition still further explains the results.

It is remarkable that during the long period of inaction Buller should have taken no measures to obtain, by careful reconnaissance, a clear insight into the strategic situation. Had he done so, he would have seen that an advance on Colenso laid him open to being cut off by an advance of the Boers at Springfield and Weenen against his lines of communication, which would have put him into the same plight as White at Ladysmith. But, after neglecting all proper reconnaissance, that he should advance to the attack without properly securing his flanks is simply incomprehensible.

The first condition for forcing the passage of the Tugela was the capture of the Hlangwane Hill and the expulsion of the Boers from the trenches on the south bank. But apparently the British did not even know that these points were occupied In force.

In the face of these disasters England ordered out all her reserves, proceeded to mobilize the 8th division, and appointed Field Marshal Lord Roberts commander-in-chief in South Africa, with General Lord Kitchener of Khartoum as second in command. The total losses of the British up to this time (not including deaths from disease) were 7,630.

COMMENTS.

Let us review briefly the causes of the events up to the present:

The main causes of the late disasters to the British arms in South Africa are readily traceable to grave mistakes made early in the campaign, and now difficult to remedy. Minor errors have marked the course of the operations, but they were due largely lo haste and a natural desire to overcome by extraordinary exertions the difficulties of a situation which was rendered dangerous by the earlier and graver errors in training, preparation, recruitment, material, organization, strategy and tactics.

First, as regards strategy. The wedge of Natal, projecting as it does into the Boer country, would appear at first to offer the great advantage of enabling an army always to operate on interior lines. With such a position a comparatively small force is able to fall on the fractions of the enemy, as his separate columns cross the passes of the border, and destroy them in turn. But in order to do this, the force in the wedge must be at least stronger than any one of the enemy's columns. The only way the British could have taken full advantage of their advantageous position would have been by concentrating their forces at some one point just north of Ladysmith; instead they divided them into two forces, one at Glencoe—Dundee, the other at Ladysmith. The result was, when White moved out from Ladysmith to pre vent the union of two of the Boer columns coming over the mountains, he had but 3,000 men available, which was much below the strength of either of the Boer columns. If the troops had been concentrated in one place, he would have had 10,000 men available, a number which would have been far greater than either Boer column.

It is only fair to state that when Sir George White arrived, he found the situation created for him, and that he desired to withdraw from Glencoe to Ladysmith at once, but for political reasons he had to hold on to it. Moreover, by permitting Symons to occupy Glencoe, the occupation of Ladysmith became a necessity.

In the defense of Dundee and Ladysmith the British showed too great a tendency to be tied down to localities, when the only proper course would have been to retire before superior forces and try to hold the Pietermaritzburg—Durban railroad, so important as a line of advance. Their tenacity and pluck in defending the places referred to are to be commended as such, but, although inspired by quite a different motive from that which induced Bazaine to hold on to Metz in 1S70, the ultimate effect on the general situation was similar. The same may be said of the defense of Mafeking and Kimberley. Instead of adding to the strength of the British attacking forces, they weakened the strategic plan, because there can be little doubt that Buller's

Horatio Herbert Kitchener, 1st Earl Kitchener (1850-1916). Officially holding the title of chief of staff, he was in practice a second-in-command, and commanded a much-criticised frontal assault at the Battle of Paardeberg in February 1900. Kitchener succeeded Roberts as overall commander in November 1900.
This is probably a photograph of a portrait by Heinrich von Angeli.

subsequent movements were greatly influenced by the desire to relieve these besieged garrisons; whereas, had they retired, they would now be available to assist the advancing columns, instead of being held in check.

Turning now to General Buller's plan of campaign, he seems, at first sight, to have followed good strategic principles in dividing into two main columns, one over Durban—Estcourt, the other over Cape Town—Orange River Station, concentrating on the Boer country, with Pretoria as the ultimate objective. But, if we examine more closely, we find that the total strength of his command does not warrant any division, because neither column is strong enough to cope with the enemy immediately in its front or to keep up proper communication between the far separated columns for effective mutual support or combined action. His entire force should have been sent to Durban and concentrated on the main Boer army in Natal, if rapid and decisive results were expected. Of course, the desire to relieve the garrisons at Kimberley and Mafeking had a great influence, and no doubt the strength and ability of the Boers were greatly underrated, but judgment and decision on such points are factors in generalship and constitute the elements of strategy.

Although these early battles prove the high quality of the British soldier in battle, they also indicate a lack of mobility, and a too great dependence on their base of supply, especially the railroad.

Secondly, as regards training. The best training is, of course, actual war, but the late wars of the British have not been of a character to teach them what an active and well-trained enemy is liable to do on the battlefield. Next to actual war come field exercises or maneuvers, and it appears from what the British officers themselves say that this kind of peace training was inadequate: first, in that it did not include on a sufficiently large scale flanking movements by the troops representing the enemy; secondly, in that the maneuvers were not conducted on a scale sufficiently extensive to make the officers familiar with the handling of large bodies of troops on the battlefield. The former explains why the British are continually surprised by the flanking movements of the Boer lines, and the latter may account for some of the tactical errors about to be considered.

Thirdly, let us analyze the British tactics. In the early part of the campaign they were very deficient in cavalry, but light infantry, properly trained, especially as opposed to such slow-moving and deliberate enemies as the Boers, should have done excellent service on reconnaissance, notably in the rough country in northern Natal, which is in reality more favorable for infantry than for cavalry scouts. But even later on, when French had an entire cavalry division at Naauwpoort, Gatacre was surprised in his advance from Queenstown. Of course the British are under the great disadvantage of operating in country where the natives sympathize with the enemy, but this does not satisfactorily explain all the deficiencies in reconnaissance work. For example, even on the battlefield, patrol duty to keep up intercommunication between the parts of a line seems to have been neglected, as at Nicholsons Nek, where one column of a small command was allowed to get so completely separated as to be captured, never having been informed of the repulse of the adjacent portions of the general line.

The cavalry failed entirely in its reconnaissance work, and the brigade commanders did not take up the work, when the cavalry retired from the front, by advancing their lines of infantry to force the enemy to develop his position.

The defeat of General Buller's army at Colenso appears to be another case in point. It is to-day considered to be no dishonor to lose a battery on the battlefield, provided its sacrifice is demanded by the general situation; but from the official report it appears that when Colonel Long advanced close to the river in his desire to be within effective range, it "proved to be full of the enemy." Now the artillery's duty was to get within effective range, but it is someone else's business to see that the bank of the river is not full of the enemy before the artillery is ordered to the front. Again, imperfect reconnaissance appears to be at the bottom of the trouble.

However, there is another point that demands consideration here. For some years the continental armies have been training special artillery scouts—that is, mounted men, selected from the field artillery batteries, whose duty it is to precede a battery, clear up the ground along the road of advance, look up the enemy's position, note points of value to the artillery commander, and report promptly whatever demands reporting, but remain constantly in touch with the enemy. These scouts are usually formed into patrols, under particularly efficient officers or non-commissioned officers. The British field artillery appears not to have put in practice this most effective means of protecting the artillery from surprise.

Another tactical weakness seems to be the failure to occupy positions properly, it is incomprehensible why Talana Hill (which cost so dear to retake after the Boers occupied it) was not occupied in the first place.

Moreover, the tendency of the British to make simple frontal attacks, is to be condemned as too great a waste of life in these days of enormous strength of the defense. The mistaken ideas of tactics, which induced the British to make such purely frontal attacks, in great measure necessitated that exposure of the officers and men which resulted in such great losses. Wherever they tried pressure on the flanks (as at Elandslaagte and Rietfontein) they were successful.

It will suffice to pass in rapid review the other elements of weakness.

As regards preparedness, it is only necessary to refer to the weak garrisons at Kimberley and Mafeking, guarding the important railroad from Cape Colony to Buluwayo, to the insignificant forces on the Orange River, covering the Port Elizabeth railroad, and to the comparatively small force at the keystone in Natal at the outset of the campaign. At home, the unreadiness of the Admiralty promptly to transport the reinforcements was severely commented on, and the length of time allowed for recruiting the army corps was probably necessitated by the lack of a full supply of clothing and equipment in the store-houses. The conditions in South Africa demanded prompt relief, and every moment of delay increased the gravity of the situation, as soon became fully apparent.

The greater part of the cavalry division of the army corps and the field artillery arrived after the infantry, which was a great disadvantage.

The want of artillery material, both field and siege, in sufficient quantity, made itself felt very early in the war. But this was not due to an actual want of such material at home, only to a deficient organization—the lack of a chief of artillery, who could demand that the proper artillery guns be sent, and who could be held responsible for not having them on hand in time. Another deficiency in organization was the mixing up of the units in the two main armies, by which one brigade of a division would be in one army, another in the other, so that Clery's column had parts of four different divisions.

The English had known for years that a collision with the Transvaal would occur sooner or later, but they closed their eyes to the strategical facts of the situation, and the military forces in South Africa were kept at an insufficient strength. The 6,000 miles separating the latter from the mother country seem never to have been considered.

Former governments and parties must, of course, take their share of the blame. The Cape garrison had always been weak, and originally it was probably sufficient to overawe the natives; but between 1881 and 1886, when there was constant friction between England and the Transvaal, some attempt to provide for the impending crisis should have been made by reinforcing the garrisons, and this would have been possible even up to 1896, but after that any such increase would certainly have led to war.

The chief of all these elements of British weakness is, of course, the strategy of the campaign-the great superiority of the Boers in strategic deployment and strategic advance, due to their unity of plan and action being everywhere manifest. The original inferiority of the British in numbers is also a prime cause; but each of the other elements has had its effect on the preliminary situation and the subsequent events.

The early operations of the Boers are marked by good strategy, and their tactical applications of their forces in battle, especially on the defensive, by considerable skill, but they lacked the spirit of the initiative and the power of the tactical offensive. The attack of the several columns on Dundee was not simultaneous; at Elandslaagte the advanced force was not properly supported; after the battles of Dundee and Elandslaagte their forces became too cautious in their advance and so allowed Yule to escape; they failed to push their advantage and to attack Ladysmith vigorously in the proper direction, before the British could have time to strengthen their position, but preferred to occupy a strong position to the north of the town; and finally, after the battle of Colenso, they failed to pursue.

PART III.

The British defeats at Magersfontein, Stormberg and on the Tugela closed the second epoch of the war. They were followed by a period of comparative inaction.

The mistakes in strategy of the second epoch, in trying to operate on three distinct lines, separated by from 150 to 300 miles—one for the relief of Kimberley, another for the direct offensive from Queenstown towards Bloemfontein, and the third for the relief of Ladysmith—and in splitting up the reinforcements for all these widely separated columns, instead of concentrating on one, brought their natural consequences, and the situation for the British became a very difficult one.

The tactical errors in applying an obsolete method of attack, in failing to develop a proper system of reconnaissance, and in neglecting to support field artillery by infantry or cavalry, the inferiority of the British artillery material at the opening of the campaign, the greater mobility of the Boer troops, as well as the inexperience of the British officers in exercising the higher commands, are the principal additional factors that have determined the events.

The obsolete method of attack consisted (on the Tugela, for example) in not preparing for the attack by a proper artillery bombardment from guns placed in well-covered gun-pits; then following the artillery duel (insufficient in every case thus far) either too soon (before proper preparation) by the infantry attack (as on the Tugela), or leaving too long an interval (as at Magersfontein); finally, in deploying an insufficient number of skirmishers for the firing line, in line, firing volleys, against an invisible, well-intrenched enemy, and making only frontal attacks on the position.

Both sides were compelled to inaction for a long period: the British for want of complete trains, for laying bridges and to enable them to cut loose from the railroads; and the Boers for lack of any further reinforcements, which compelled them to economize their troops, and consequently prevented them from taking Ladysmith or Kimberley by storm, or from advancing any farther into the British domain.

The total number of British troops in South Africa on January 1,

1900, was about 103,400, of which 83,000 were unmounted and 19,800 mounted. The position of the troops was as follows:

Lord Methuen was in an intrenched position between the Modder and Riet rivers, just east of their point of junction, and covering a bridge over the two rivers as well as the railroad bridge. He had about 13,000 men. The Boers, under Cronje, Delarey and Prinsloo, about 20,000 strong, occupied a fortified position at Spytfontein—Magersfontein, both flanks resting on the Modder River, the left extending across the river to Jacobsdal. They were gradually closing in on Methuen, and stray parties threatened his line of communications, so he made an effort to clear up the situation to the southwest, and on the 1st of January sent General Babington with a part of the 1st cavalry brigade from the main camp and Colonel Pilcher with a small detachment from Belmont, towards Douglas. Pilcher surprised a Boer detachment at Sunnyside, and pushed on to Douglas, but the approach of a commando (500) of Boers along the Riet induced him to leave Douglas on the 3d and return to Belmont. Babington also returned to the main camp without accomplishing his object.

A mixed force occupied Zoutpans Drift, about 20 miles east of Orange River Station on January 6th.

Griqualand West and British Bechuanaland have practically joined the Boers, and Kuruman, the capital of the latter, surrendered on January 2, with 12 officers and 108 men.

On the southern border of the Orange Free State, Gat-acre had retired towards Sterkstroom, French was at Arundel and Rendsburg, and Naauwpoort and De Aar were occupied by British reserves. On December 31st, leaving in Rendsburg a half-regiment and a section of horse artillery, French advanced with 5 squadrons of cavalry, 80 men, mounted infantry and 10 guns against Colesberg. He occupied a position to the west of Colesberg and made a demonstration in the direction of the railroad junction north of Colesberg. The Boers (1,000) retired in the direction of Norvals Pont, but on the morning of the 3rd of January, being reinforced, they returned and forced French to retire. He took up a position about 5 miles southeast of Colesberg. On the 6th he sent out Colonel Watson with a half-battalion of the Suffolk regiment, to occupy a small height about 2 miles-west of Colesberg, commanding the road to Philipstown. Colonel Watson advanced in close column to the top of the hill, and there, while giving his orders for the occupation of the position to the assembled officers, was surprised by the Boers and lost one-third of his force. French remained operating in the vicinity of Colesberg.

In Natal the situation remained practically unchanged. Joubert, who had been absent, ill since December 6th, had resumed command of the Boer forces north of the Tugela on December 18th.

The Siege of Ladysmith.

Before proceeding to consider Buller's third attempt to relieve Ladysmith, let us interrupt the narrative of events in the active armies and cast a glance at the military situation in and about this beleaguered city.

Ladysmith, on account of its natural advantages, its position on the railroad and its situation (well to the north) in Natal, was long ago selected as a depot of supply and point of support for this colony. Had it been properly fortified and adequately supplied with supplies and material, as well as with a strong infantry garrison, in addition to the necessary artillery; it would probably never have been besieged, or, if so, it could have held out indefinitely. As it was, there were, at the outbreak of the war, only four months' provisions on hand, and about three hundred rounds of ammunition per piece. A few batteries of heavy guns on the surrounding hills, with strong bridge heads on the Tugela at Colenso and on the Bushmans and Mooi rivers, would have protected the city as well as the line of communications. But the British underrated the power of the two Republics, and so were loath to make the proper preparations. Had the Boers been trained in siege operations, the place would probably have fallen.

The town lies in a valley, on both sides of the Klip River, and is commanded on all sides by high hills, which, on the north, run in a ridge close to the river, on the south consist of more isolated hills, separated from Ladysmith by a broad plain. Outside of this nearer chain of hills is another line encircling them, but rising somewhat higher.

The position of White was on a ridge beginning at Helpmakaar Hill east of the town (nearly half-way between the town and Lombards Kop), and running in a horseshoe bend to the north of it, bending in the west and around by the southeast of the town, near the railroad bridge over the Fouries Spruit. In front of this general ridge on the south side, several other points were occupied: Maiden Castle, Besters

Hill and Waggon Hill. The British position encircled Ladysmith—on the east at about 1½ miles, on the north close against the town, on the west at over 2 miles, and on the south at about a mile. The entire line measured about 13 miles, for the occupation of which White had originally about 12,000 troops, but this strength rapidly diminished to 9,000.

Outside of White's lines there was no high ground nearer than about 6,000 yards from the center of Ladysmith, which was a great advantage for the British. The Boer lines occupied the nearest chain of hills outside of the British lines, and this was about 3 miles on the north of Ladysmith, and 5 miles on the west and south.

The 14 works composing the British line were occupied as follows:

Helpmakaar	1st battalion Devonshire Regiment.
Cemetery Hill	1st battalion Liverpool Regiment.
Tunnel Hill	
Junction Hill	1st battalion Gloucestershire Reg't.
Gordon Hill	1st battalion Leicestershire Reg't.
Leicester Hill	
Cove Redoubt	Naval Brigade (Powerful).
	2d battalion Rifle Brigade
King's Post	King's Royal Rifles.
Range Post	2d battalion Royal Dublin Fusiliers.
Red Hill	1st battalion Royal Irish Fusiliers.
Highlandman's Post.	2nd battalion Gordon Highlanders.
Maiden Castle	
Caesar's Camp	1st battalion Manchester Regiment
Waggon Hill	2 squadrons Imperial Light Horse

The guns were distributed as follows:

Cove Redoubt (opposite Pepworth and Isimbulwana Hills)	One 4.7-in. navy gun.
Junction Hill	One 4.7-in. navy gun.
Gordon Hill	Three navy 13-pounders.
Ladysmith	6 field batteries (3G guns).
	Several 3-pdr. Hotchkiss guns.
	Two mountain guns.
	One machine gun for each infantry battalion and cavalry Reg't.

The Boer lines were 24 miles in extent, and were occupied by a force varying continually between 10,000 and 20,000 and by 22 guns:

Pepworth Hill (4 m. north of the town)	Long Tom (15.5 cm. or 6 in.).
	Two 12-pdr. field guns.
	Two 37 mm. R. F. guns.

"Long Tom," rendered unserviceable by the British, was replaced by another piece of the same kind.

Isimbulwana Hill	Slim Piet (6-in. Creusot).
Valley bet. Pepworth Hill and Surprise Hill	2 British guns captured at Nicholsons Nek.
Surprise Hill	One 4.7-in. howitzer. (Destroyed by the British.)
Lombards Kop	One 4.7-in. howitzer.
Between Lombards Kop and Isimbulwana Hill	Three field guns.
	Two 75 mm. mountain guns.
Beyond Caesar's Camp	One 4.7-in. howitzer.
	One field gun.

Other guns were behind the kopjes west of the town, and were moved about from point to point as required.

In reserve	One 37 mm. R. F. "Pom-Pom."
	Several Maxim guns.

The British had, therefore, but five guns which could reach the Boer guns of position, and these were the navy guns. Without them they would have been helpless.

Communication from Chieveley Camp with Ladysmith was kept up by means of a heliograph station on Mount Umkolumba, near Weenen, under Captain Kayser. The latter was in almost daily communication, and by the middle of January had sent over 41,000 words. There were also several balloons in Ladysmith, which did excellent service.

On January 6th the Boers made a strong attack on the British lines, especially on the outlying heights of Waggon Hill and Besters Hill. Some of the positions were taken and retaken three times during the day, but the Boers were repulsed. The British lost in this action 14 officers killed, 25 wounded; 135 men killed, 244 wounded.

The Boers lost (according to their own reports) 54 killed (including 5 field cornets) and 96 wounded; total 150.

It is remarkable that Buller did not attack the enemy with more energy at the same time that the latter attacked White, for Buller and White still communicated by heliograph, but he contented himself with a demonstration towards the Hlangwane Hill (east of Colenso), consisting merely in an artillery bombardment of the Boer position, to which the Boers did not even reply. His only chance of helping White effectively was by way of Springfield, for White's attack was towards the south, and he would naturally avoid the enemy's strong position at Colenso, in case he broke through the lines in his front, and strike westward.

This is the military situation at the beginning of the third act of the war.

Two grand movements open the third act. In Natal, General Buller decided on turning the right flank of the enemy's position by an advance over Springfield, Potgieters Drift and Trichards Drift on Acton Homes and Dewdrop; and in the west General Roberts developed his plan to turn the Boer position in his front.

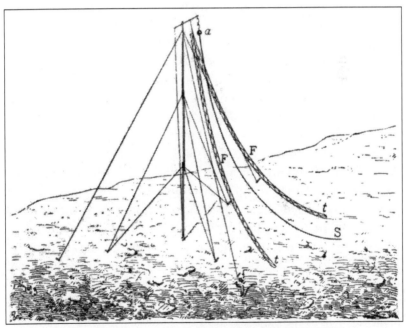

RECEIVING STATION, WIRELESS TELEGRAPHY.

THE CAMPAIGN IN NATAL.

The Second Attempt to Relieve Ladysmith.
Battles on the Upper Tugela.

The Boers occupied the plateau and rugged ridges constituting the foot-hills of the Drakensberg Mountains, from Acton Homes, over the Tabamyama Hills and Spion Kop to Grobelaars Kloof, and after the battle of Colenso had remained behind the Tugela, merely sending out patrols from the fortified Hlangwaneberg, and in the west over Springfield.

For some time after the battle of Colenso, General Buller had devoted his time to drawing in his reinforcements, concentrating at his headquarters in Frere all available forces, a large supply train, and a number of traction engines for the transportation of his artillery. The country as far as Springfield was carefully reconnoitered. A narrow-gauge road was also laid from Frere to Springfield. The enemy was deceived by feints indicating a projected advance around his left flank over Weenen.

General Buller's entire force comprised about 25,000 men.

Leaving only Barton's brigade (and several navy guns) at Frere to hold the enemy in front, and cover his lines of communication, he directed the rest of his command (about 20,000 men) westward towards the upper Tugela. The advance guard cavalry brigade of Dundonald and Warren's division left Estcourt on January 10th, and the brigades of Lyttleton and Hart (under General Clery) left Frere on the 11th, Hildyard's brigade following on the 12th. On account of the long train of 400 wagons and 5,000 draught and pack animals, and the precautions taken to insure safety, as well as the bad condition of the roads from heavy rains, Buller did not reach Springfield till the 13th, where a day's halt was ordered. Clery's Division was then sent on the road to Potgieters Drift, Dundonald and Warren on the western road to Trichards Drift, Buller's headquarters being located at Spearman's camp, a farm on the southern slope of the Zwarts Kop. His general plan was to hold the enemy in front at Colenso by means of Barton's brigade, to attack his right flank by Clery's Division in a northerly direction over the road between the Arnot Kop and the Brakfontein Kopjes or over the plateau to the east of Arnot Kop, pressing forward towards Ladysmith, but first to turn the Boer right flank by means

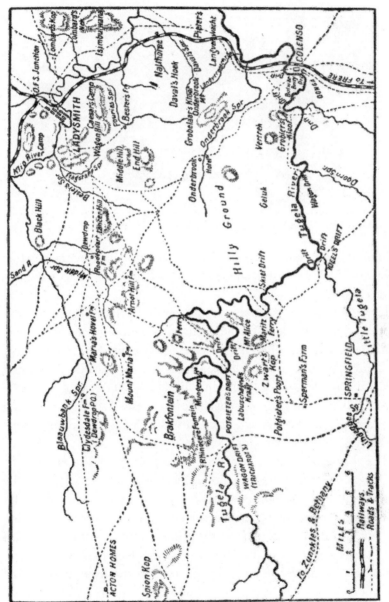

THE UPPER TUGELA.

TRACTION ENGINE WITH DYNAMO AND SEARCH-LIGHT.

of Dundonald's and Warren's columns, roll it up, secure the roads to Oliviers Hoek and the Bezuidenhout Pass, and join Clery's division over Dewdrop.

General Buller's operations, in spite or all the difficulties in the way, were so well concealed that the enemy was not aware of his real plan until he had crossed the Little Tugela and occupied the Zwarts Kop, although the movement of his columns had been noticed and in a general way preparations to receive his attack were made.

At Springfield provisional magazines were established for supplying the troops, and the enemy's position was carefully reconnoitered by means of anchored balloons.

The ford at Potgieters Drift was secured on the 11th, and on the 16th half of Lyttleton's brigade and a howitzer battery crossed the Tugela there. Six howitzers were promptly placed on One Tree Hill and the latter occupied, while the heavy guns were taken up Zwarts Kop on the south bank to cover the position on the north. Coke, with part of his brigade, was placed below Zwarts Kop to observe Schiets Drift; the remainder of his brigade guarded the train and lines of communication. The advanced position of the Boers on the spurs of Brakfontein Kopjes, immediately in front of Lyttleton, separated him completely from General Warren, who, after constructing a pontoon bridge at Trichards Drift, crossed there on the 18th. Warren had also part of the 2d and 3d divisions. Dundonald moved rapidly to the left and cleared the western side of Acton Homes, but Warren decided that the position of the Boers was too strong to turn, so he ordered Dundonald to fall back to Trichards Drift on the 19th, and directed his attention to the Spion Kop, which appeared to be the key to the position.

Action at Venter Spruit.

General Warren, on January 19th, had decided to modify his orders. Meanwhile, the Boers were making preparations to meet his attack. General Botha at Colenso received orders on the 19th to repair to the Upper Tugela and assume command. He rode all night and at 3 a.m. on the 20th arrived in the camp of General Schalk Burgher. The position was inspected and the disposition of the troops made.

On January 20th, General Warren placed two brigades (Woodgate's and Hart's) and 0 field batteries under General Clery to attack the Boer position. The latter was in the form of a semicircle around an amphitheatre containing Three Tree Hill. The Boers had not had time to construct trenches, but they built up with stones rude ramparts on their lines of defense.

The British advanced in two columns. One (comprising the 1st battalion South Lancashire Regiment and the 2d battalion Lancaster Regiment of Warren's brigade) deployed and moved out against two kopjes—Three Tree Hill and another to the east of it. The other (comprising the rest of Woodgate's brigade and all of Hart's) advanced to the west of Three Tree Hill and remained massed under cover. Hildyard's brigade remained in reserve.

The ascent of the kopjes was very difficult, and it was not until 7 a.m. that the artillery came into action on Three Tree Hill, at about 2,500 yards from the Boer defenses. At 7:30 a.m. the hill to the east was occupied by the British, when the Boers opened a heavy fire of musketry. At 11 a.m. the west column received orders to advance.

The Boer position was naturally very strong. The ground was broken and covered with rocks for the first part of the British advance, but for 1,000 yards from the Boer lines there was an open, gentle slope down toward the British position. The artillery of the latter also had very little effect against the Boer defenses.

At 3 p.m. the British artillery opened a rapid fire, and then the entire line started to advance over this open ground. The attacking

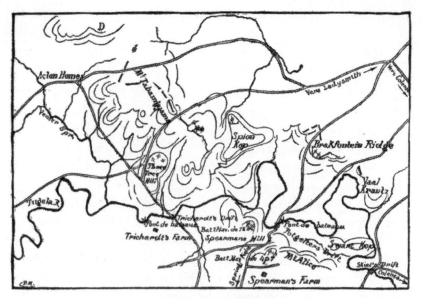

THE BATTLE OF SPION KOP.

troops, however, could make no headway, and gradually turned into the valleys instead of going up the slopes, and so the order to halt was given. At 7:30 p.m. fresh battalions from Hildyard's brigade were sent in to relieve the Lancashires.

The artillery of the Boers replied only at intervals to that of the British, constantly changing its position, and rarely firing more than three shots from any one.

Meanwhile, Dundonald's mounted brigade was active on the left of Hart's brigade, and took a hill about 1,700 yards to the west of the latter, holding it all night.

The troops bivouacked in their positions at night. On the extreme right Lyttleton made a demonstration in force against the Boer position opposite Potgieters Drift, but found the latter still strongly occupied. On the morning of the 21st it was found that the Boers on the right of their line had retired to a second line of crests defended like the first. The British occupied the line abandoned by the Boers.

The British artillery had great difficulty in coming into action on this day, because the position on Three Tree Hill was now out of range of the Boers, and there was no nearer position (except on the plain) available. Two field batteries were sent by Warren to strengthen the left, and four howitzers were sent by Buller to reinforce Warren.

Nothing was accomplished on the 21st. The two field batteries and the howitzers were placed on the plain between the Venter Spruit and the road to Acton Homes, and bombarded the Boer lines during the 22d and 23d, but produced no effect.

The troops in Ladysmith made sorties on the 20th and 22d, but without result; and Barton, at Chieveley, made a weak demonstration on Hlangwane Hill.

Action on the Spion Kop.

On the 23d, since the Boer lines appeared to be very thin, an attack on Spion Kop was decided upon in order to break through them.

General Woodgate was designated to command the forces, comprising the advance under Colonel Thornycroft (6 companies mounted infantry, 194 men and 1 company of engineers) and a reserve of two companies of the South Lancashire and the Imperial Light Infantry.

The height was scaled in the night of the 23d and 24th, and at 3 a. in. the troops arrived at the summit, where they surprised and drove off a small Boer outpost. They at once intrenched, but a heavy fog prevented them from appreciating their real position. At 8 a.m. the fog raised, and they found themselves enfiladed by the Boers.

The outpost of Boers, driven off by the British, had given warning, and in the fog the Boers managed to bring five guns to bear on the British position, as well as two Maxim-Nordenfelts, and had sent up two strong columns to retake the position, so that when the fog raised at 8 a.m. they opened with artillery and musketry, on the British trenches, and by 10 a.m. the British were driven to the southern extremity of the plateau. General Woodgate fell mortally wounded, and was succeeded by General Coke, who arrived in the afternoon with reinforcements, but later Colonel Thornycroft was assigned to the chief command. The two battalions of Coke's brigade were sent as reinforcements and arrived about noon.

The extreme right, under Lyttleton, continued its efforts against Brakfontein, and also sent reinforcements to Thornycroft: the Scottish Rifles and the 60th Rifles back over Potgieters Drift, and up stream to a ford, where they again crossed to the north side, then the former went up Spion Kop by the same path as the original troops, while the latter followed along the foot of the Spion Kop, then up to the north salient of the east side.

British soldiers lie dead on the battlefield after the Battle of Spion Kop, 24 January 1900

The arrival of these reinforcements during the afternoon (4:30 p.m.) enabled the British to hold out till evening. Preparations were being made to send up the 4th mountain battery and two naval 12-pounders, and part of Hildyard's brigade was assembled at the foot of Three Tree Hill, with orders to attack Tabamyama in the morning, but Colonel Thornycroft was not informed of these measures.

The troops on the plateau on the Spion Kop had suffered severely, and therefore Colonel Thornycroft decided to abandon the position in the night, commencing his retreat at 8:30 p.m.

On the 25th Buller arrived in person at Trichards Drift, and gave orders to retire over the Tugela.

On the 27th, General Warren's troops were taken to the south bank of the Tugela. The passage was accomplished without accident or loss, and the command deserves high praise for this feat, for, besides the troops and the guns (6 field batteries, 4 howitzers and the machine guns), there were 489 wagons—namely, 232 ox-wagons, 98 ten-mule teams, 107 six-mule teams, 52 four-mule teams.

Lyttleton's brigade was also partly drawn to the south bank, but the Zwarts Kop was held, as well as One Tree Hill.

Buller's plan was evidently to begin the turning movement at Acton Homes, but Warren, not being able to make any progress on the extreme flank of the Boer position, and recognizing the importance of

Spion Kop, decided to fall back and take that first, with a view to then advancing on the Fair View—Rosalie road (branching to the right from the Trichards Drift—Acton Homes road). In other words, he converted Buller's plan for a turning movement into what practically became again a purely frontal attack. He reported his decision at once to his superior, but the latter was too far away to control his actions in time. In a similar way, after Spion Kop was taken, it was abandoned, without consulting General Warren, by the immediate commander, Thornycroft (Woodgate having been wounded). In both cases orders were given by subordinates entirely upsetting the main plans of their superiors.

The forces at this time were distributed somewhat as follows:

The Boers had in all about 30,000 men—12,000 at Lady-smith, 3,000 at Colenso, and about 15,000 on the heights of the Tabamyama and Brakfontein.

The British had for the turning movement about 12,000 in all—Lyttleton 3,000, Hart 2,000, Hildyard 3,000, Wood-gate 4,000 and Dun do raid 800.

The losses of the British in this turning movement were 216 killed, 671 wounded and 315 missing; that of the Boers is reported at 1,200. Buller's total losses between the 17th and 24th amounted to 87 officers and 1,652 men.

The Boers at Spion Kop

THE THIRD ATTEMPT TO RELIEVE LADYSMITH.

Battle of the Vaal Kranz.

On January 30th Dundonald's cavalry, in order to draw the attention of the Boers to their western flank, made a demonstration towards Hongers Port (11 miles above Waggon Drift), still further destroying the bridge there.

On February 3d the British artillery on Zwarts Kop and Alice Hill opened a heavy fire on the Boer position north of the Tugela. Buller's object was to prepare for his advance over Potgieters Drift and Mole Drift, just below, his most direct route towards Ladysmith.

Opposite Potgieters Drift the first line of hills is that of One Tree Hill, and beyond that rises another ridge (a spur of the Brakfontein Kopjes) called the Vaal Kranz. To the east of these hills, near the bend of the Tugela, rises the Mole Spruit Kop and further north the Dornkloof Berg, the latter permitting of a flank fire on the Vaal Kranz, and being itself flanked by the western spurs of the Onderbrook Plateau (especially the Kranz Kloof).

The only position north of the Tugela held by the British after the retreat of Warren over Trichards Drift was the One Tree Hill ridge, about LJ miles northeast of Potgieters Drift, which Lyttleton's brigade had occupied. The rest of General Buller's army was encamped between Spearman's Farm and Springfield.

On February 4th the British troops broke camp, Clery's Division marching towards the valley behind the Zwarts Kop, while Warren's moved towards Potgieters Drift. Wynne's brigade (11th) and 6 field batteries crossed the Drift on the evening of the 4th and relieved Lyttleton's brigade.

The plan of attack was as follows:

Wynne's[2] brigade, with the field batteries, was to move over One Tree Hill and demonstrate against the Brakfontein Heights, while the main attack was to proceed over a second pontoon bridge (to be constructed farther east), directed against the southern spur of the Vaal Kranz. The batteries with Wynne were to retire in echelon, and then support the main attack. In support of the general movement a

---

2 Wynne succeeded Woodgate, the latter having been wounded.

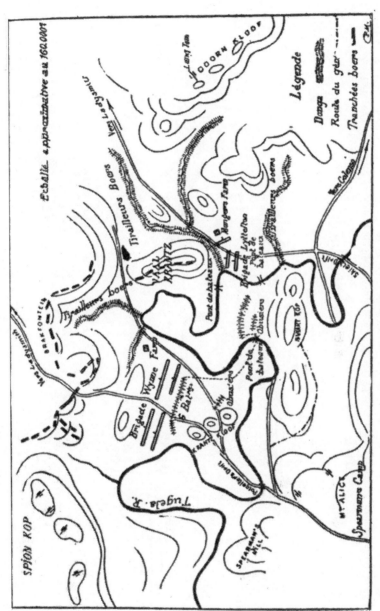

BATTLE OF THE VAAL KRANZ

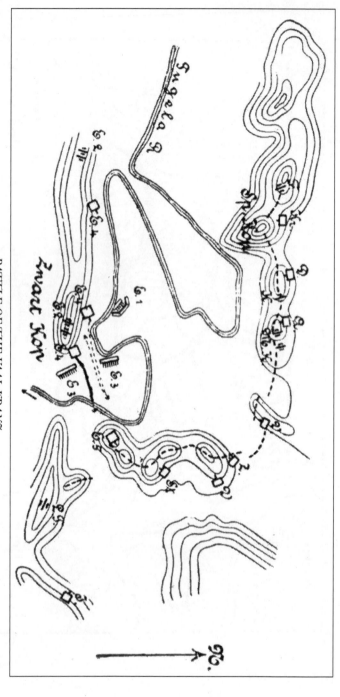

BATTLE OF THE VAAL KRANZ

----- Boer trenches.

L. T. - Long Tom, arrived from Ladysmith on night of February 6.   M. K. - Maxim and Krupp guns, brought from Spion Kop.
K. - Krupp gun.   F. - Schneider gun.   J., St., V, V, Z., A, D, Kr., - Boer Laagers.   E 1 - British battery, entrenched.   E 2 - British howitzer battery.
E 3 - British field batteries (4).   E 4 - British infantry advancing.   E 5 - British infantry on evening of February 5.

battery of six 4.7-inch guns had been established on Mount Alice, and six navy 12-pounders and two field 15-pounders on the Zwarts Kop.

The 1st brigade of cavalry (13th and 14th Hussars and a horse battery under Burn Murdock) was to attack the Brakfontein Plateau on the right of Clery's division, while the 2d brigade (volunteers with a battery of machine guns under Dundonald) was to protect the right flank against a Boer advance from the Doom Kloof; Coke's brigade was held in reserve. Buller had been reinforced by eight G-inch howitzers from the siege train, and three batteries of naval guns.

On the morning of February 5th, about 7 o'clock, the British field batteries (five) moved out and took position, in front of One Tree Hill Ridge, and opened fire, together with a howitzer battery farther in rear, and the six 4.7-inch guns on Alice Hill.

Wynne's brigade advanced slowly in open order. At 1,600 yards from the enemy's position the advanced line halted.

Meanwhile Lyttleton's brigade moved along the foot of the Zwarts Kop, and the engineers laid the second pontoon bridge.

At 10 a.m. the first British battery limbered up and proceeded along the Tugela to the first pontoon bridge and crossed over; the other batteries followed at intervals of half an hour. As soon as the artillery began this movement, the Boer artillery opened at about 5,000 yards. At 1 p.m. Wynne's brigade received orders to retire.

The second pontoon bridge was completed at 12 m., practically without any losses. The batteries took position northeast of the Zwarts Kop, and, after felling trees to mask their position, opened fire and continued the bombardment for two hours, when the principal attack began.

Lyttleton's brigade crossed first and advanced against the Vaal Kranz. Monger's Farm on the British right flank was taken. Meanwhile, the artillery (70 guns) concentrated on the left flank, opened at 2,400 yards on the Vaal Kranz Ridge. The Boers were taken completely by surprise and the ridge was captured by the Durham battalion. But the Boers promptly took measures to meet the British advance, and guns were rapidly placed on the Brakfontein spurs. The Boer infantry, rapidly concentrating at the northern end of the Vaal Kranz, drove the British from the east side of this ridge. By evening of February 5th, Lyttleton occupied about 1,000 yards of the west side of the Vaal Kranz. The tactical value of the Vaal Kranz had been greatly overrated, and it was now seen that, from their position on it, it was impossible to take the Boers in flank.

At sunset Hildyard's brigade relieved Lyttleton's. An attempt was made to capture the British position, but it was repulsed. During the night the Boers placed a 6-inch Creusot gun on the Doom Kloof, and on the morning of the 6th opened on the British with musketry, and shell fire. The position of the Boers was exceedingly strong, as the British advance would have been practically through a defile between the Spion Kop on the west and the Doom Kloof on the east, both almost impregnable. Buller, instead of outflanking the Boer position, found himself outflanked, and since it became known through balloon reconnaissance that the Boers had placed a Cinch gun in position on the Doom Kloof, and it was recognized that the latter must be taken by a frontal attack to clear the road to Ladysmith, Buller gave orders at 9 p.m. on February 7th for the retreat over the Tugela to Spearman's camp. Two days later the main part of the army was back in Chieveley.

The British lost 2 officers killed, 16 wounded; 24 men killed, 280 wounded and 5 missing.

In consequence of Buller's defeat the Boers began a number of demonstrations indicating a projected strategic advance against the British lines of communication. Joubert pushed out a considerable force over the Tugela towards Chieveley, occupying Bloy's Farm and the Doom Kop; other troops crossed at Bridle Ford m miles west of Colenso) and at Robinson's Ford (6 miles west of Colenso), threatening Buller's line of communication. Cavalry skirmishes took place beyond the east and west flanks of the British at Chieveley and Springfield.

In Zululand a Boer column of about 2,000 men pushed on from Vryheid through Nqutuland and Ingogo, capturing the police station at Nqutu, and early in February took the Inkandhla magistracy, and threatened a move on Eshowe, the capital, 30 miles distant. Colonial scouts from north Zululand, however, occupied Eshowe.

THE CAMPAIGN IN THE SOUTH AND WEST.

Preliminary Movements.

During the period from the 6th of January to the 12th of February few movements of any importance took place in the southern and western theatres, but reconnoitering was carried on continually, and led to many minor engagements.

Colonel Pilcher stationed at Belmont, to secure the railroad there, was ordered to Sunnyside on January 1st to prevent the reported assembly of hostile troops in that vicinity. He surprised 200 Boers, taking 40 prisoners. The rest retired on Douglas, followed by Pilcher, but on the approach of Boer reinforcements down the Riet River, the latter returned to Belmont.

General Babington, with the 12th Lancers, sent to support Pilcher on the 2d, also returned to the camp on the Modder River on the 4th.

Lord Roberts arrived at Cape Town on January 10th, but awaited there the arrival of the 6th and 7th divisions.

General French, near Colesberg, displayed the greatest activity. His efforts were directed to taking Colesberg and securing the crossings of the Orange River at Bothos Drift and Norvals Pont, but he only succeeded in establishing himself on the heights south of Colesberg.

The British position at Colesberg was in the form of a wide semicircle, south of the town, with the Coles Kop (900 feet high) in the center, occupied by two 15-pounder guns. About 1,000 yards southwest of the Coles Kop the British held a small kopje, occupied by the Berkshire regiment, and 2 miles southwest of Coles Kop they had Porters Hill, occupied by two guns supported by a company of mounted infantry, while 2 miles farther south was the Rensburg camp; and about 3 miles northwest of Coles Kop two squadrons of Lancers were posted. The Boers at Colesberg were commanded by De Wet. French's activity resulted in causing 1,000 men to be drawn from the forces besieging Ladysmith and 600 from Magersfontein under Delarey, to strengthen De Wet.

On the 12th of February the Boers made an energetic attack and drove the British back to Rensburg. On the 13th the Boers continued the attack and forced the British (under Clements) to Arundel. French was ordered to the Modder River to command the newly formed cavalry division.

On the 26th of January the 6th division (Kelly-Kenny) arrived, and was sent over Port Elizabeth to Steynsburg and occupied Thebus, on the Rosmead (Middelburg)—Stormberg line (about 40 miles west of Stormberg). The 7th division (Tucker) arrived at Cape Town early in February, and was sent towards the Modder River.

On January 30th, Prieska, on the Orange River, 100 miles west of

Orange River Station, was occupied by a British force.

Colonel Plumer was encamped, early in February, at Krokodil Pool (about 65 miles north of Mafeking), with a strong Boer commando in his front, which held the kopjes commanding the road and river.

The Boers had abandoned their positions at Graspan and Belmont, in rear of Methuen's army, but on February 4th General Macdonald was sent with the Highland Brigade, the 9th Lancers and a field battery to Koodoos Drift, in order to prevent at that point the union of two Boer commandoes, which were advancing with a view to reoccupying Belmont. Macdonald would probably have succeeded in his attempt, but was recalled by Lord Roberts. He lost 3 officers and 5 men killed, 4 officers and 35 men wounded. On the 9th he was ordered back to the camp on Modder River.

LORD ROBERTS' CAMPAIGN.

The problem which Lord Roberts had to solve was by no means a simple one, but, for several reasons, he adopted the plan to take the 0th and the 7th division, as well as French's, and move to the east over Klip Drift, around Jacobsdal, on Bloemfontein, with a view to the speedy relief of Kimberley.

In the first place, Kimberly had nearly reached the limit of its powers of resistance, and although its garrison held 6,000 Boers to the spot, and not available for the active field army, still its loss would add this force to the Boer Army and deprive the British Army of the garrison of 2,600 men and 78 guns, not to mention the necessity for saving the valuable diamond-fields. In the next place, after the failure of Buller's third effort to relieve Ladysmith, it seemed useless to reinforce him and attempt any further movements in that difficult country, whereas an advance as projected in the western part of the Orange Free State would be over ground which would be in every way advantageous to the British. Moreover, such an advance would probably soon draw Boer troops, from in front of Ladysmith, and at least improve the chances of Buller's breaking through their lines.

The difficulties of the situation are traceable to the original splitting up of the forces, in consequence of which the British are now in four columns separated respectively by 240, 64 and 144 miles, or 448 miles between the extreme columns, and they are tied to these lines on account of the extreme difficulty of withdrawing the immense trains

TRACTION ENGINE AND STEEL CARS.

(2,000 transport animals and several hundred wagons per division) as well as the magazines of supplies and materials established on these lines. In addition, if an attempt were made to withdraw on any one of these lines, the Boers would promptly advance, and so threaten the communications on the others.

Moreover, Lord Roberts could not await the arrival of the 8th division (expected about the end of March), in order to build up an army of 50,000, and then advance into the Orange Free State according to the original plan, but was compelled to act promptly for the relief of the besieged places and of the general situation, with what forces were available for an advance—viz., the 6th and 7th divisions and Brabant's colonial troops, either against Cronje's army on the Modder, or against the Boer forces at Colesberg (Arundel) or Sterkstroom, leaving Buller in Natal to hold as many Boer troops as possible in front of him and away from the decisive theatre in the west.

On the 10th of February Lord Roberts arrived on the Modder River, and immediately proceeded to organize his army, gathering in all available cavalry and placing it under French, and filling up with volunteers and local troops, to form of the 6th and 7th divisions, recently arrived, together with the 1st division (Lord Methuen's) and the 9th brigade, an army of about 50,000 men, for an offensive advance for the relief of Kimberley against Cronje's army and Bloemfontein.

General Roberts formed his army into four divisions: 1st, Lord Methuen's; 6th, Kelly-Kenny's; 7th, Tucker's; 9th, Sir A. Colville's (formerly commanding Guard Brigade) and French's cavalry division, which had been ordered from Colesberg, Clements relieving French there.

The Guard Brigade was placed under the command of Pole-Carew (previously commanding the 9th brigade), while Colonel Douglas was given the 9th brigade. The 18th brigade was formed of volunteers and colonial troops (under Stephenson).

His train consisted of 700 wagons and 9,000 pack and draught animals.

General Roberts' Army.
9th Division: Colville.
    3d Brigade: Macdonald
    19th Brigade: Smith-Dorrien.

7th Division: Tucker.
   14th Brigade: Chermside.
   15th Brigade: Wavell.
6th Division: Kelly-Kenny
   13th Brigade: Knox.
   18th Brigade: Stephenson
1st Division: Methuen.
   1st Brigade: Pole-Carew.
   9th Brigade: Douglas.
Cavalry Division: French.
   3d Brigade: Gordon.
   2d Brigade: Broadwood
   1st Brigade: Porter.

His preparations were kept perfectly secret, and the activity of Buller in Natal, the appearance of Brabant's volunteers in front of Dordrecht, General Gatacre's movements and General Clements' resistance at Colesberg, all served to keep the enemy occupied, attracted his attention to other points in the theatre of operations, and prevented him from sending timely reinforcements to the Modder River.

The direction of Lord Roberts' attack was well considered. A front attack on Cronje's strongly fortified position at Spytfontein—Magersfontein was out of the question. A flank movement around Cronje's right flank, while it might relieve Kimberley, was tactically and strategically false: first, because Macdonald's operations near Koodoos Drift undoubtedly attracted the attention of the Boers in that direction; and secondly, because, even if successful, it would merely force Cronje back on his line of communications. An attack on Cronje's left flank had first to be directed on Prinsloo's strong position at Jacobsdal, then after that was taken, Cronje's position would be flanked, but in the meantime the latter would hare had plenty of time to change front, so that Roberts would have been compelled to make xi frontal attack after all.

In view of these considerations, Roberts decided to go around Cronje's left flank, and advance over Waterval and De Kiel's drifts (on the Riet) and Klip Drift (on the Modder) over Olifantsfontein, a maneuver which was both tactically and strategically sound, and promised great results. Tactically, it took the British army over open ground, and gave the relief column a direct and unoccupied route to Kimberley, and strategically it cut Cronje's line of communications with Bloemfontein.

Lord Roberts' plan was to leave Lord Methuen with the Guards Brigade at the junction of the Riet and Modder rivers in order to support the turning movement by a frontal attack on Cronje's position, while he with the cavalry under French, the Highland Brigade, the divisions of Kelly-Kenny and Tucker, as well as the new division, passed around Cronje's left flank. This involved a division of his forces, and, of course, gave the enemy an opportunity to attack the separated parts in detail, but his superior strength and the great results promised warranted his taking the risk.

On the 12th of February, French, moving over Enslin, Graspan and Ramdam, crossed the Riet at Waterval and De Kiels drifts, and after a march of 37 miles, the Modder at Klip Drift on the 13th. On the 14th he had an action with a Boer force at Roodekalkfontein, and, carefully reconnoitering on the way, passed between Olifantsfontein and Alexanderfontein into Kimberley on the 15th. The siege of Kimberley had lasted 122 days (October 15, 1899, to February 15, 1900). To cover his left flank, a detachment under Colonel Gordon was sent over Rondevals Drift (west of Klip Drift), which, after some slight engagements with Boer detachments, turned to the left and reconnoitered in rear of Cronje's position.

The 6th division, followed by the Highland Brigade, crossed the Riet at Waterval Drift on the 14th, reaching Klip Drift on the 15th. The other two divisions and Roberts' headquarters also crossed the Riet on the 14th, but at De Kiels Drift. A Boer commando of 2,000 men under De Wet, coming from Colesberg to reinforce Cronje, advanced from Koffeyfontein (9 miles below Waterval Drift) and captured a large British wagon train. Roberts, with his two divisions, turned on Jacobsdal, but found it abandoned and the Boers in retreat.

Cronje, it appears, was completely surprised by Roberts' movement, and not until reports of French's fight north of Klip Drift reached him did he have any clear idea of the situation. He promptly gave orders to retire from the Magersfontein position and to raise the siege of Kimberley, directing all the troops in this vicinity towards Bloemfontein. The interval between French (at Kimberley) and Kelly-Kenny (still south of the Madder River) enabled him to slip through.

On the 15th of February he assembled his troops, and on the 16th commenced his retreat eastward. His plan was first to move along the north shore of the Modder, and cross to the south at Paardeberg Drift. On the 16th Lord Kitchener (who was with the 6th division at Klip Drift) saw at daybreak immense clouds of dust moving eastward and at once concluded it was Cronje's army in retreat, and decided to pursue, sending the mounted infantry after his train. The British scouts found his rear guard at Roodekalkfontein, and Kelly-Kenny (who had crossed the Modder) hastened after him with Knox's brigade and captured a part of his train. On the 17th, French's cavalry division started from Dronfield to the Modder River in pursuit of Cronje. Stephenson's brigade was sent back over Klip Drift, along the southern bank of the Modder River to cut off Cronje's retreat in that direction. The two divisions with Lord Roberts were ordered to move on Bloemfontein, French was directed to hang on Cronje's rear, while Lord Methuen was sent up to Kimberley to restore the communications there.

Lord Roberts had in all about 53,000 men, but for his offensive movement only 40,000; Cronje had in all about 35,000 men: 5,000, which were moving from Jacobsdal on the southern road; 8,000, his main army, north of the Modder at Koodoos Rand Drift; 0,000 at Stormberg, and 10,000 from Colesberg, at this time near Koffeyfontein, marching against Roberts' right flank. About 6,000 had retired to the north and northeast.

Cronje reached Driput on the 16th, halted to rest, and continued his retreat in the night along the north bank of the Modder to Wolvekraal Drift. He was followed by Knox's brigade, which joining Stephenson's on the 17th at Klipkraal Drift, continued its advance thence along the south bank, towards Paardeberg Drift.

Battle of Paardeberg.

Cronje halted at Wolvekraal Drift (half-way between Paardeberg Drift and Koodoos Rand Drift), intending to cross there on the morning of the 18th. On the north side he was already cut off, as Broadwood's brigade and a horse battery (from Kimberley) had reached Koodoos Rand Drift on the evening of the 17th and occupied the heights there, and French with his other two brigades struck Cronje's wagon park at noon near Kameelfontein (north of Wolvekraal Drift).

Lord Kitchener, with the 6th division, accidentally passed

BOER TRENCHES AT PAARDEBERG

Paardeberg Drift, and so reached the point (on the south bank) just opposite Cronje's camp (on the north bank). The 9th division (over Weydrai) reached Paardeberg Drift in the night of the 17th, Smith-Dorrien's brigade crossing there to the north bank, while Macdonald's joined the 6th division on the south bank.

The British attacked from the south bank on the 18th, but could not take the Boer positions along the river bank, which had been intrenched during the night. On the 19th the 7th division and the naval brigade arrived. Lord Roberts decided to prepare for any further attacks by artillery fire, and located his artillery, consisting of about 50 guns, to shell the Boer laager, posting three field batteries and two naval 12-pounders south of the Modder at 2,000 yards from the laager; 1 howitzer battery and 3 4.7-inch naval guns on the north bank, enfilading the river-bed, in which was the laager, at 1,000 yards range. A concentric fire was thus brought to bear on Cronje's camp, which was kept up for several days, the infantry gradually drawing up closer by trenches thrown up at night.

The balloons did good service in locating vulnerable points not visible to the gunners. On the 24th they located the Boer caissons, which were promptly blown up by the artillery.

Several attempts were made by commandoes of Boers (under Botha and others from Natal) to break through the British lines, and reinforce Cronje, but they were all repelled with heavy loss. French's cavalry division was entrusted with the duty of warding off these attempts, and took position on both banks, facing east, supported by a part of the 7th division.

Cronje lost about one-fourth of his command during his week of heroic resistance. On the 26th he made a desperate effort to break through, but was repulsed, and on the morning of the 27th (the anniversary of Majuba Hill, where Cronje defeated the British) he surrendered.

The forces which capitulated amounted to 4,100 men, with 4 Krupp guns, 2 Maxim guns and 9 1-pounders. Among the officers who surrendered, besides Cronje and his brilliant chief of artillery, Major Albrecht, there were 10 commandants and 18 cornets.

The fruits of the victory were rapidly reaped in other quarters. Barkly West on the Vaal was occupied by a force detached from Methuen's command at Kimberley, and the country around Kimberley was gradually taken under British control again. Colonel Plumer received reinforcements from Rhodesia, to enable him to attack the Boer position at Crocodile Pools.

General Roberts moved his headquarters to Osfontein, his main army facing eastward, on both banks of the Modder River, while his cavalry under French scouted towards Bloemfontein. The main Boer position was between Abrahams Kraal and Aasvogel Kop, behind the Kaal Spruit. General Joubert came with the reinforcements from Natal and had the supreme command. The advanced Boer line was held by Lukas Meyer, extending over Petrusburg, Bosch-kop and Wolvespruit.

THE SOUTHERN THEATRE OF WAR.

The effect of Cronje's surrender made itself felt at once in the other theatres of operations, in spite of the great distances separating them. The central position of the Boers gave them the advantage of interior lines, and enabled them to transfer quickly troops from one part of the general theatre to another, where they were most needed at the time; but the strategic advance of the Boers was too extended for the forces at their disposal, and they tried to cover too great an extent of country; consequently, when the British gained the superiority in numbers, they could no longer weaken any part to reinforce another temporarily, because the distances were so great that they could not hope to bring such troops back in time to meet a British advance at the depleted point.

About the time that Roberts began his advance, the Boers under Delarey, in the southern theatre, gained some marked successes, forcing the British first from Colesberg and then from Rensburg back to Arundel. But just as they were ready to threaten Roberts' line of communications, reinforcements had to be sent to Cronje: De Wet from Colesberg, and others from Dordrecht, Molteno and Naauwpoort. His entire force was about 10,000 strong, and after leaving 2,000 at Arundel, he sent the rest to threaten Roberts' right flank, and, if possible, reinforce Cronje.

On the 18th of February General Brabant entered Dordrecht, and the British forces advanced to the line Barkly East—Jamestown—Colesberg. Lord Kitchener, after Cronje's surrender, came in person to this portion of the theatre to direct the advance.

'The Relief of Ladysmith' by John Bacon
Sir George White welcomes Major Hubert Gough with these words "Hello Hubert, how are you?" Shortly afterwards, moved by the ovation given him by his soldiers and townsfolk, he acknowledged their support and ending with these words "Thank God we have kept the flag flying".

On February 27th General Clements reoccupied Rensburg and Colesberg, and on the 28th Colesberg Junction, the enemy retreating on Norvals Pont.

On the 22d and 23d Gatacre reconnoitered towards Stormberg and had a severe skirmish there.

THE SITUATION IN NATAL.

The Fourth Attempt to Relieve Ladysmith.

In order to prevent the Boers in Natal from sending reinforcements of the western theatre, and if possible to relieve Ladysmith, Buller began a new offensive movement on the 17th of February. This time his attack was directed on the Hlangwane Berg, east of Colenso, in order to gain possession of the nearer bank before attempting to cross the Tugela. As early as the 12th of February he had made a reconnaissance of Hussar Hill, 6 miles northeast of Chieveley, and finding the Boer lines marked by Colenso, Hlangwane Hill, Green Hill, Monte Christo and Cingolo, he determined to turn the left flank of this position; on the 14th he had directed his troops on Hussar Hill,

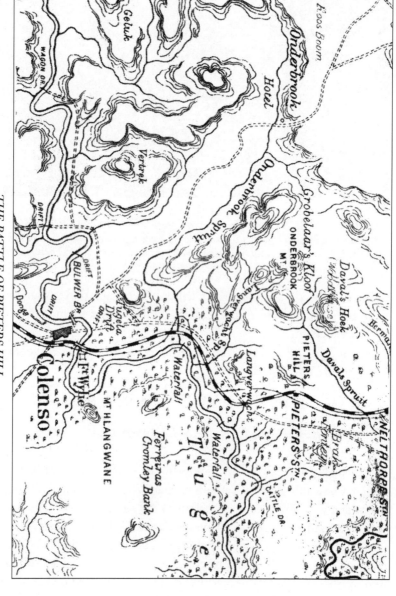

THE BATTLE OF PIETERS HILL

the irregular cavalry supported by two infantry battalions covering the left flank, Dundonald's cavalry covering the front of advance. The latter had taken Hussar Hill after a slight skirmish at 8 a.m. on the 14th, and by night the British troops were intrenched in the position. The 15th was devoted to artillery fire on the enemy's line.

On the 16th the real advance began. The 2d division (Lyttleton, who had replaced Clery, the latter being ill) and Wynne's brigade were to march eastward and make a grand turn to the left, while Dundonald's cavalry brigade, crossing the Blaauwkrass River, was to pass farther to the eastward and scale the hill of Cingolo; Barton's brigade was to remain with the artillery, and the latter (66 pieces) was to prepare the advance by firing on Green Hill, where the Boers had a heavy gun and two light ones. Hart's brigade was to guard the railroad.

Cingolo was occupied by a Boer outpost only, and was quickly taken by Hildyard's brigade. It became evident in this attack that the Boers were still in force here; consequently, on the 17th, three brigades were ordered to attack the heights: Barton's on the left, to demonstrate; Hildyard's on the right, to make the principal attack; the 4th brigade (Norcott's) in reserve on its left rear; Dundonald covering the right. The ascent was very difficult. The troops bivouacked on the ground gained. On the 18th the attack was resumed. The artillery opened at 8 a.m., and Hildyard's brigade (with Norcott's on its left) advanced against Monte Christo, which was taken by 11 a.m. The Boers, being taken in flank, were compelled to evacuate Green Hill and Hlangwane Berg, which were occupied by Barton's brigade, the artillery moving up.

Buller's troops gradually forced the Boers back, and on the 20th the latter evacuated the south bank of the Tugela, and a battalion of Hart's brigade (from Chieveley) occupied Colenso. where they found the bridge destroyed.

The Battle of Pieters Hill.

On the 21st of February Buller threw a pontoon bridge over, below Colenso. The British troops crossed the Tugela and attacked Grobelaars Kloof on the 21st of February, but without much success. The British artillery, posted on Green Hill and the Hlangwane Berg, supported the advance.

The mounted infantry occupied the hills north of Colenso, and at noon the 5th division crossed the pontoon bridge, followed by Hart's brigade, while a battalion of the 10th brigade (Coke's) advanced against Grobelaars Kloof. The Boers, however, forced back the attack. On the 22d the struggle was renewed. This time the attack was directed on Pieters Hill, but again without success. The whole of Buller's army was now over the Tugela near Fort Wylie, the Boer position in a semicircle before it. On the 23d another effort was made to take Pieters Hill, but this also failed. Buller intrenched his infantry, and on the 24th moved with his artillery back over the Tugela, followed by the infantry; he destroyed this pontoon bridge, and in the night threw another pontoon bridge over the Tugela nearer Pieters Station at the mouth of the Langverwacht Spruit. On the morning of the 27th, Barton's brigade crossed the bridge and stormed Pieters Hill. Meanwhile, Warren (with the 4th and 11th brigades) attacked the western heights, and Dundonald, with four squadrons of cavalry, moved on to Ladysmith, which he entered on the 28th, thus relieving this city after 120 days' investment.

The Boers retired from their positions in the vicinity of the town towards the mountain passes, and Buller moved on Nelthorpe on the 28th. The Boer forces had been greatly weakened by reinforcements sent to the western theatre.

Buller's losses between February 16th and 27th amounted to 1,859: 252 killed, 1,512 wounded and 95 missing.

The total casualties in Ladysmith during its investment were 24 officers and 235 men killed, 70 officers, 520 men wounded, 6 officers and 340 men died of disease.

On February 27th Hart was placed in command)f the 2d Division, Clery having been injured; Colonel Kitchener (a brother to Lord Kitchener) received the 11th brigade, Wynne having been wounded; and Colonel Norcott the 5th brigade in place of Hart, promoted.

Buller moved his troops up to Nelthorpe on the 28th of February.

COMMENTS.

In this campaign the great principles of strategy and tactics appeared in some cases to be violated at the outset, but closer inspection and further developments invariably showed the fallacy of such a conclusion. One of these great principles is the old-established maxim that, in spite of all the boasted defensive power of modern intrenchments and the immensely increased effect of modern fire-arms, only the offensive (strategical and tactical) can lead to decisive results.

With the British the spirit of the strategical and tactical offensive was innate, and the 'reason it did not make itself felt in the earlier stages of the campaign was due to several causes. In the first place, their entire system, both as regards organization and practical field training, was somewhat imperfect. Their field maneuvers were inadequate to teach practically either the proper tactical employment of the separate arms, or that of the three arms combined, to impart knowledge of correct estimation of their own or the enemy's fire-effect, or to impress the troop leaders with the necessity for flank attacks in proper form in modern battle tactics.

This accounts for the fact that the offensive of the British was strategically unsound, in that the forces were too much subdivided, too greatly scattered, and not applied with the best effect; and in that the enemy was greatly underrated and the general situation very imperfectly known. Moreover, tactically the execution was poor, in spite of great bravery on the part of the officers and men, on account of antiquated battle formations and tactics.

The service of reconnaissance and the mobility of the troops were no doubt affected by the climate and the terrain, and the difficulties of the former were greatly increased by the character of the ground, the lack of good maps, the use of smokeless powder and the manner of fighting of the Boers, and these causes also interfered with the best use of the artillery; nevertheless, as will appear later, the well-planned and prepared offensive advance (that of General Roberts), executed with rapidity and energy, promptly compelled the Boers to give up their fastness at Magersfontein, so that it was evidently previous mistakes in strategy and tactics that caused the failure of so many efforts, not the climate or the terrain, much as they may have increased the difficulties.

The Boers, on the other hand, in spite of their original offensive advance with its brilliant results, do not really possess the spirit of the offensive strategically, and are not capable of executing the offensive tactically, as shown by the subsequent events. On a small scale there were, on the part of the Boers, occasional offensive attacks and pursuits, as in some of the actions in Cape Colony, but never with large bodies of troops. For cohesive attack they lack the necessary leaders, training, discipline and tactical organization, and for energetic and prompt pursuit they lack cavalry, for although every Boer is mounted, he is not in a true sense a cavalryman.

The Defensive and the Offensive.

At first sight it would appear that the plainest lesson taught by the Boer war is the apparent impossibility of attacking successfully in front a fortified position—in other words, the impossibility of so silencing even a weak artillery on the defensive, and so demoralizing a good infantry line on the defensive, as to enable the attacking infantry, without too great loss, to move to the attack over open ground.

Both at Magersfontein and at Colenso the English artillery was superior to that of the Boers, and especially was this the case in the later actions on the upper Tugela and on the Vaal Kranz. In all these cases the British artillery could not dominate that of the Boers, and in the first two actions referred to the British greatly overrated the effect of their artillery. At the last mentioned action the infantry advance was indeed prevented by the Boer artillery alone.

Many authorities conclude, therefore, that our ideas on this point of tactics must be modified accordingly. It is at present stated in all tactics that the first duty of the attacking army is to silence by means of its artillery that of the enemy; then to concentrate its artillery fire on the enemy's-infantry at the point of principal attack. But from the above it appears that the artillery of the defense may withdraw temporarily (be apparently silenced) and then turn up in full power at the moment of the decisive infantry attack. But these conclusions must not be arrived at hastily. There are many considerations that must first be settled before we can determine whether the English artillery actually followed modern tactics in its employment of this arm. It appears, on the contrary, that the batteries were brought into action separately, and seldom really attained concerted fire-action on the decisive point of attack; moreover, they had at first no pieces for curved fire (recognized everywhere as essential nowadays in the attack on intrenchments), and finally, the difficulties of the ground were such as to exclude anything approaching ideal action as a general rule. Consequently, it is better to wait till more complete data are available, before laying too great stress on the power and advantages of the defensive.

In fact, if there is one lesson that does stand out prominently and definitely, throughout the Boer War, it is the necessity for adopting the offensive in order to secure decisive results. In other words, the exact opposite of the conclusion above suggested, which would give the preference to the defensive.

The indecisive results even of the Boer victories can only be attributed to their lack of offensive power, either in attacking the British in intrenched positions (as at Ladysmith), or, after defeating the British attack (as at Dundee, Colenso and Magersfontein), in taking up a proper offensive counterattack, thereby making their victory complete. An active and energetic offensive at Ladysmith and on the Tugela would have led to results very different from the passive defensive actually adopted, and the Boers could have met the advance of Roberts with very different forces from those which they were actually enabled to assemble. Moreover, a more energetic offensive south of the Orange River would have made it possible to penetrate farther into the British domain, and would have afforded a better chance of encouraging the Dutch inhabitants to rise and join their Boer countrymen.

The old principle of strategy, therefore, still holds true; viz.: that the best mode of action for decisive results is the strategical and tactical offensive. The resorting to mere frontal attacks and the remaining on the tactical defensive and indulging in mere position actions are signs of mediocre ability. If the enemy adopts the tactical defensive, the advantages of his mode of action must be overcome by proper strategic deployment and advance and by increased mobility, to force him from his positions, to obtain the superiority in numbers, not at all points of the line, but at the decisive points, and to keep him moving, thus preventing him from occupying continually strong positions. All this requires a well-trained cavalry for reconnaissance, an artillery with proper material as well as one trained in the correct tactical employment of this arm and in hitting, and, finally, an infantry instructed to shoot accurately and move rapidly.

Railways.

One of the characteristic features of modern warfare is the part played by railroads. The power of effecting rapid concentration which they confer causes their direction and location to determine the lines of advance of the main armies, and their points of crossing or branching fix the strategical points in the theatre of war where the great battles must be fought. The side that possesses or commands the

A British armored train

main lines at the opening of a campaign has an immense advantage, and this advantage in the present war was with the Boers.

Pretoria, the Transvaal capital, has radiating from it three main lines: one to Lorenzo-Marques, one to Durban, and one to Port Elizabeth; the latter with a branch from north of the Orange River to East London; a fourth main line runs west of the two Republics from Buluwayo to Cape Town. There are also two minor lines, one from Pretoria northward to Pietersburg, and one from Johannesburg southwestward to Klerksdorp.

The Boers, of course, made full use of these lines in their strategic deployment on the border, and in their subsequent advance, but the original disposition of their troops resulted mainly from the British forces at Dundee, Ladysmith, Mafeking and Kimberley; hence they concentrated the bulk of their armies on the Natal and the western frontier, neglecting the important points on the Orange River border. Had the British been able to conduct their campaign on purely military principles, untrammeled by political reasons for relieving these isolated points (Ladysmith, Kimberley and Mafeking), this neglect might have been at once fatal to the Boer strategy, for the military plan was, it is stated, to advance from the south directly on Bloemfontein and Pretoria over the Orange River.

The holding on to the isolated points above mentioned, had the same crippling effect on the Boers, therefore, that it had on the British movements, for it prevented the former also from carrying out their original plan of invading Cape Colony, concentrating in Natal at Pietermaritzburg, and forcing the point of main attack in the West far south of Kimberley. Had they carried out this plan, the problem for the British would have been a far more difficult one.

The Strategy of Buller's Campaign.

General Buller's plan to turn the Boer right flank over the upper Tugela is based on a correct strategical principle, but its success must depend on the forces available, for this was not a mere tactical maneuver, but a strategic operation on a large scale, involving an extension of the British base from Frere over Springfield to Trichards Drift, about 20 miles, before the actual turning maneuver can begin.

The Boer position was, moreover, naturally very strong and was occupied in force. Ultimate success in the turning movement depended on the rapidity of its execution, and this, in the face of all the difficulties of the situation, was practically impossible.

However, the left flank was the critical point of the British line, and there, north of Trichards was Buller's place, and not at Spearman's camp. The tactical value of that part of the Spion Kop which was the object of the attack was greatly overrated, on account of imperfect reconnaissance and poor maps, and, had Buller been originally with Warren's force, he probably would not have permitted the assault on this point.

The Boers, after Warren's failure, again neglected a splendid opportunity to reap the rewards of success in not pursuing. Even admitting that they were economizing their men, it is plain that an energetic pursuit might have almost annihilated Warren's command, in which case the Boers would have been spared the battles of the 5th and 7th of February, which also involved considerable losses to them. As it was, Buller's plan failed, but his strength was not broken, and he immediately proceeded to make and execute other plans for breaking through the Boer lines.

The Tactics of Buller's Campaign.

General Buller's third attempt to relieve Ladysmith was justified by the circumstances, for it promised success, and even if it failed, it held a certain number of Boers in Natal, and therefore away from

Roberts' front. Nevertheless, there are several points in the plan and its execution which are subject to criticism.

Once more imperfect reconnaissance led to overrating the tactical value of the Vaal Kranz, and consequently it was not known until after it was taken that it could not be held.

The two key points to the Boer position on the upper Tugela were the Spion Kop and the Doom Kloof, and yet in the two separate attacks on these points Buller did not put in all his available forces, nor did he act with the requisite energy in pushing the attack. In both cases the Boers were at first surprised, but the inadequacy of the forces employed prevented a rapid advance and gave them time to reorganize their lines, and repel the attack.

Buller's attack, moreover, does not appear to have been supported in the least by any demonstration on the part of Barton in front of Colenso.

This appears to have been the fault with all of Buller's battles. When he attacked the key point of a position he made no general attack along the entire line to prevent the enemy from reinforcing the threatened point—in fact, he allowed them every opportunity to do so at their leisure—Spion Kop, at the Vaal Kranz, at Pieters Hill. An energetic attack along the entire line would have prevented that constant shifting of forces by the Boers which enabled them to make such good use of their small force and their interior lines.

The Boers took no measures to reap the rewards of their victory. They neither pursued Buller's army over the Tugela, nor made any effort to defeat Barton and so cut off Buller's line of retreat.

The Strategy and Tactics of Roberts' Campaign.

General Roberts could have divided the reinforcements he received in the 6th and 7th divisions, but it would have been another case of splitting up the forces, so he decided to add them all to the left column.

The new troops amounted to 30,000 men and 9 batteries. Had one division only been added to Lord Methuen's army, he would have had 25,000 men and 78 guns; and had the other division been assigned to French's command, and Gatacre's also added, this column would have had 24,000 men and 60 guns; Brabant's division would have been available to reinforce either column. The total of the British field forces in this theatre would have been about 60,000 men and 138 guns.

The Boers had about 20,000 at Magersfontein, 15,000 at Colesberg, and 6,000 at Stormberg, or a total of 41,000.

Evidently, Roberts could have advanced on both lines, but by combining all his reinforcements on one the results were more decisive and also more rapid.

General Buller on the Tugela was compelled to inaction. It was very difficult for Roberts to leave this army of 30,000 men and 78 guns inactive, but had Ladysmith fallen, the besiegers, 20,000 in number, would have been at once available in other theatres and the British would have lost the chance of having the garrison of 8,000 added to their ranks in case of a successful sortie. Therefore, there was nothing else to do but let Buller detain as many of the enemy as possible in his front.

The results of Lord Roberts' victory stand out in marked contrast with the early successes of the Boers on the Modder, at Colenso and at Stormberg: whereas the latter were isolated successes, with no decisive effect on the general situation, the former entailed the retreat of the Boers along their entire line of defense as far east as Natal. The cause is not far to seek, and illustrates on the one hand the weakness of the purely defensive, and on the other the power of the strategical and tactic offensive combined with a definite plan of action.

The Strategy and Tactics of the Boers.

The strategic deployment of the Boers and their advance over such widely separated lines (Natal, Cape Colony and the West) was in accordance with sound principles of strategy. The advance into Natal was demanded because of the presence there of the main British force and the shortness of their line of communications; that into Cape Colony and the West was necessitated by the immense importance of gaining possession of the railroad net-work, which was so essential for the rapid advance of the British, and also the desire to gain reinforcements from the Afrikaner population in these districts. Nevertheless, the three lines should have been treated differently in a tactical sense, for, while a tactical, as well as strategical, offensive was quite in place in Natal, the southern and western theatres warranted (and in view of the limited Boer force, commanded) the tactical defensive, provided the strategic measures were sufficient. But the latter was hardly the case, for the Boer efforts against the line De Aar—Kimberley were not on a scale corresponding to its vast importance to the British. In the early stages of the campaign this line was occupied by such weak British forces that it would have been very easy to have destroyed considerable stretches of it; moreover, even in the later stages there were many points vulnerable to such attacks. An effective destruction of this road, requiring considerable time to repair, might have fatally delayed Roberts' advance, or caused him to alter his plan. In addition, constant attempts to interfere with this all-important line would have revealed to the Boers the plan of the British, and probably prevented Cronje's surprise.

However, the fact that in general the tactical defensive was the proper role for the Boer troops in the West, should not have prevented them from taking up the tactical offensive after the defeats of Lord Methuen on the Modder River. Such an offensive after the battle of Magersfontein, when Lord Methuen still had the river in his rear, promised decisive results, and his further defeat would have prevented Lord Roberts from assembling his army in Cronje's immediate front, and would consequently have prevented him, from surprising Cronje by his flank movement.

The great weakness of the Boers, however, was the lack of the tactical offensive in Natal, where it was more particularly in place. This lack of the tactical offensive neutralized all the advantages of their strategical offensive advance, and enabled the British to transfer the decisive theatre to the West. Had the Boers followed up their strategic deployment and advance in Natal with an energetic tactical offensive, the British would have been forced to accept Natal as the decisive theatre, and all the advantage of topography and situation of the troops would have been with the Boers; or, in case the Boers won a decisive victory there, sufficient Boer forces might have been liberated to turn the tide in the West.

This tendency of the Boers to avoid the tactical offensive is apparent even in the selection of their defensive positions, which rarely admit of easy advance toward the front, and is further emphasized by their neglect of proper pursuit after victory.

The offensive requires a far higher capacity in the troop leaders than the defensive, and the Boer commanders were evidently not sufficiently trained in the art of war to meet these requirements. The defensive may be the stronger form, but the offensive is, nevertheless, the most effective. So long as the Boer defensive remained intact at all points of their line it succeeded, but the moment the British offensive broke that line at a single point the entire line was broken.

The Artillery Tactics of the Boers.

It is a principle, definitely established long before, but especially emphasized by the experiences of the Franco-Prussian war, that artillery fire, to be effective, must be concentrated.

The Boers seem at first sight to have upset this principle. They were able to select their ground, conceal their guns, and prepare their positions, and this, combined with the use of smokeless powder, which assisted the concealment, and the longer range of their guns, gave them such an advantage that military men began to think that isolated guns in well-concealed positions were better than masses of artillery, But, in reality, the old principle is still true, and it is only a question of modifying the application. The Boers, although adepts in hiding their artillery, never succeeded in concentrating its fire, and this is one of the secrets of their want of success.

PART IV.

The third act in the drama has closed, the decisive battle of the war has been fought, but there are still many elements of strife to be subdued, and finally the contending elements must be harmonized to restore peace and quiet permanently.

The third act closed with the defeat of Cronje, the advance of the British into the Orange Free State from the west, the relief of Kimberley, the retreat of the Boers from Cape Colony and in Natal, and the relief of Ladysmith.

The weakening of the Boer forces in Natal was very poor policy, for it failed to help Cronje on the one hand} and left the road to Ladysmith open on the other; moreover, it indicates a weakness in the leadership of the troops, for the proper course was undoubtedly to fall upon General Buller with all available forces, and to strike a blow there to counteract the disastrous events in the West. This separation of the forces was a serious mistake in strategy, but may have been called forth by the fact that the coalition between the Transvaal and Orange Free State was none too strong, and the discipline of the Boers comparatively weak, so that the Orange Boers preferred to protect their own land rather than help the Transvaal Boers to finish the campaign for both.

The forces at the opening of the fourth act (about the beginning of March) were distributed as follows:

In the Western Theatre.

Lord Roberts, after Cronje's capitulation, took up a position fronting to the east, on both sides of the Modder River, his headquarters at Osfontein (about 5 miles east of Paardeberg), the 6th division (Kelly-Kenny) on the right holding all kopjes to a distance 5 miles south of the Modder, the 7th division (Tucker) at the center close to the river, the 9th division (Colville) on the north bank, the cavalry (French) on the extreme left, and the mounted infantry (Colonel Ridley-Martyr) on the right. The troops were given a rest of several days, with a view to supplying them with full rations once more, reestablishing the communications and preparing for the advance on Bloemfontein.

The reconnaissance of the cavalry had developed the fact that the Boers were intrenching themselves on a series of kopjes about 8 miles east of Roberts' position, their position extending several miles north and south of the Modder. These troops were under the command of Delarey and De Wet, and numbered about 14,000. Other Boer columns were reported coming from the northwest of Kimberley and from the southeast towards Petrusburg.

Lord Methuen, from Kimberley, had occupied Boshof on the road to Bloemfontein, and had sent a column to relieve Mafeking.

In the Southern Theatre.

In Cape Colony the Boers (8,000) retreated towards the Orange River, followed by the columns of Generals Brabant, Gatacre and Clements. The forces confronting Roberts were partly these troops from the south. West of the De Aar—Hopetown line and in Griqualand West a serious uprising of the inhabitants took place, but Lord Kitchener, who was in charge of the lines of communication, with headquarters at De Aar, readily suppressed it.

In the Eastern Theatre.

In Natal, General Buller rested and reorganized his troops in Ladysmith camp, assembling a large force near Helpmakaar with a view to resuming the offensive at an early date, as soon as White's division would be ready for service again. The Boers under Joubert (20,000) occupied a position on the Biggarsberg, north of Ladysmith, their left near Dundee, with detachments in the passes of the Drakensberg as far south as Bezuidenhout Pass. This was still the main Boer army.

***

Such was the general situation at the opening of the fourth act. The country between Osfontein and Bloemfontein is not especially favorable for the Boer tactics, but their purpose probably was to delay Roberts as much as possible along this route, thus giving time for the main army to reorganize and establish itself on more favorable ground north of Bloemfontein, where the country is more hilly and broken, the crests often rising to a height of 8,000 feet above the sea.

For the British the campaign thus far had been a very severe one, especially on the horses of the cavalry, and some time was needed for their recuperation; moreover, the supplies had been short, owing to the loss of a considerable part of their train as well as the natural

Frederick Sleigh Roberts, 1st Earl Roberts, by John Singer Sargent

consequences of such strenuous efforts as the army recently made in the way of marching and fighting, and time was required to bring the supply of food and forage to the normal state again. The country was very poor in water and the army was therefore tied to the vicinity of the river.

The natural consequence of the British invasion of the Orange Free State was that many of the burghers left the Army to defend their own houses, and thus the Boer Army was greatly reduced in a comparatively short time, and the resistance to Roberts' advance was gradually weakened.

GENERAL ROBERTS' CAMPAIGN.

Battle of Poplar Grove.

On March 7th General Roberts continued his advance. French's division, composed of 3 brigades of cavalry, 2 of mounted infantry and 7 batteries, started at 1 a.m. in a southeasterly direction, followed by Kelly-Kenny's division, and at daybreak struck the left of the Boer lines, posted on a group of seven hills, hear Poplar Grove. French attempted to turn the left flank of the Boers by means of Porter's brigade and several guns. The British guns soon silenced those of the Boers, and Porter continued his advance, but came upon a second Boer position, farther to the rear, from which he received heavy musketry fire. He sent cavalry and mounted infantry against this position, but he had the enemy on two sides of him and so found himself in a difficult situation. However, the howitzers and guns of Kelly-Kenny's division came into play soon after this and forced the enemy in the advanced position, to retire from the hills in a northerly direction, thus freeing Porter.

The artillery of Kelly-Kenny advanced and attacked the second or actual Boer position, while the cavalry worked on the flanks. The Boers were gradually driven back, and, finally, when the cavalry threatened their line of retreat, they fled in confusion towards the north and east, pursued by the cavalry.

The British lost 1 officer killed and 4 wounded, 3 men killed, 46 wounded and 1 missing.

The British horse artillery did excellent service, and the fighting was practically confined to the cavalry, which was very nearly exhausted. The British captured 1 gun and great quantities of forage, stores, tentage, etc.

Roberts moved his headquarters to Poplar Grove.

The infantry on the north of the Modder River crossed to the south at Poplar Drift (opposite Poplar Grove), and General Roberts' further advance was continued along the south bank. The 7th division (Tucker) on the right, moving on the Petrusburg, road towards Aasvogel Kop; the left of the Boer position covering Bloemfontein. The 6th division (Kelly-Kenny) in the center, over the open country. The cavalry division (French) on the left close to the river, followed by the rest of the troops.

The Battle of Driefontein.

On the morning of March 10th Broadwood's brigade of French's division came in contact with the Boers at Driefontein, 8 miles south of Abrahams Kraal, and drove their outposts back, attempting then to outflank the position. The Boers kept up a heavy artillery fire. About 1 p.m. Kelly-Kenny's division arrived before the center and left of the Boers, and then Broadwood took his brigade to his left, made a wide detour and came upon the rear of the enemy before nightfall. Meanwhile, Kelly-Kenny's division attacked at the center and worked around the enemy's right flank. By 2 p.m. the horse batteries cleared the way for the infantry, which advanced to the attack. Finally, they stormed the kopjes at the charge, and took the heights at the point of the bayonet, but not until after a hard fight, lasting six hours.

The Boers were commanded by Delarey, and were mainly those from Colesberg. They had no time to intrench, although the heights afforded good natural positions,, and scattered rocks gave some shelter.

The British lost 7 officers killed and 10 wounded, 66 men killed and 313 wounded. The Boers left 173 dead on the field and 20 prisoners.

The strength of the British forces was about 45,000; that of the Boers about 12,000.

Lord Roberts reported to the Presidents of the two Republics that their troops had abused the privilege of the white flag, and of the signal of holding up the hands in token of surrender; and also that he had captured large quantities of explosive bullets, which are being used by the Boers. Lord Roberts reported to the War Office that the wounds, as a rule, are more serious than usual, owing to expanding bullets having been freely used by the Boers.

The Occupation of Bloemfontein.

After the battle Driefontein, Lord Roberts, instead of following, the retreating Boers, turned to the southeast, along the Kaal Spruit, in the direction of Bloemfontein, the capital of the Orange Free State. On the 11th he reached Aasvogel Kop, and on the 12th Venters Vallei,

18 miles southwest of the capital, and about 10 miles west of the railroad. The cavalry division was ordered to push on and seize the railroad station and its rolling material. French struck the railroad six miles below Bloemfontein in the morning, and by evening succeeded in taking two hills close to the station, which commanded the town. On the morning of the 13th, the 3d cavalry brigade and mounted infantry from the 7th division were sent to support French, and the town was called upon to surrender, on pain of being bombarded; the white flag was raised at noon, and a few hours afterwards Lord Roberts entered and took possession.

The President, Mr. Steyn, and the officials fled to Kroonstad, which was proclaimed as the new capital.

The British captured 8 locomotives and much rolling stock.

Lord Roberts set to work at once to reestablish the government of the district south of the Modder River. General Pretyman was designated as military governor. The civil affairs were turned over to Mr. Fraser, a member of the former government, but a friend of the English. Many of the former officials who remained were retained, and the burghers were allowed to retire peaceably to their homes on condition that they would not take up arms again in the present struggle.

The result of this tolerance was that the Boer line on the Orange River broke down at once. Of course, the fact that Lord Roberts had penetrated to the rear of this line had its natural effect, but its immediate collapse was due to the fact that many of the burghers preferred to accept Lord Roberts' conditions.

The moral effect of the occupation of Bloemfontein was of course very great, not only on the Boers of the Orange Free State as well as the Transvaal, but also on the native uprisings in western and northern Cape Colony; but the strategic effect was far greater, as it gave the British control of the important—nay, indispensable—railroad line from Colesberg to Bloemfontein, a line not only necessary to supply the army in its present position, but absolutely required for any further advance northward. Besides, Bloemfontein, with its natural advantages and its generous water supply, formed an excellent base of supply for the subsequent movements of the army.

Lord Roberts had another problem to solve before he could advance; viz.: to transfer his base at Modder River Station and his overland line of communications to the railroad. The Boers had destroyed the bridge at Norvals Pont, but as the British had previously prepared the necessary parts for repairing it and held them all ready to ship to that point, this work would not require over two weeks. Meanwhile, 2,000 Kaffirs had been ordered there to effect the transportation of supplies and material over the Orange River.

The security of the lines of communications was left to Lord Kitchener, a master in that art. Lord Roberts also recognized the danger of the uprising in the Southwest, and on March 19th sent Lord Kitchener to the Prieska and Carnarvon districts to suppress it. General Settle was sent to Prieska (85 miles west of Hopetown) on the Orange River) with a force of mounted infantry, and Sir Parsons to Van Wyks Vlei (215 miles west of Colesberg).

Another care of General Roberts was to insure his junction with Generals Brabant, Gatacre and Clements, coming up from Cape Colony, to facilitate which he sent General Pole-Carew with a brigade by rail to Springfontein, the junction of the railroads from Norvals Pont and from Bethulie, where the advancing British troops could be sup ported against any Boer resistance on the Orange River by threatening the rear of the enemy.

The troops were greatly in need of rest and reorganization, especially the arm in which the British Army excelled, and which had increased in importance as the army advanced—viz., the cavalry; moreover, the supply trains, on account of the great loss of pack animals en route from Modder River Station, were not in condition for any farther advance, and so, for all these reasons, it became imperative to give the troops a long rest, in spite of the fact that such a delay would also afford the Boers time to gather their forces at some advantageous point and prepare a strong defensive position. The raid to Kimberley broke down nearly 20 per cent of the British horses, and over 1,700 horses were disabled. On the way from Kimberley to Bloemfontein, over the hot plain, a large number were foundered or died, so that in all the cavalry was short about 10,000 horses, and remounts had to be awaited.

EVENTS IN THE SOUTHERN THEATRE.

At the beginning of March Generals Brabant, Gatacre and Clements, meeting with no resistance in their front, began to advance from Jamestown, Molteno and Colesberg behind the retiring Boers. They moved slowly in order to take on the way the measures necessary for quieting the inhabitants of the districts through which they passed.

General Brabant moved from Dordrecht on the 3d, with about 1,800 men, on the 4th took possession of the Boer position at Labuschagues Nek, about 6 miles north of Dordrecht. On the 5th he attacked the Boers north of this position, and, after an all-day light, defeated them. The British lost about 30 killed and wounded, and captured wagons, rifles and cattle in large quantities.

General Gatacre reoccupied Stormberg on the 5th of March, and thus came in railway communication with General Clements at Colesberg; on the 7th he occupied Burghersdorp, while Brabant reached Jamestown, and Clements advanced to Norvals Pont, on the south bank of the Orange River. At the last-mentioned place the enemy, after retiring over the river on the 6th, blew up the bridge.

On March 12th, Brabant was at Aliwal North, Gatacre at Bethulie bridge and Clements at Norvals Pont. When Gatacre reached the Orange River, the railway bridge had been destroyed, and the enemy were preparing to demolish the road bridge, but were driven off before they could accomplish their purpose. On the 15th he occupied Bethulie. Patrols of Clements' force effected a juncture with Gatacre's troops near Burghersdorp, and a patrol from Bethulie bridge effected a union with Brabant's column.

On March 4th, on which day Brabant defeated the rear guard of the Boer column from Dordrecht at Aliwal North, the three columns were practically in touch with one another. It appears that the Boers in their retreat had become demoralized, failed to take proper measures to insure the service of security and information, and were consequently completely surprised by the rapid advance of the British. As a result, they were unable to make a firm and concerted stand on the Orange River. On the 16th the three British columns crossed the river without opposition.

The Boer column retiring over Aliwal North, commanded by Grobeler, assembled at Smithfield; that over Bethulie, under Olivier, joined them at Smithfield, thus combining to a force of about 5,000 men and 16 guns. The combined columns, under Olivier, then moved over Wepener on Winburg, to join the Boer forces there. The column over Norvals Pont (600), under Van der Post, assembled at Fauresmith,

On the 18th, Clements was advancing on Philippolis and

Fauresmith; Gatacre was established at Springfontein, with a detachment at Springfield and the Scots Guards holding the railway at Edensburg; and Brabant occupied Rouxville, preparing to move along the Basutoland border.

EVENTS IN THE WESTERN THEATRE.

Lord Kitchener remained in the Prieska and Carnarvon districts, southwest of Orange River Station, pacifying the uprisings kindled by roaming bodies of Boers, until March 27th, when he returned to De Aar. About 200 rebels made their submission, and others retired over the Orange River.

Cronje left Modder River Station on March 4th for Cape Town. He was to be held a prisoner at St. Helena till the close of the war.

The Transvaal Boers, augmented in number since the relief of Kimberley, reoccupied Griquatown. Bodies of rebels were reported at various points, commandeering and looting. A body of 800 Boers with 4 guns held the north bank of the Vaal at Fourteen Streams, and attacked the British at Warrenton, but without success. Lord Methuen, who had gone to Barkly West to restore order, returned to Kimberley on the 27th.

General Snyman was still investing Mafeking in the month of March. Colonel Plumer's force was checked at Lobatsi by an offensive advance of the Boers on March 16th; whereupon he made a raid to within 12 miles of Zeerust against the line of communications of Snyman's force, and returned to Ramathlabama, only six miles from Mafeking. The Boers, however, drove him back with heavy loss to Gaberones.

EVENTS IN NATAL.

The relieving force under Sir Redvers Buller marched through Ladysmith on March 3d. On the 9th the naval brigade of the Powerful returned from Ladysmith to Durban. The line between Colenso and Ladysmith was clear, but the Boers began entrenching on the Biggarsberg, as proven by a reconnaissance to Pomeroy on the road to Helpmakaar, by Bethune's Horse.

The British army occupied a line extending from Acton Homes and Dewdrop in the west to Elandslaagte and Sundays River in the east, with outposts along a line from Van Reenens Pass to Helpmakaar.

This photograph shows General Piet Cronjé (1836-1911) as prisoner of war on Saint Helena where he remained until the conclusion of the war on 31 May 1902.

The Boers occupied the Biggarsberg with about 14,000 men and 20 guns, and had strong detachments in De Beers, Tintwa and Van Reenens passes. The cavalry of Dundonald reconnoitered continually on the left flank, while Bethune's Horse guarded the right, and felt its way forward.

Pomeroy, on the Zululand border road, was burned by the Boers on March 23d.

LORD ROBERTS' CAMPAIGN.

Pacification of Conquered Territory.

As soon as the army had rested and sufficiently recuperated, and the system of supply was in normal working order again, Lord Roberts directed his attention more particularly to pacifying the conquered territory—the southern part of the Orange Free State—and to secure his lines of communication.

His first move was to intercept, if possible, the retreating Boer columns from Cape Colony, the principal of which was that under Olivier (5,000 men with 16 guns) retreating over Smithfield and Wepener towards Winburg. For this purpose Lord Roberts sent General French with his division to cut Olivier off on the Thaba 'Nchu—Ladybrand road. A brigade of cavalry had been sent to Thaba 'Nchu as early as March 18th, to quiet the inhabitants, but on the 26th General French's division advanced towards Ladybrand, which his advance guard occupied. He was too late, however, as Olivier had already passed that point on his way north, gathering to his standard many of the Boers who had returned to their homes.

The rejection of the peace propositions of Presidents Krüger and Steyn by the British government was followed by flaming proclamations by both these rulers calling upon the Boers to continue the struggle to the end. In consequence of this, many returned to the army.

French's movement was observed by a Boer outpost near Brandfort, and a commando under Crowther was promptly sent to Ladybrand to hold the road open for Olivier. Crowther drove French's advance guard back and compelled him to give up his mission, as he had no infantry with which to dispute the ground. French left Broad-wood's brigade at Thaba 'Nchu, and returned with the rest to Bloemfontein.

The Boer force at Fauresmith, under Van der Post, slipped through to the north at Petrusburg and Poplar Grove, reaching the Boer lines at Bultfontein.

The British columns from Cape Colony, after uniting with Pole-Carew's brigade, moved northward on a broad front, taking all necessary measures to pacify the inhabitants and to restore peace and order. One of the great objects of Lord Roberts—the junction of his main army with the scattered columns in Cape Colony—had thus been accomplished.

Clements entered Fauresmith and Jägersfontein on the 27th, and, leaving a garrison at the latter place, reached Bloemfontein on the 8th of April; Gatacre made his headquarters at Springfontein, and Brabant remained at Aliwal North. Gatacre and Brabant were required to preserve order in this portion of the captured district, and to secure the lines of communication.

Preparations for Advance.

Depressing as were the consequences of Cronje's surrender for the Boers, there were many indications at this time that their spirit was not yet broken, and that Lord Roberts had still a numerous and active enemy to contend with.

The first element was the Afrikander uprising, which was still going on in the rear of Roberts' army, and along his long lines of communication. In the next place, the success of Olivier in eluding the British, combined with President Steyn's determination to stand by the treaty of alliance with the Transvaal, and President Krueger's to carry on the war to the end, had given the Boers new courage and inspired them with a new enthusiasm. Their numbers, due to the return of many on the call of the Presidents, had risen considerably, and but few of the reinforcements Lord Roberts received had been available at the front. As regards war supplies, arms and ammunition, the Boers were well prepared and had enough for a long war. In losing Joubert and Cronje, on the other hand, they suffered most, for they had no leaders to fully replace them, although Botha and De Wet, for the kind of warfare they decided to wage, were remarkably well fitted. Finally, their tendency to assume the tactical offensive in small bodies seemed always to have been greater than on a large scale; consequently their new mode of warfare benefited thereby.

Before resuming his advance, therefore, it was not only necessary to reorganize the troops, remount the cavalry, and secure the lines of communication, but also to quell disturbances in and to pacify the conquered districts, to clear the country of the numerous smaller bodies of Boers, or at least to locate them and determine their strength, with a view to leaving behind detachments to watch them, and to counteract the effects of Krueger's and Steyn's proclamations by such measures of leniency or severity as might be found most effective.

Evidences of this new energy of the Boers were felt in all directions. Some of these have already been referred to; namely, the repulse of

Methuen at Fourteen Streams, and of Plumer at Lobatsi, the attack on French's advance guard and its expulsion from Ladybrand, and, in Natal, the burning of Pomeroy. Other evidences made themselves felt, and gradually on a larger and larger scale.

On March 20th the two railroad bridges north of Bloemfontein (over the Modder and the Vet rivers, respectively) were destroyed by the Boers.

Roberts' army near Bloemfontein was posted as follows: 7th division, 1st and 3d cavalry brigades, at Glen, near the Modder River; 6th division in Bloemfontein; 2d cavalry brigade at Thaba 'Nchu; 9th division in Bloemfontein; 1st and 2d brigades mounted infantry near Karree Siding, with portions at Thaba 'Nchu and other points.

On March 25th the British reconnoitering towards Brandfort had a small skirmish with the Boers.

Action at Karree Siding.

On the 31st General Roberts found it necessary, in consequence of the activity of the Boers, under General Smets, in his immediate front, to drive them from some kopjes they occupied near Karree Siding Station, a few miles south of Brandfort. The operation was conducted by the 7th. division, assisted by the 1st and 3d cavalry brigades under French, and Le Gallais' regiment of mounted infantry.

The group of isolated hills at Karree Siding trends east and west, extending over about 5 miles of ground. The line was occupied by about 3,000 Boers.

Tucker's division was sent to Glen. French, with his cavalry division, was sent to the west to turn the Boer position, while Le Gallais, with the mounted infantry and 3 guns (37 mm.), was to do the same by the east. Tucker' was to attack in front after the turning movements were completed.

At 10 a.m. French sent a heliograph message that he was in position in rear of the hills, and Tucker advanced to the attack.

The infantry pushed the Boers back gradually, but they resisted with some energy till about 4 p.m., when French's artillery opened on them from the rear. The Boers then retired precipitately. The mounted infantry did not reach their rear in time to cut them off.

The British took the kopjes after a six-hour fight and held them. They lost 2 officers killed, 7 wounded; and about 100 men killed, wounded and missing.

The success of the British was due to the enveloping attack {around both flanks) made by the cavalry, but the fact that no pursuit was attempted indicates that the latter was not yet in proper condition for active operations.

Action Near Bloemfontein Waterworks, on the Koorn Spruit.

On March 30th, Broadwood, who had been left at Thaba 'Nchu, 38 miles east of Bloemfontein, having received information that two strong forces from the north and east were approaching his position, retired to the waterworks, which were 17 miles nearer Bloemfontein, and where he had a detachment of two companies of mounted infantry for the protection of the works, near Sanna's Post. General Roberts sent the 9th division to his support.

Broadwood's force consisted of the Household Cavalry, the 10th Hussars, Q and U batteries horse artillery, and Pilcher's battalion mounted infantry, in all about 1,400 men.

De Wet, hearing on the 30th that Broadwood had retired from Thaba 'Nchu. decided to intercept him, and by a, forced night march, with a force of about 8,000 men, reached the British camp before daybreak, and made his dispositions, for attack.

At dawn Broadwood found himself attacked on three sides. He immediately despatched his two horse-artillery batteries and his baggage towards Bloemfontein, covering them with his mounted troops. At the point where the road crosses the Koorn Spruit about 2 miles from the waterworks, a Boer force was so well concealed that the scouts had not discovered them, but as the artillery and the train entered the drift, the Boers opened fire at short range, shooting down drivers and horses. Such as were able galloped away, covered by Roberts' Horse. Meanwhile, another passage was found where the remainder of Broadwood's force crossed and re-formed. The horse-artillery guns that got out formed at Klip Kraal, a group of ten houses over the Koorn Spruit, and opened on the Boers, but they were soon driven back by cross-fire. The 9th division, after a magnificent march, arrived on the scene of action at about 2 p.m. French with 2 brigades had also been ordered up, but did not arrive in time to take part in the action.

The Boers retired towards Ladybrand, leaving 20 wounded officers and 70 wounded men. Broadwood lost 7 guns and all his baggage, about 150 killed and wounded, and 200 missing.

Action at Pietfontein, Near Boshof.

The column of Boers under Van der Post, which slipped through the British lines from Fauresmith north, remained in that vicinity and sent out detachments from Koodoos Band, in the direction of Poplar Grove, to disturb the British communications between Modder River Station and Bloemfontein. One of his outposts, to protect his rear in the direction of Kimberley, 70 men strong, was surrounded by Methuen's troops from Boshof on April 5th and captured, the French colonel of engineers, Villebois, being among those who fell in the attack. The British lost 1 officer and man killed, 10 men wounded. The Boers lost 8 killed, 8 wounded and 54 prisoners.

Action at Reddersburg.

The Boer columns under De Wet and Olivier again took up their offensive movement southward early in April. On the 3d De Wet reached Reddersburg, where he fell upon a small British force and captured it.

This force, composed of 3 companies 2d Royal Irish Rifles and 2 companies 9th Regiment Mounted Infantry, had been sent to Dewetsdorp, 40 miles east of the railway, to receive arms of the burghers, and on the way back to Bethany it found its way intercepted a few miles east of Reddersburg by a large force with guns. The British detachment rushed to a kopje near by, and held it for 18 hours, when, all hope of reinforcement being abandoned, they surrendered. The battle opened in the afternoon of the 3d, and the English, without artillery, defended themselves until 2 a.m. on the 4th, at which time all their ammunition was expended. At daybreak, therefore, they were compelled to surrender.

Gatacre, at Springfield, in spite of the thunder of the Boer artillery all the afternoon, was not informed of the battle until late in the evening, when he received an order from Lord Roberts to send reinforcements. The latter he took by rail to Bethany, and then marched across country, but did not reach the field till noon of the 4th—too late to be of any use. He therefore retired to Bethany.

In consequence of this mishap, General Gatacre was relieved from command on the 9th and ordered home. General Pole-Carew was placed in command of his troops.

The British lost 2 officers killed, 4 wounded and 9 captured; 10 men killed, 33 wounded and about 400 captured.

THE GENERAL SITUATION.

Before discussing the movements of Olivier's column, which began at the same time as those of De Wet's against Reddersburg, and which resulted in the siege of Wepener, a glance at the general situation will enable us to obtain a clearer understanding of Lord Roberts' preliminary movements and his resumption of the advance.

The Boers were distributed somewhat as follows: around Ladybrand, 10,000; on the Vaal, from Fourteen Streams to Christiana, 0,000; at Brandfort, about 6,000; near Boetsap (Barkly West), 400; near Witrand (Barkly West), 700; about Kroonstad, 5,000; and in the eastern theatre (Natal), about 14,000.

The general plan of the Boers was evidently to attack Roberts at the center near Brandfort, and at the same time to make a raid around his right flank over Wepener against his communications in rear, and another against his left flank over Paardeberg, and to threaten the extreme left at Kimberley by an advance from Barkly West and Fourteen Streams.

The British had nearly completed their reorganization and remounts, the bridges at Bethulie and Norvals Pont had been repaired, and the uprisings in Cape Colony subdued. General Clements had reached Bloemfontein, while Generals Gatacre and Brabant were moving gradually on Ladybrand to secure Roberts' right flank.

In Natal, Botha held his intrenched position in the Biggarsberg with about 12,000 men, his main body north of Helpmakaar, with strong detachments at Glencoe and One Tree Hill (Road Junction Pass), while 2,000 Orange Boers held the Drakensberg passes.

General Buller, with 40,000 men, occupied a position north of Elandslaagte and on the Sundays River. His advanced position was of great importance, as it was geographically 60 miles farther north than Bloemfontein.

In the north of the Transvaal a new movement was being planned. With the consent of Portugal, the Rhodesian Feld Force, under General Sir F. Carrington, 5,000 strong, composed of Colonial Horse, mostly Australian bushmen, was to land at Beira and be transported by rail to Rhodesia.

The army was entirely reorganized, both the divisions under General Roberts and those in Natal (see Appendix); and Hart's brigade was sent from Natal to reinforce Brabant in the Orange Free State, while Barton's was sent to the extreme west at Kimberley a little later.

Lord Roberts' original plan appears to have been to advance from Bloemfontein with the main army against the left flank of the enemy at Kroonstad, uniting on the way with a part of Buller's army, opening a way from Natal through the Drakensberg passes, while Methuen was to advance over Boshof and Hoopstad on Kroonstad, thus making a concentric march in three columns. But the enemy's dispositions showed that a very small force was concentrated at Kroonstad, whereas the right flank of the British was seriously threatened, and in Natal, as soon as they learned of the transfer of a part of the 10th division (Hart's brigade) to the western theatre, the Boers, on the 10th of April, attacked Buller, and took Clery's camp, on the south side of Sundays River, completely by surprise, only the arrival of reinforcements saving the situation, but not until after a three-days struggle.

Methuen's force, it is true, advanced on its route towards Hoopstad, and reached Zwartskopjefontein. His march was opposed by a detachment of 2,000 under Delarey. On the 20th Lord Methuen retired, followed by Delarey, a serious skirmish taking place between the latter and Methuen's rear guard.

Evidently, then, Lord Roberts could not count on a junction with Buller from Natal, and even Lord Methuen would have difficulty in taking part in the march northward. Moreover, the main force of the Boers, now east of Bloemfontein, demanded attention before any march north could be made.

The total British forces in South Africa numbered at this time about 200,000 men, distributed over a front of 300 miles, and guarding nearly 1,800 miles of railway. Lord Roberts' army at the center was posted in and around Bloemfontein, occupying also other strategic points, and numbered about 60,000 combatants with 216 guns and howitzers ($3\frac{1}{2}$ guns per 1,000 men). The army of Natal numbered about 36,000 combatants, with 96 field guns and howitzers ($2\frac{3}{4}$ pieces per 1,000 men), besides a number of naval guns.

Lord Methuen, in the extreme west, had about 14,000 combatants. The railways and towns of Cape Colony and Natal were protected by about 35,000 combatants. The other fighting forces were those of General Brabant in southern Orange Free State, Colonel Plumer at

Gaberones, the garrison of Mafeking, Colonel Parsons at Carnarvon in western Cape Colony, and the new force under Carrington landing at Beira.

The Siege and Relief of Wepener.

At the same time that De Wet fell upon Reddersburg (April 4th), Olivier with his column arrived before Wepener. The latter had been occupied by a detachment of Brabant's force under Dalgetty, composed of a company of Scotch mounted infantry, the Cape Mounted Scouts, the 1st and 2d Kaffrarian Scouts—about 2,000 men in all, with 7 guns. The success of De Wet at Reddersburg should naturally have led to an attempt on Roberts' communications on the Springfield—Bloemfontein railroad, but the appearance of small detachments from Brabant's force, and the approach of the new 3d division under Pole-Carew, induced the Boers to turn eastward.

Olivier, finding Wepener already occupied, left a detachment in front of it, which was joined by two other commandoes retiring from Rouxville and Smithfield, respectively. With the rest of his force Olivier moved southward, and on the 6th of April attacked a detachment of Brabant's troops, composed of 4 companies Irish Fusiliers, 2 companies volunteers and 2 squadrons border scouts, between Bushmans Kop and the Caledon River, the Witte Spruit and the Basutoland border, opposite Mafeteng, and forced them back on Aliwal North, reoccupying Smithfield with a detachment of his force. On the 9th the Boers besieging Wepener began the attack on that place, the British force occupying: the town and the Jammerberg Drift. On the 10th the latter made a spirited sortie, inflicting severe loss on the Boers. The attack of the Boers was continued, however, and was covered by Olivier at Rouxville and Smithfield against Brabant at Aliwal North, and by De Wet, who concentrated his force at Dewetsdorp after the action at Reddersburg, against a British approach from the northwest.

Meanwhile, for the relief of Wepener, Roberts ordered Bundle's 8th division by rail to Bethany, thence due east over Reddersburg, by way of Rosendal and Vorlogspoort, on Dewetsdorp; while Brabant, recently reinforced by Hart's brigade from Natal, was directed over Rouxville on Boesmans Kop to force back Olivier's troops. To cover Run-die's left flank, Chermside's division (stationed between Bloemfontein and Bethany) was concentrated at Reddersburg and ordered to Marshoutfontein (17 miles east of the railroad), Knox's brigade holding the railroad in rear, in support.

Rundle left Bethany on the 13th of April, and Reddersburg on the 16th, but heavy rains made the roads almost impassable, so that he did not reach Wakkerstroom till the 19th, and only come in contact with the Boers (4 miles south of Dewetsdorp) on the morning of the 20th. Chermside occupied Marshoutfontein on the 14th. Brabant reoccupied Rouxville on the 15th.

The vicinity of Dewetsdorp is comparatively high ground, containing the sources of the Modder, the Kaffir, the Koorn Spruit and of several branches of the Caledon emptying into the Orange River. It is much cut up, very difficult for cavalry, favoring the defense and offering many obstacles for the attack. The Boers recognized the fact that it covered their line of retreat to Thaba 'Nchu and Ladybrand, and consequently fortified it with great care. The right of their position was protected against an attack from Bloemfontein by the Leeuw Kop (16 miles southeast of Bloemfontein), which was occupied by the left flank of the Boer forces encircling Bloemfontein on the east. The front of their position at Dewetsdorp faced southwest. The total Boer forces at Wepener and Dewetsdorp amounted to 8,000 men, with 15 guns.

Rundle, deciding that the position was too strong to attack in front, deployed the mounted infantry and yeomanry in front, and sent Brabazon with the cavalry to outflank the left of the Boer position. The Boers retired their left wing, but took up a new defensive position, while Rundle entrenched on the ground gained.

Meanwhile, Brabant reached the enemy's position at Bushmans Kop, 18 miles south of Wepener, on the evening of the 21st.

De Wet's force at Dewetsdorp resisted Rundle's advance; consequently Roberts despatched Pole-Carew's division from Bloemfontein on the 22d, and two brigades of cavalry under French, to relieve the situation. They reached Leeuw Kop (near Bloemfontein) the same day, the latter being abandoned by the Boers on their approach, and continued to Tweede Geluk (24 miles northwest of Dewetsdorp).

Brabant turned the flank of the Boers at Bushmans Kop and pushed on to within 8 miles of Wepener.

At this time (23d) General Roberts instituted a general movement against the Boer position to the east of Bloemfontein, sending the mounted infantry under Hamilton against the waterworks and Thaba 'Nchu, supported by Smith-Dorrien's brigade.

To occupy the enemy in front and to prepare for his advance toward Kroonstad, Maxwell's brigade of the 7th division at Karree Siding moved eastward and took possession of the hills commanding the wagon bridge over the Modder River at Kranz Kraal, 8 miles east of the railway, on the 23d of April.

On the 24th Hamilton occupied the waterworks at Sanna's Post, Smith-Dorrien's brigade 10 miles in rear, the rest of the 9th division in Bloemfontein ready to march eastward, the object being to cut off the line of retreat of the Boers in the south. Brabant made little progress, the Boers holding their own against him and renewing the attack on Dalgetty. Pole-Carew reached Roode Kop, 14 miles from Dewetsdorp, on the 24th, French pushing on to the east as far as Grootfontein, in order next day to seize the Boer line of retreat on Thaba 'Nchu at Vaalbank, 9 miles northeast of Dewetsdorp. Rundle's scouts also came in touch with Brabant's outposts on the Caledon.

The Boers, on the night of the 24th, however, abandoned their positions at Dewetsdorp and Wepener and retired on Thaba 'Nchu and Ladybrand, respectively. Brabant pursued along the Basutoland border, while French and Rundle followed along the Dewetsdorp—Thaba 'Nchu road. Pole-Carew returned to Bloemfontein, as reserve. On the 27th French reached Thaba 'Nchu, joining there the forces of Hamilton and Smith-Dorrien, Bundle also arriving later in the day. The Boers, however, made good their escape and joined their forces near Ladybrand.

The pursuit of the Boers was continued during the 26th and 27th of April. The district of Moroka, through which the Thaba 'Nchu—Ladybrand road passes, is mountainous country in the form of a bastion with its base and higher ground near Ladybrand, its point and lower ground towards Bloemfontein. East of Thaba 'Nchu the ground changes from its comparatively low hilly character to the westward to broader and higher reaches to the eastward, the latter forming excellent defensive positions, very difficult for cavalry. In the latter the Boers (under De Wet), retiring from Thaba 'Nchu, took up a strong position. French, with his usual energy, attacked, but was compelled, after a fruitless engagement, to retire on Thaba 'Nchu.

On the 28th and 29th the advance was continued, but this frontal attack was effectively resisted by the Boers. The British attempted to turn the Boer left flank, but the right flank of the latter was so active that little headway could be made, until the British decided to make a wide detour and attempted to strike through the Houtnek Pass, about 12 miles north of #Thaba 'Nchu, which was held by a Boer force under Botha. This was accomplished by Hamilton with the mounted infantry, supported by Broadwood's brigade, and Bruce Hamilton's infantry brigade (21st), on the 2d of May, and the Boers retired towards Winburg. In this action the Boers lost 12 killed, 40 wounded and 26 prisoners. Hamilton rested at Jacobsrust by Lord Roberts' orders, as he had been fighting for seven days out of the past ten.

Meanwhile Roberts resumed the general advance on Kroonstad, and these troops joined his right flank. The Boers, on the 3d and 4th, retired over the Leeuw River (east of Thaba 'Nchu), followed by Rundle and Brabazon to that stream, when the latter came in touch with Brabant. The parts of the 3d division left at Thaba 'Nchu returned to take charge of the line of communications.

LORD ROBERTS' CAMPAIGN.

The Advance on Kroonstad.

The country between Bloemfontein and the Vaal River is a rolling plain, with low ridges crossing in the northern-portion, showing occasionally the characteristic South African table mountain.

The railroad runs in a northeastern direction for 125 miles without a curve, over nearly level country, which is treeless, with streams only in the rainy season, and only grass and low bushes visible over the broad plain. Few houses, and these only isolated dwellings and kraals, are met with, and the country furnishes nothing for the support of troops.

But, while the British army will have to depend entirely on the supplies it carries along, the advance offers no difficulties, since the railroad, wherever it has been destroyed (as at the low bridges over the Modder, Vet and Zand rivers), is easily repaired. There are no places for defensive positions except at Brandfort, Winburg and Ventersburg, where there are considerable elevations; but all these can be turned, especially since the entire country is practicable for cavalry or mounted infantry. The innumerable spruits are far more troublesome to an army than the kopjes, because in the rainy season they swell so suddenly, and are rarely bridged, while in the dry season they form excellent defensive positions for the Boers.

The total number of British troops in South Africa on the 21st of April amounted to about 210,759, including officers, but after deducting the non-combatants (13,000), the troops on the lines of communications (40,000) and the sick (about 23,670), the total fighting strength was about 134,000, stationed as follows:

- Under Roberts, directly in Orange Free State (including garrisons): 66,000
- Under Methuen and Hunter, at Kimberley, Boshof and Fourteen Streams: 20,000
- Under Parsons, in western Cape Colony: 10,000
- Under Plumer, north of Mafeking: 2,000
- Under Baden-Powell, in Mafeking: 1,000
- Under Carrington, in Rhodesia: 5,000
- Under Buller, in Natal: 30,000

The total Boer forces in the field amounted to about 50,000 men, distributed as follows:

- Southeast of Bloemfontein: 8,000
- At Smaldeel: 3,000
- At Brandfort and Karree Siding: 5,000
- Ladybrand: 1,500
- East of Bloemfontein—Springfontein R. R: 2,000
- Between Kroonstad and Winburg: 5,000
- Total: 24,000

The rest at Fourteen Streams (6,000), in Natal (14,000), in Barkly West and in reserve.

Roberts' immediate army was posted as follows, previous to the resumption of the advance from Bloemfontein:

- 7th Division, 14th Brigade (Maxwell) at Modder River bridge, beyond Glen.
    15th Brigade (C. E. Knox) between the Modder River and Karree Siding.
- 6th Division, 12th Brigade (Clements) on outpost duty.
    13th Brigade (Wavell) north of Modder River, south of Karree Siding.

- 11th Division, in Bloemfontein.

    21st Brigade (newly formed), at Glen.

The position of the cavalry and mounted infantry changed constantly.

The Boers were known to be in force at Karree Siding and on three kopjes southeast of that point, guarding the road to Winburg.

On April 30th Maxwell's brigade, assisted by Broadwood's cavalry brigade, then at Holzhuisfontein, was ordered to take these kopjes, which was accomplished before nightfall.

Broadwood's brigade was then directed to move out well to the east, while Hutton was sent to the west, to outflank the Boer position at Brandfort. The 6th and 11th divisions and the 21st brigade were ordered to advance, following the general direction of the railroad, and to attack the enemy at Brandfort.

On May 2d Broadwood reached Isabelfontein, 16 miles east of Brandfort, and the Boers retired. The British occupied the position on the 3d.

The 9th division, Hamilton's mounted infantry and French's cavalry, which had moved on Houtnek Pass and compelled the Boer forces there to retire on Winburg, having accomplished their purpose, joined the movement of advance of Roberts' main army. Hamilton reached Welcome (12 miles south of Winburg) on May 4th, and had a skirmish with a retiring Boer column there; on the 5th he crossed the Little Vet and took Winburg.

Meanwhile, Roberts had engaged the Boers at the railroad crossing of the Little Vet, south of Winburg. Pole-Carew's division (11th) was deployed for the attack, the Boers (under Delarey) on the right bank opposing its advance, bringing several guns in position. The British developed a superior artillery fire, bringing 2 batteries of field guns, 4 navy guns and 2 siege guns into action, and soon silenced the Boer artillery, but kept up the fire all the afternoon (May 5th). Roberts again turned the enemy's flank, without making a strong frontal infantry attack, by sending Hutton with his mounted infantry and some cavalry and artillery down stream to a ford. The latter was held by a small Boer force with 2 field guns, a howitzer and a Maxim gun, but their artillery was silenced by the British guns, and the Boers retired, losing their Maxim gun and a number of prisoners.

Hamilton reached Winburg about the same time as Broadwood

(who advanced along the Bloemfontein—Winburg road). The Boers united their forces, however, and in the night, with the aid of the railroad, effected their retreat. On the morning of the 6th of May Hutton's patrols destroyed the railroad at Smaldeel, but his force was too late to cut off the Boers, although it secured some rolling material for Roberts' further advance.

At Smaldeel the British were compelled to halt for a short period, in order to repair the bridge over the Little Vet, to rearrange the strategic front and the columns of march, and to await supplies. Hamilton with one brigade of mounted infantry, Broadwood's cavalry brigade and the 9th division constituted the right wing and moved over the Winburg—Kroonstad road; the 7th and 11th divisions and the 21st brigade formed the center along the railroad; and Hutton's brigade of mounted infantry and the other three cavalry brigades under French, the left, west of the railroad.

On May 7th Roberts had the entire country to the Zand River cleared up by his cavalry and mounted infantry, and found the Boers strongly intrenched on the north bank of the Zand; but indications of retreat induced Hutton to attack with his artillery at Virginia, near the railroad, south of the river, and established the fact that the Boers were abandoning the position.

On May 9th the general advance was resumed by Roberts' army, and on the 10th the Zand was crossed, the troops advancing that day to Ventersburg. On the 11th the army reached the Bloem Spruit, and on the 12th Kroonstad. The Boers retired over the Vaal. President Steyn moved the seat of government to Heilbron.

EVENTS IN THE SOUTH.

The 8th division (Rundle's), it will be remembered, followed the retiring Boers east of Thaba 'Nchu as far as the Little Leeuw Spruit. On the 9th of May, not being able to penetrate to Ladybrand eastward, Bundle turned north along the Leeuw, and after a number of minor affairs with stray Boer commandoes, reached Mequathings Nek (18 miles northwest of Ladybrand) on the 16th, and Clocolan (20 miles northeast of Ladybrand) on the 17th. After these points were taken, Brabazon with the yeomanry was able to push forward to Ladybrand.

EVENTS IN NATAL.

Buller also resumed the offensive on the 9th, and advanced against the Boer position in the Biggarsberg. The 2d division and Dundonald's cavalry marched towards Helpmakaar, while Bethune's mounted force was sent in the direction of Greytown to mislead the enemy. On the 12th, the 5th division moved eastward from Elandslaagte and occupied Indoda Mountain, 11 miles away, to cover and support Buller's movement, while Bethune, turning northward, made for Pomeroy

The enemy's position was a few miles southwest of Helpmakaar. On the 13th the British infantry attacked it in front, the cavalry turning the right flank, and Bethune's force operating on the left and rear.

The Boers (now about 7,000 strong) retired over Helpmakaar, firing the dry grass as they went. Dundonald's cavalry pursued, and the army occupied Dundee and Glencoe on the 15th; on the 17th it reached Dannhauser, with its advanced patrols at Newcastle. The Boers fell back over Laings Nek and De Jägers Drift on the Buffalo River. They destroyed the waterworks at Newcastle, and the bridge over the Ingogo, and blew up the tunnel at Laings Nek. Buller sent Clery and Dundonald as advance guard towards Laings Nek (Clery detaching Hildyard's brigade towards Utrecht), and ordered Lyttleton towards Vryheid to turn the Boer left flank.

EVENTS IN THE EXTREME WEST.

Towards the end of April Douglas' brigade, which had advanced as far as Zwartskopjefontein had been forced to return to Bosh of by Delarey, and Paget's brigade was still striving to force a passage over the Vaal near Fourteen Streams. Meanwhile, a detachment of mounted troops, about 1,500 strong, under Colonel Mahon, attempted to cross the Vaal below Barkly West, in order to turn the Boer west flank and thus reach Mafeking by forced marches; this force reached Taungs on May 7th, and Vryburg on the 9th.

Colonel Mahon's force consisted of picked cavalry and included a detachment of Queenslanders and Canadians drawn from Carrington's Bushmen at Beira. This detachment left Beira on May 5th went by rail to Salisbury and by coach to Buluwayo, where it arrived May 8th, then by train to Oatsi, arriving May 11th, then marched for twenty-two hours to join the main column on the 12th.

Early in April Hunter's division (10th) was taken from Natal and transferred to the western theatre, Hart's brigade sent to reinforce Brabant at Aliwal North, while Barton and the artillery were sent to Kimberley, where they were joined by Hart after the relief of Wepener. The object of thus rein-forcing Methuen was to enable him to cross the Vaal and relieve Mafeking.

While Paget made a demonstration at Warrenton, Hunter endeavored to cross the Vaal farther west, at Windsorton, about 27 miles below Fourteen Streams, then to turn on Fourteen Streams and roll up the Boer position. On the 5th of May he effected a crossing, and on the 9th he attacked the right flank of the Boer position at Fourteen Streams, while Paget advanced against its front at Warrenton. The Boers were forced to retire. Hunter sent Barton's brigade towards Mafeking, while he with the other brigade moved towards Bloemhof, and at the same time Methuen advanced in the direction of Hoopstad. Delarey from Zwartskopjefontein moved north towards Mafeking, while the Boers from Fourteen Streams retired on Klerksdorp. Hunter occupied Christiana on the 13th of May.

The Relief of Mafeking.

Meanwhile, the column under Mahon advanced by forced marches to the relief of Mafeking. After passing Vryburg, the column made a detour to the west to avoid a Boer force at Pudimoe Siding, 10 miles north of Taungs, and again on the 13th, at Setlacoli, a similar detour was made to avoid a column from Maritsani Station, which was that of Delarey,' who had moved north to cover the siege. At Kraaipan the British column was heavily attacked, but the Boers were finally repulsed. On the 15th Mahon joined Plumer at, Janmasibi, 20 miles west of Mafeking, and on the 16th they attacked a Boer force of 1,500, 9 miles west of the investing lines. The Boers were defeated and retreated eastward, and on the 17th Mahon entered Mafeking. The Boers had made a last attack on Mafeking on the 12th, in which they were completely defeated, El off, the commander, and 120 men being taken prisoners.

The siege of Mafeking had lasted 217 days.

On the same day, May 17th, Methuen entered Hoopstad, and Hunter left Christiana for Bloemhof.

LORD ROBERTS' CAMPAIGN.

The Advance on Pretoria.

At Kroonstad the army of invasion rested in order to secure its lines of communication, first, as regards their organization; secondly, as regards their protection, since a number of commandoes still hovered about the flanks of the British front as well as their line of advance.

In the movements instituted for the protection of the flanks, Hutton on the left succeeded in capturing a small Boer detachment at the mouth of the Olter Spruit, on the Vaal, while Broadwood on the right occupied Lindley on the 17th. These mounted troops on the extreme flanks pushed out detachments toward the Rhenoster River, and found the Boers on its north bank. Hamilton and Broadwood moved out from Lindley on the 9th and had a series of engagements with a Boer force under De Wet retiring before them, reaching Heilbron on the 22d. French and Hutton on the left reached Borman on the Rhenoster on the same day, and Prospect, 5 miles north of the river, on the 23d.

At the same time Hunter in the West advanced to Vryburg, which he reached on the 23d.

The general advance was resumed on the 22d, the army reaching Honing Spruit Station, 20 miles north of Kroonstad, on that day, and continuing the advance on the 23d. The Boers, threatened on both flanks, retired, after destroying the Rhenoster bridge and the railroad.

After passing the Rhenoster, Lord Roberts decided to concentrate his army more, and to put all the cavalry on the left flank. The interval between the two flanking columns (nearly 50 miles) had proven too great for concerted action, so that, although the Boers were easily maneuvered out of their positions, they were always enabled to retire with all their artillery and baggage. Hamilton and Broadwood were directed to join French and Hutton on the left wing, the right being covered by Colonel Henry's mounted infantry only.

French and Hutton reached Parys on the 24th, and part of their forces crossed the Vaal there; Hamilton and Broad-wood stood at Wolvehoek north of Heilbron Station, and Roberts was close up to Wolvehoek. On the 25th the main part of the forces of French and Hutton crossed at Lindequees Drift, 10 miles west of Vereeniging, Broadwood crossed at Wonder Water Drift north of Boschbank (8 miles west of Vereeniging), while Hamilton stood at Boschbank; Roberts swung away from the railroad, moving on Boschbank. Broadwood's brigade secured Wonder Water Drift, 3 miles above Lindequees Drift, and there covered the passage of Hamilton's column on the 26th.

Colonel Henry, constituting the advance guard, seized Viljoen's Drift (south of Vereeniging), but one span of the railway bridge was blown up by the Boers, here commanded by Lemmer. On the 27th Roberts' army crossed the Vaal there, the 3d cavalry brigade (Gordon), which had crossed at Engelbrecht Drift the day before, covering the right flank.

The extent of the front of Roberts' army by these movements was reduced to 25 miles.

Immediately after passing the Vaal, and entering the Transvaal or South African Republic, Lord Roberts announced the annexation by Great Britain of the Orange Free State under the name of the Orange River Colony.

On the 27th French and Hamilton, operating to the westward, reached Vanwyksrust, 30 miles southwest of Johannesburg, while Roberts' main army on the 28th advanced to. Klip River, 15 miles from Johannesburg, continuing on the 29th to Germiston, 10 miles east of Johannesburg. There-Roberts secured possession of the junction of the road to Natal over Heidelberg, and that of the Johannesburg—Klerksdorp road.

Colonel Henry with his mounted infantry, supported on the right by the 3d cavalry brigade, had orders to seize Natal Spruit and Elandsfontein at all cost. Pole-Carew and Tucker advanced along the railroad. Natal Spruit was first taken, then Elandsfontein, thus turning the Boer right.

Roberts here detached the 9th division for service in guarding the communications, retaining only the 11th and 7th divisions.

On the 30th Lord Roberts' army surrounded the city: the 7th division and Gordon's cavalry on the north, Hamilton on the west at Florida, French on the northeast, the 11th division and the heavy artillery remaining in Germiston. On the 31st the city surrendered, Roberts having agreed to allow its complete evacuation by the armed burghers. The Boers had left much rolling material and even a train-load of coal in their hasty retreat, and the mines were found undisturbed.

The British army had covered the distance between Kroonstad and Germiston, nearly 100 miles, in 8 days, at the rate of nearly 20 miles a day, repairing roads, railroads and bridges as they went, a remarkable performance.

In Pretoria Lord Roberts' victorious advance created consternation. President Krüger and the principal officials fled on the 29th of May to Machadodorp, a station on the railroad to Lorenzo-Marques. General Botha, however, was in Pretoria on the 31st, encouraging the Boers and endeavoring to incite them to further resistance, but with poor success.

Roberts, therefore, hastened his advance in order to take advantage of the confusion and to prevent the Boers from forming and executing new plans of resistance. His army rested on June 1st, and on the 2d, leaving the 14th brigade (Wavell's) in Johannesburg, he resumed his advance, the left flank covered by Hamilton, the extreme left guarded by French and Hutton pushed out towards Schoewan.

On June 4th the British came in contact with the Boers at Six Mile Spruit (Hennops River), just south of Pretoria. The mounted infantry and yeomanry dislodged the Boers from their first position, but, after pursuing them for nearly a mile, came upon their real position, protected by guns. The British heavy guns, which had been placed well to the front for that purpose, came into action, supported by Stephenson's brigade, and drove the Boers out of their position.

The latter then attempted to turn the British left flank, but were resisted by the mounted infantry and yeomanry and Maxwell's brigade, and finally Roberts directed Hamilton, 3 miles to the west at that time, to turn into the gap between the two columns. The Boers were driven back to Pretoria. Roberts bivouacked on the field, 4 miles from Pretoria. French, with the 3d and 4th cavalry brigades and Hutton's mounted infantry, was north of Pretoria, Broad-wood between French and Hamilton, and Gordon was watching the right, near the railway bridge at Irene Station, which had been destroyed by the Boers.

The strength of the latter at Six Mile Spruit was still about 10,000.

Hamilton pursued the Boers on the evening of the 4th to within 2,000 yards of the town, through which they retreated. In the morning the town was surrendered. The Boer forces, under Louis Botha, taking their guns with them, had retired to the eastward and northward.

Most of the English prisoners (4,500) were left by them at Waterval.

The surrender of the Transvaal capital closes the fourth act of the drama.

EVENTS IN THE SOUTH.

The guarding of the railway south of the Vaal was conducted by Rundle, Brabant, Clements and Methuen, holding a chain of posts from Heilbron to Ficksburg, 110 miles.

Kelly-Kenny remained at Bloemfontein.

Rundle and Brabant continued maneuvering against the Boer commandoes between Ficksburg and Bethlehem. On May 24th, Colville standing at Winburg, they reached Trommel, and on the 28th they had a sharp engagement with a Boer force at Senekal. On the 29th Rundle advanced southeast from Senekal to draw the Boer forces from Lindley, where a force of yeomanry was hard pressed. Lindley was occupied by the British, but on the 31st of May the 13th battalion yeomanry under Colonel Spragge was surrounded and captured by a superior Boer force. Methuen from Kroonstad had been ordered to the rescue and marched 44 miles in 25 hours, but arrived too late. He attacked the Boers, however, and routed them.

EVENTS IN THE EXTREME WEST.

In Griqualand West a revival of the rebellion so recently stamped out took place. Warren, with 700 men, was surrounded at night on May 29th, surprised and attacked by 1,000 rebels, while encamped at Faber Spruit, 12 miles from Douglas. The Boers were finally repulsed, but with heavy loss to the British.

Hunter was occupied in repairing the railway to Mafeking. On May 24th Hart was at Fourteen Streams on the Vaal, Barton at Taungs, Hunter at Vryburg, Baden-Powell at Mafeking, and Carrington at Marandellas. On May 28th Plumer occupied Zeerust, and on the 30th Hunter was at Khunwana, 40 miles south of Mafeking, and early in June was marching unopposed over Ventersdorp on Pretoria.

EVENTS IN NATAL.

Buller was detained at Newcastle repairing the railroad.

On May 18th a squadron of Bethune's horse (500 men) was detached to march from Dundee by Vantis Drift, showing their force in Nqutu, then to rejoin the main body at Newcastle. On their return they were ambushed by the Boers and lost 27 killed and 11 prisoners.

On May 19th Clery's division encamped at Ingogo, 12 miles north of Newcastle, while Dundonald reconnoitered to Laings Nek. On the 21st Butler's scouts crossed the Buffalo into the Transvaal.

Hildyard's (5th) division joined Buller at Newcastle on the 27th of May, and was at once sent out to seize Utrecht, while Lyttleton was ordered to move on Doornberg and Vryheid. The object of these movements was to turn the strong Boer position beyond Laings Nek.

The defile at Laings Nek was opened and the tunnel there repaired.

One June 2d Hildyard joined the main force from Utrecht. Lyttleton was at Coetzee's Drift, protecting the right flank.

The Boers, under Christian Botha, still numbered 10,000 men, and successfully opposed Buller's advance.

COMMENTS.

The Advance on Bloemfontein.

The battles of the war thus far, not including that of Paardeberg, fall into three groups of four each.

The first group embraced the actions in Natal at Glencoe, Elandslaagte, Rietfontein and Nicholsons Nek—three tactical successes culminating in a grave disaster. The second included the encounters in the West, of Belmont, Graspan, Modder River and Magersfontein—again three victories followed by a serious repulse. The third group comprised the battles on the Tugela, Colenso, Spion Kop, Vaal Kranz and Pieters Hill—three desperate repulses, succeeded by a final victory.

The invasion of the Free State by Lord Roberts rendered possible the forcing of the Boer lines on the Tugela, by drawing off a portion of Joubert's army, but the capture of Pieters Hill decided the campaign in Natal. In tactics this battle also illustrates the best modern ideas on the subject—namely, the combined frontal and flank attack, and is a perfect example of the proper execution of such a movement and action.

After Cronje's defeat the Boer Army should either have struck a decisive blow in Natal to counteract Lord Roberts' victory at Paardeberg, or, if they had to give up the siege of Ladysmith, their only chance for any decisive results was to concentrate all their available forces as rapidly as possible at Brandfort and Winburg in order to strike a decisive blow against the victorious army of Lord Roberts.

The occupation of Bloemfontein—turning aside from the direct route against the enemy's army—by Lord Roberts was a sound movement strategically, in which the moral effect of occupying the enemy's capital played but a secondary part. His strategic purpose was to get in communication with the columns of Brabant, Gatacre and Clements, to secure a strong base and the railroad as a line of supply and communication, and to reestablish on a normal footing the system of relays and intercommunication of the parts of his army. Moreover by taking the southerly direction along the Kraal Spruit any further intrenched positions of the enemy would be turned by the mere advance of the army.

Knowing the state of French's cavalry, it is difficult to criticise the tactics of the advance on Bloemfontein. Their deeds, considering the circumstances, are rather the subject for praise and wonder. Nevertheless, it was a mistake in reconnoissance to allow Porter's brigade at Poplar Grove to fall into the zone of a Boer position which had not been properly reconnoitered. Moreover, as another result, his turning movement was not at first sufficiently extended to strike the actual rear of the Boer flanks in the first place, so that Roberts' success was not complete, and the Boers were ready to oppose him again on the 10th.

Again, at Driefontein, the British came upon the Boer position unexpectedly, and were forced at first to make a frontal attack. They failed again to cut off the Boers, or to gain a decisive victory. One great cause of the British difficulties in reconnaissance, aside from the worn-out condition of the cavalry, is the lack of good maps, those of the Intelligence Division being remarkably poor; but the greatest element in their failure to bring about decisive actions is the remarkable mobility of the Boer troops, which they made full use of at this time in the tactics which they adopted—namely, to stand and fight till the tide begins to turn against them, and then rapidly to retire beyond reach. The forced march of the division of Kelly-Kenny across the hot plains, followed by six hours of hard fighting, was a performance deserving to rank among the finest of this kind.

After the fall of Bloemfontein there were three positions available for the Boer forces to make a defensive stand: at Brandfort, about 35 miles north of Bloemfontein; near Winburg, about 30 miles farther north; and at Ventersburg, about 30 miles still farther.

On the east these positions rest on considerable heights, but on the west they can all be turned, for which purpose the numerical superiority of the British would, of course, be taken advantage of. The first position (at Brandfort) could have been occupied immediately after Cronje's defeat, but after the fall of Bloemfontein it was no longer possible to concentrate the Boer army from Natal there, but it was still practicable to assemble it at Ventersburg or Kroonstad, holding the passes of the Drakensberg by a few thousand men. Moreover, after the occupation of Bloemfontein, the flanks of the position at Brandfort could readily have been threatened from Boshof, which Roberts had previously ordered occupied.

It is evident that, unless a decisive blow could be struck at once in Natal, it was useless for the Boers to hold on there, because the advance of Lord Roberts north from Bloemfontein would at once render the position of the Boer army on the Biggarsberg untenable, and force the latter to retreat over Laings Nek into the Transvaal domain. No doubt, the desire to hold the British beyond their own borders as long as possible influenced the Transvaal Boers to keep their main army in front of Buller, and to attempt to delay Roberts by means of a small but active force in the West.

The Strategy of the Boers.

The Boers, however, contrary to all expectation, adopted a more daring plan than that of concentrating at Kroonstad. They occupied the difficult hill country to the east and southeast of Bloemfontein, not over 40 or 50 miles from that capital. This was a bold step to take, but it promised results, for it placed on Lord Roberts' flank a force which would either compel him to give up his advance and turn against it towards Ladybrand, or, if he persists in advancing, to leave his long line of communications exposed to a flank attack. The moral effect of occupying a position so near to the British army was also very great, and restored the courage of the Orange Free State Boers.

By the death of Joubert the Boers lost their ablest general, and, coming as it did just after the capture of Cronje, the blow fell doubly hard. But the new generals, Botha, Olivier, De Wet and others, appeared to fill their places remarkably well, as shown by the actions immediately after Joubert's death and for some time thereafter;

General Christiaan de Wet 1854-1922

indeed, the fact that they were younger men in general probably was an advantage in itself, considering the new and more active mode of warfare demanded by the circumstances and adopted by the Boers.

This new strategy of the Boers led to innumerable minor engagements, but finally, early in April, they began a movement on a larger scale. While part of their forces made an attack at Brandfort against the center of Lord Roberts' line, a large force undertook a raid around his right flank towards Wepener, with a view to striking the British communications in rear and to gather up as many of the burghers as possible to swell the ranks of their army, while at the same time another force was gathering in the west at Paardeberg to move against Roberts' left flank. Moreover, farther west still, at Barkly West, Fourteen Streams, and along the north bank of the Vaal, the Boers were threatening an advance on Kimberley. Another great object of this movement to the rich country of southern Orange Free State was to gather in supplies, especially the harvest for which the district is noted.

While the spirit of this movement was strategically offensive, even to actual contact with the enemy (as at Reddersburg and Smithfield), its tactical execution failed entirely, for, instead of taking up the tactical offensive and attacking the British with determination, they split up their forces and engaged in a number of minor affairs which had no real connection with the original object of their strategical advance. Again did their tendency to a tactical defensive prevent them from reaping the rewards of their strategic offensive.

The Actions Around Bloemfontein.

The escape of Van der Post's column through the British lines at Poplar Grove, and that of Olivier's and Grobeler's along the Basutoland border must be attributed, first, to the fact that Roberts' cavalry was used up and the necessary remounts had not yet arrived, and, secondly, to the necessity of slow movement of the British columns following them from Cape Colony, this slowness being demanded in order to pacify the country passed over. The British columns were thus prevented from keeping in touch with the Boer columns, which enabled the latter to escape.

In the action at Karree Siding the condition of the cavalry evidently prevented a more complete victory.

The surprise of Broadwood's train at Koorn Spruit and his

command at the waterworks is another example of neglect of outpost and reconnaissance duty, at least of an effective kind. Broadwood knew that the enemy was in the vicinity in force, for he had himself reported the fact to General Roberts and had acted on the information by retiring from Thaba 'Nchu.

The capture of the command at Reddersburg was due to insufficient equipment at the outset, since no artillery was assigned to this column, and for this neglect General Gatacre was properly held responsible. Moreover, it would seem that with a proper system of transmitting information General Gatacre should have known of the action going on within 8 miles of one of his permanent posts (at Bethany) long before he received his order from General Roberts; and after he received that order, since he had the railroad available to Bethany, and only 8 miles to march, it would seem that the relief force should also have arrived earlier. In addition, however, there was again the usual neglect of proper outpost duty; otherwise so complete a surprise would have been impossible.

The Relief of Wepener.

The measures taken by Lord Roberts for the relief of Dewetsdorp and Wepener were finally effective so far as to cause the retreat of the Boers as soon as their line of retreat was threatened, but failed in effecting their capture. This was mainly due to the condition of the British troops, and it is to be noted that other indications point in the same direction. A careful analysis of the events will make this clear.

In the first place, the ordering of Brabant, Hart and Rundle against Wepener and Dewetsdorp was not dictated by strategical considerations, but merely to relieve the British force at the former of these two points, and to support it against great odds. The reinforcement of Rundle's troops by Pole-Carew and French was originally of a similar character.

In the next place, the movement finally made against the Boer lines of retreat (by Hamilton's command) was made by an entirely inadequate force and too late to be effective in capturing the agile Boers. It is evident that Roberts simply did not have his troops ready any sooner for taking the field, and this view is supported by the fact that the troops first selected were those which had not participated in the hard march to Bloemfontein, and also by the fact that as soon as possible Pole-Carew was sent back as a reserve to Bloemfontein to be available for any possible movement of the Boers from the northeast or northwest, or to meet any emergency in the east or southeast.

Finally, the pursuit by the British after the Boers abandoned Dewetsdorp and Wepener was too slow to insure success, and this again must be attributed to the condition of the troops, more especially as to supplies.

The explanation of this state of affairs after so long a rest in the case of the troops at Bloemfontein is to be sought not only in the effects of the hard marches from Modder River to Bloemfontein, but more especially (and this applies also to the new reinforcements recently arrived) to the fact that the British rolling material for the narrow-gauge road of supply had all to be prepared before the system of supply could be fully organized.

Nevertheless, some share of the blame must fall on the apparent lack of good training of the new troops in modern war movements.

The Advance on Kroonstad.

The decision of Lord Roberts to advance again after the capture of the kopjes southeast of Brandfort on the 4th of May was good judgment and fine strategy. The movements of his entire army were thus combined on a single object, and no time was lost in forming a new front, but the parts came up into line as they moved forward on their natural routes, and in such a way as to embody a turning movement at the same time.

But in turning the enemy's position at Vet River with cavalry (or mounted troops) on both his flanks it does not appear clear why Hamilton or Hutton did not strike the rear of the enemy and break up the railroad to prevent his retiring. In all probability Hamilton was not sufficiently informed on reaching Winburg of the position in front of Roberts, and so could not know how effective such a measure might be, and Hutton evidently obeyed his orders too literally, and did not take advantage of the opportunity offered till too late.

At Smaldeel the question naturally arose as to the propriety of attacking in rear the Boer detachments occupying the Drakensberg passes, because Winburg, on account of the connections and communications, was the nearest point along the railway from which to accomplish this. To have done this, however, would have necessitated leaving the railway again, and, besides, would have offered the Boers an opportunity to attack the British in flank. In view of these facts, then, and the additional one that Buller was holding a large Boer force idle in front of him, the strategy of Lord Roberts in continuing his advance along the railroad must be regarded as sound.

Of course, the latter movement still presented some difficulties, because the Boers retiring from the Moroka district might effect, in the vicinity of Bethlehem, a junction with those opposing Roberts' advance directly, and then compel the British to fight with their front to a flank. But the character of the opposition thus far met with did not indicate such mobility, determination or strategic ability on the part of the Boers. It was with a view to preventing such action on the part of the latter that Roberts, on May 7th, had such an extended reconnaissance made by his cavalry and mounted infantry to make sure that the Boers were retiring northward beyond the Zand River.

The prompt advance of Lord Roberts beyond Smaldeel was masterful strategy. The moral effect was in itself very great: most of the Orange Boers returned to their farms, and the Transvaal Boers declined to fight any longer in the Orange Free State. But the strategic results were greater still, because it gave Roberts practically control of the lines Durban—Bethlehem, and Durban—Johannesburg. The advance, moreover, put these three theatres in actual strategical relation with one another, for Buller in Natal, and Hunter and Methuen in the vicinity of Kimberley, moved out at the same time, and Roberts' short halt in Kroonstad was mainly to adjust the parts of this line.

The Advance on Pretoria.

The advance of Roberts from Kroonstad to Johannesburg was conducted at first on a broad front (about 50 miles), but it soon became evident that, while such an extent of front facilitated the turning of the Boer positions strategically, it did not fulfill the tactical conditions necessary for capturing the Boers or for forcing them to stand and fight a decisive action, because concerted action between the turning wings was impossible. Consequently, after passing the Rhenoster, the width of front was reduced to 25 miles, and all the cavalry was put on the left flank. The Boers then could escape only by giving up practically all resistance.

This march to Johannesburg, considering its distance, the character of the country, the size of the army and the destroyed bridges, railroads and roads, was a splendid achievement, and illustrates the grand qualities of the British in marching capacity in their ability to repair bridges, railroads and wagon roads, in their utter contempt for the danger of an enemy hovering on their lines of communication in rear, and in their determination to reach their objective.

The turn to the west before crossing the Vaal was sound strategy, for the Vaal, unlike other rivers in this section in the dry season, is not fordable except at a few points, and the position at Vereeniging was a very strong one to force, and required passage over the bridge there.

The strategy of Roberts' campaign was brilliant and effective, and the opening of Laings Nek by Buller and the advance of Hunter over Ventersdorp on Pretoria promised to furnish him the necessary reinforcements. Nevertheless, the escape of the Boers at Johannesburg and again at Pretoria give to the results an element of incompleteness, especially as the enemy retired to the difficult mountain country—the Lydenburg District.

Roberts' turning movement in both these cases was by his left; had he turned to the east, he would have forced them to fight at both places. However, it must be remembered that Roberts counted on Buller's advance from Natal, which the latter was unable to effect; moreover, his main object was to keep the Boers moving by the rapidity of his strokes, and at both the above mentioned places the turning of the western flank was far the easier, hence the more quickly accomplished.

Strategically, then, his march marked the great commander who takes a comprehensive view of the entire situation, and retains his object, in spite of mishaps in isolated parts of the theatre. Tactically he could not reap the full harvest of his strategy because of Buller's difficult advance from Natal and the disturbances around Lindley threatening his line of communications in rear: the necessity for rapidity of action was greater than that for perfection in tactical disposition.

PART V.

The fourth act in the South African war closed with the brilliant campaign of Roberts, ending with the occupation of Pretoria, the Transvaal capital.

Pretoria had been well fortified with seven strong forts, but only five of these had their armament. Fort Signal, about 5½ miles south of Pretoria, commanded the railroad to Johannesburg, and was well armed, and at the outbreak of hostilities fully garrisoned; and Fort Wonderboom, about 5 miles south of the capital, was one of the best of modern forts. The garrisons, however, had been sent into the field, and were never replaced. Moreover, the entire line of defense was too extended for the 10,000 men left to hold it. For these reasons the Boers gave up this important point, and retired to Middelburg on the railroad, leaving a strong rear guard at Hatherley, 12 miles east of Pretoria.

They had decided to defend the mountain district of Lydenburg, and had for some time been sending daily from Pretoria 50 trains with supplies into this region. Nevertheless, they had not yet made up their minds to limit themselves to guerrilla warfare, but proposed to make a stand at any good available defensive positions, such as Hatherley, Middelburg and Volksrust.

In the northern part of the Orange Free State their resistance was not yet subdued, but there guerrilla warfare was exclusively adopted, and proved effective.

EVENTS IN THE ORANGE RIVER COLONY.

Lord Roberts reached the end of his march with about 25,000 men— 10,000 cavalry and 15,000 infantry, so that he still had enough to cope with Botha, and had reason to hope that Buller and Hunter could advance to Pretoria. But the great danger was that threatening his lines of communication, especially as Buller's advance was too slow to enable him to count on a line through Natal in time, and to dispense entirely with the line through Kroonstad.

Roberts took with him into the Transvaal about 46,000 men. Hunter,

Mahon and Plumer had about 11,500. In Orange River Colony there were about 41,500.

His immediate army comprised Pole-Carew's (11th) division, Smith-Dorrien's brigade of Colville's division, and Maxwell's of Tucker's division; also French's cavalry, and Hamilton's mounted infantry.

The following troops had been assigned to the protection of the lines of communication in rear of Roberts' army, viz.:

- 1st division, Lord Methuen, on the Rhenoster (Paget's Brigade at Lindley).
- 3d division, Chermside, near Senekal.
- 6th division ($\frac{1}{2}$), Kelly-Kenny, at Bloemfontein.
- 8th division, Rundle, at Hammonia.
- 8th division, Colville, at Heilbron.
- Colonial division, Brabant, at Ficksburg.

West of Johannesburg the detachments of Hunter and Colonel Mahon had joined forces at Ventersdorp. Troops from Cape Colony and half of Kelly-Kenny's division (Maxwell's brigade from Johannesburg) had been sent to Kroonstad to strengthen the line of communications.

Buller in Natal had Clery's, Lyttleton's and Warren's divisions, as well as three Natal cavalry brigades.

The Boers were still about 27,000 strong: 10,000 at Hatherley—Middelburg (east of Pretoria), 8,000 under Stein at Heilbron—Bethlehem—Harrismith—Ficksburg— Vreede, 9,000 at Laings Nek.

De Wet, who had retired into the Elandsberge, between Lindley and Frankfort, soon began to display great activity. Utilizing the difficult mountain district as his base, he made constant forays against the railroad between Kroonstad and Vereeniging. In the early art of June he succeeded in destroying the telegraph line and the railroad, near Roodeval and American Station, for a distance of 20 miles.

The advance of Methuen from Lindley towards Heilbron, and of the troops of the lines of communication under Lord Kitchener from Vereeniging, prevented their gaining a permanent foothold, but constant forays were made against this long line of railroad. Lord Kitchener joined forces with Methuen at Heilbron, and the united forces marched to the Rhenoster River, where they completely defeated De Wet, and then marched to Kroonstad. During the repair of the road between Roodeval and American Station the Boers captured a number of workmen, detachments of troops, convoys, and in one case even an entire battalion —the 4th of the Derbyshire Militia Regiment. The Boers were especially active against Honing Spruit Station. Whenever successful they retired to their fortresses in the Elandsberge.

On June 19th, De Wet with 5,000 men attacked Methuen's force, escorting a transport train to Heilbron, but was defeated. Nevertheless, on the 23d, he cut off a British detachment on the Kroonstad—Honing Spruit Section, attacked the camp of the Shropshire Regiment and the Canadian Contingent, captured a train going south, tore up the track for some distance, and only retired before superior forces coming from Kroonstad.

In the vicinity of Ficksburg, where General Brabant had remained, and at Hammonia, whither Bundle was hastening in support, the Boers under De Villiers were also active. In the middle of June, Brabant disarmed a Boer commando of 1,500 men near Ficksburg, but the Boers received considerable reinforcements from the northern part of the Orange River Colony. President Stein had moved his seat of government to Bethlehem, so as to be between De Wet and De Villiers, in order to incite both to desperate and constant resistance.

These engagements have no effect on the general situation, and the fact remains that a large part of the inhabitants of the Orange River Colony have retired to their farms, leaving the forces in the field too weak to accomplish anything decisive.

EVENTS IN NATAL.

The advance of Buller in Natal against the extremely strong position of the Boers had been necessarily slow, so that he was not able to take part in the proposed concentric advance on Johannesburg. His efforts were directed to turning the Boer position, and in this he showed that he had learned well the lesson of the Tugela.

His attempt to turn the Boer left flank, by detaching Lyttleton to Vryheid and Hildyard to Utrecht, failed. His next step was to secure favorable artillery positions to command Majuba Hill and Laings Nek, operating against the right flank of the Boer position.

The advance of Lord Roberts to Johannesburg had had its effect on the Boer troops, and their forces, previously given at 10,000, were considerably reduced. Their leader, Christian Botha, had asked

General Louis Botha, taken c. 1900

for a three-days cessation of hostilities, but Buller's demand for unconditional surrender ended the correspondence.

On June 3d, Buller resumed his advance, his plan being to hold the Boer front and to roll up the flanks. For this purpose he made a reconnaissance over Botha's Pass towards Gansvlei Spruit, a branch of the Klip River, and then assembled his forces behind his left wing for a decisive attack.

Meanwhile, Lord Strathcona's Horse (from Canada) was sent out to the north to threaten the rear of Botha's force and his railway communications with Delagoa Bay over Komatipoort.

General Coke, with the 10th brigade and the South African Light Horse, took the Van Wyk Berg, a spur of Mount Prospect, with little loss; and in the night of the 7th the Van Wyk Berg and the southwestern spurs of the Inkwelo Berg were occupied by artillery. Under the protection of the fire of the latter, General Hildyard on the 8th attacked, the heights between the Inkwelo and Botha's Pass and carried them in excellent form, winning thereby his promotion to lieutenant-general. Almonds Nek, the last pass before Charlestown, was taken, and the road to the enemy's rear was opened.

On the 9th Buller resumed the offensive, moving in the direction of the Gansvlei valley, pushing along the Transvaal and Natal border in a northeastern direction, to turn Laings Nek. The Boers in his front retired towards Paarde Kop and on the 11th of June, after the further advance of the British on Volksrust, the Boers (3,000), occupying Laings Nek and Majuba Hill, abandoned this strong position, retiring on Wakkerstroom. They were thus separated into two parts, but in spite of the success of Buller's strategical maneuvers, the Boers were enabled to retire without loss, taking their artillery and train with them.

On June 12th Buller, on account of the scarcity of water, retired from Volksrust to Charlestown, where he joined Clery, who had come from Ingogo.

The interruption of the railroad at Laings Nek was soon repaired, and by the 17th of June the first train was running through this point.

On the 19th Lord Strathcona's Horse (sent out about the 9th) destroyed a railway bridge near Komatipoort, cutting Botha's communications in that direction.

EVENTS IN THE TRANSVAAL.

First Campaign Against Louis Botha.

Reconnaissances from Roberts' main army at Pretoria had established the fact that Louis Botha's army was at Eerste Fabrieken (Hatherley and DonkerhoIk), about 16 miles east of Pretoria, on both sides of the Middelburg road. The position was a strong one, but too

The Coldstream Guards at Diamond Hill

extended for the troops occupying it—about 12,000.

In spite of the fact that everything was quiet and peaceful in Pretoria and Johannesburg, the close proximity of so strong a Boer army was a constant menace, and Roberts decided to attack it. Reinforcements could not be expected for some time, as Buller was still at Laings Nek, Hunter at Potchefstroom, Baden-Powell at Rustenburg, and no troops could be spared from the line of communications. He therefore decided to make the attack with what troops he had in hand.

The Battle of Diamond Hill.

Botha had concentrated his forces on the flanks of his position, leaving the center comparatively weak. Roberts, following his usual course, advanced on the 11th of June with a broad front, intending to enclose the Boers with both flanks; French's cavalry division on the left to turn the Boer right flank; Hamilton, with the mounted infantry and Broadwood's brigade on the right, to turn the Boer left; while Pole-Carew, with some mounted infantry, under Colonel Henry, held the enemy at the center. Roberts, however, soon found Botha's flanks too strong, and directed his efforts on the center, ordering Hamilton to attack Diamond Hill, which was accomplished with little loss on the 12th by the aid of Pole-Carew's division, the Boers retiring towards Middelburg. The British troops did not pursue, but returned to Pretoria.

Roberts decided to await the arrival of reinforcements before inaugurating a definite campaign against the forces in northern

Orange River Colony, threatening his line of communications. With this object in view, he drew in the Natal army along the Laings Nek—Johannesburg railroad, to separate completely the Transvaal and Orange Boers. Buller reached Standerton on the 17th, and Hunter turned off at Krügersdorp (west of Johannesburg) towards Frankfort. Baden-Powell reached Pretoria on the 18th. On the 21st Buller reached Paarde Kop; Hamilton's column from Pretoria reaching Springs on the same day, ready to join hands with Buller at Heidelberg on the 24th of June, but Buller was forced to halt at Standerton, which he reached on the 23d, because the Boers had destroyed the bridge there, and their forces to the eastward threatened his line of communications.

EVENTS IN ORANGE RIVER COLONY.[3]

Roberts, towards the end of June, directed his attention to the Boers under Steyn and De Wet, threatening his line of communications. The enveloping movement already begun was gradually completed.

A glance at the general situation at this time will aid materially in comprehending the movements about to follow:

Baden-Powell, Hutton and Plumer held Rustenburg; Pole-Carew, Tucker and French formed the garrisons of Pretoria and Johannesburg; Smith-Dorrien was at Vredefort (southwest of Johannesburg), to guard the west of the railroad; Methuen, Knox, Kelly-Kenny, Clements, Paget, and Colville were stationed at Rhenoster, Kroonstad, Bloemfontein, Senekal, Lindley and Heilbron, respectively, to guard the railroad on the east; Rundle and Brabant completed the cordon along the northwest border of Basutoland, at Hammonia and Ficksburg, respectively; Hamilton and Hunter occupied Heidelberg; and Buller had reached Standerton.

The Boers, still numbering 20,000, had about two-thirds of their forces south of the Vaal, divided into four commandoes, under Piet and Christian De Wet, Limmer and Olivier.

Buller, after occupying Standerton, sent mounted troops forward to Greylingstad. Viljoen's commando, which had held the place, retired towards Middelburg. Buller had left a strong detachment under Hildyard at Volksrust and Laings Nek to guard the pass and railroad against any efforts of the Boers who had retired from that point on

---

3 In Cape Colony, on June 23d, De Villier's commando, 200 men, 280 horses, 18 wagons, 260 rifles, and over 100,000 rounds of ammunition, arrived at Blikfontein and surrendered to Sir Charles Warren. De Villiers in person escaped eastward.

Wakkerstroom. During his advance his outposts had met numerous small bodies of Boers, indicating the presence of the latter on all sides. A Boer force of 1,000 from Wakkerstroom took up a strong position at Gras Kop, northwest of Volksrust, and fifteen miles from Sand Spruit Station, threatening the railway line.

On June 20th General Coke, sent on a reconnaissance with the 10th brigade to Amersfoort (12 miles north of the railroad), discovered a force of 2,000 Boers with, guns in a strong position there, which he did not attack. In view of these facts, Buller strengthened his outpost at Greylingstad with a brigade on July 3d, and early in July pushed out Clery to the vicinity of Heidelberg, where he joined Hart's brigade on the 4th. Thus it is evident that nearly all of Buller's troops were needed to guard the railroad. However, on July 7th, he reported that the railroad was serviceable as far as Pretoria.

Buller's position along the railroad completed the separation of the Orange from the Transvaal Boers and brought his forces in contact with those of Roberts.

The Campaign Against De Wet.

As soon as Roberts had organized his cordon around the Orange Boers, and had completed their separation from the Transvaal Boers, he proceeded to institute a decisive campaign against De Wet, ensconced in the Elandsberge, whence he had made numerous successful sorties against the troops guarding the lines of communication.

The general movements were inaugurated on July 1st by sending Hunter (exclusive of Hart's brigade, which was left at Heidelberg), as well as Broadwood's and Little's cavalry brigades, to Frankfort.

As soon as these troops were in position, the following changes in organization and command were instituted:-

Colville's division (9th) was broken up, and its commander relieved; Macdonald's (Highlander) brigade being assigned to Hunter's (10th) division, in place of Hart's, joining Hunter on July 3d in Frankfort; Smith-Dorrien's being transferred to Methuen's (1st) division, then at PaardeKraal, north of Kroonstad, the latter sending Paget's brigade to operate against De Wet. Broadwood's and Little's brigades, first attached to Hunter's division, were now attached to Paget's brigade, which was to constitute Hunter's advance guard. The mounted infantry, which had been sent from Roberts' immediate command, reached Heilbron on the 8th of July, but was afterwards called back to relieve Methuen on the lines of communication, when the latter was sent on July 11th to the relief of Rustenburg.

The general plan was a concentric advance of Hunter from Frankfort, Paget from Kroonstad, and Clements from Winburg, against De Wet, in order to surround and capture him in the mountains near Lindley.

Paget moved rapidly, reached Pleiserfontein, east of Lindley, on July 3d, and had an engagement with the Boers there. The latter were defeated and followed by Paget on the 4th to a point half way between Lindley and Bethlehem (the temporary seat of the Orange Boer government, which was now moved to Reitz). De Wet had taken up a strong position at Bethlehem, consequently Paget hesitated to attack him, and decided to await the arrival of Clements. On the 7th their combined forces continued the advance, and compelled the Boers to retire into the mountains south of Bethlehem.

Meanwhile Broadwood and Little arrived at Bethlehem, while Hunter was still on the march from the north, some distance away. The original concentric advance of three columns had thus become the simple advance of a single column.

De Wet, after retiring into the Roode Berge south of Bethlehem, found himself between the forces at Bethlehem and the Basutoland border, threatened in his left flank by Brabant and Rundle, and cut off in the west.

Meanwhile, Rundle and Brabant continued their advance, reaching Rooikrans (northwest of Ficksburg), where they drove off a small Boer detachment, and establishing the fact that a strong Boer force was posted east of that place.

On July 16th, meeting with little resistance, De Wet was enabled to break through the left flank of Rundle's line, with 1,500 men and 5 guns, marching on Lindley.

Broadwood and Little (from Bethlehem, where Bruce Hamilton had now arrived) followed in pursuit, and struck De Wet on the 19th at Palmietfontein, just west of Lindley, and defeated him. But on the 22d he turned up at Serfontein, just north of Honing Spruit, took a transport train with its guard (1 officer, 100 men), continuing his march to Vredefort, where he halted on the 23d and prepared his position for defence.

The Boers again displayed considerable activity at other points. A reconnoitering party with a battery, sent out from Bethlehem by

Hunter on July 21st, came upon a strong position held by Boers about 20 miles west of Bethlehem, and was forced back. On the 22 minor engagements took place with Boer forces south of Bethlehem, and on the 23d Hunter moved out with stronger forces, but failed to carry the Boer position on that day. On the 24th, however, he succeeded in turning the Boer flanks, the latter retiring before him. He moved south in pursuit, reaching Fouriesburg on the 27th.

Meanwhile Bundle continued his advance, pushing the retiring Boers in his front before him towards the same point. He occupied Kommando Nek, and the two forces of Boers found themselves between Hunter and Rundle. The result was that Prinsloo with about 4,140 men surrendered on July 30th. Among the captured were commandants Villiers and Crowther, and three other commandants of less note. General Olivier, with his commando and five guns, however, succeeded in breaking through in the direction of Harrismith.

The renewed activity of the Boers was made evident not only along Roberts' line of communications, but also on his immediate front and flanks. The flanks of the British army at Pretoria are covered by detachments at Rustenburg (50 miles west of the capital), near Bronkhorst Spruit (35 miles east) and at Springs (the terminus of the branch line from Johannesburg), and at all these points, as well as at others, the Boers made more or less energetic attacks, besides that already referred to at Greylingstad.

Actions at Rustenburg and Olifants Nek.

On July 8th Lemmer with a commando of Boers suddenly appeared before Rustenburg, occupied the heights commanding the town, and demanded its surrender. Major Tracy, in command there, refused, and opened an attack on the Boers. Part of Carrington's force from Zeerust arrived in time to take part in the action, and Lemmer was forced to give up the siege and retire. A few days later, however, after this relief force moved on to join Lord Roberts, the Boer leader Delarey appeared before Rustenburg and resumed the siege. The garrison was too weak to resist him for any length of time, so Roberts, to relieve his threatened left flank and restore communication with Mafeking, was forced to draw Methuen from Paarde Kraal (north of Kroonstad) to Rustenburg. The latter reached on the 21st the vicinity of Rustenburg over Krügersdorp, struck the Boers at Olifants Nek, and dispersed them.

Lord Roberts had at this time decided on a grand right wheel of his army, advancing on Middelburg, and Methuen was left at Rustenburg to cover his rear. But on the 25th he was ordered to march over Potchefstroom towards the Vaal, to join Broadwood and Little against De Wet, who had intrenched himself at Vredefort.

In Roberts' immediate front the army of Louis Botha had again grown to a strength of 15,000 men, and had taken up its position at Bronkhorst Spruit, 35 miles east of Pretoria.

Action at Springs.

Colonel Mahon had occupied with his own troops and portions of Hamilton's mounted infantry, which had been left in the Transvaal, the important end station, Springs, on the Johannesburg branch. He was the first to feel the pressure of this strong Boer army in such close proximity to Roberts' front. On July 6th, about 3,000 Boers attacked his position, and could only be forced back over the Bronkhorst Spruit after a hard fight on the. 7th. But this attack was evidently merely a diversion to cover a more determined advance of the Boers by the north and west of Pretoria to act on the flank of Roberts' line and gain touch with the Boers around Rustenburg.

Action at Uitvals Nek.

In anticipation of such a movement Roberts had sent five companies of the Lincolnshire Regiment, and a squadron of Scots Greys, with several guns, to occupy Uitvals (Massilikatz) Nek, a pass about 18 miles west of Pretoria, to cover his left flank. These troops reached their destination on July 10th, and occupied a position directly covering the pass with three companies, the other two being left on the plain. On the 11th, at dawn, Boers to the north of the pass opened fire on the British outposts, and at the same time a heavy fire was opened by Boers from kopjes to the east of the pass, or in rear of the British. These Boers were part of Delarey's force. The fight lasted all day, and although reinforcements were sent, they arrived too late, the three companies in the pass having been surrounded and captured. The British lost 90 prisoners, besides the killed and wounded. The latter amounted to 1 officer and 15 men killed; 3 officers and 51 men wounded.

Action at Derdepoort.

On the same day, July 11th, Roberts' outpost at Derdepoort (5 miles northeast of Pretoria) was surprised and attacked by the Boers under Delarey, resulting in the retreat of the British with considerable loss, viz.: 1 officer and two men killed; 2 officers and 4 men wounded; and 10 men missing.

Another Boer subdivision occupied a ridge running east and west, about 10 miles north of Pretoria, but retired before a strong detachment[4] sent out by Roberts on July 16th, since it had accomplished its object of drawing British troops in that direction, in order to prepare the way for a direct attack on Roberts' front.

The latter was directed on Pole-Carew's left flank and the left wing, commanded by Hutton, but the excellent handling of the British artillery resulted in the defeat of the Boers. An attack on Springs, at the same time, was repelled by the fire of the Royal Irish Regiment.

Numerous sallies were also made against the British detachments at Krügersdorp.

All these operations of the Boers indicated their presence on all sides of Roberts' army, and demanded some decided action at once.

CAMPAIGN OF MIDDELBURG.

Second Campaign Against Louis Botha.

Roberts determined to move against the strongest and most active of the Boer armies—namely, that of General Louis Botha, in the direction of Middelburg.

On July 19th the movement began. The British line was formed just east of Pretoria, facing eastward: French on the right at Treneestate, Pole-Carew in the center, Hutton's mounted infantry on the left, including Hamilton's mounted infantry and Mahon's brigade, which had been sent to Springs.

The British forces numbered about 22,000; the Boers had about 12,000 men in position.

He first moved along the railroad to Bronkhorst Spruit; during the advance Hutton was sent to reinforce French's right wing, while Hamilton's and Mahon's mounted infantry moved to the left flank behind Pole-Carew's division.

On July 22d the right wing was south of Prinsloo, on the Bronkhorst Spruit, its center at the station; the left flank at Russfontein (6 miles north of the station); giving Pole-Carew a very advantageous position

---

[4] A new brigade under Colonel Cunningham was formed, comprising 1st battalion King's Own Scottish Borderers, 1st battalion Royal Berkshire Regiment, 1st battalion Argyll and Sutherland Highlanders. Hickman's mounted infantry (1,800) was attached.

at the center. On the 23d, when the general advance began, the Boers retired eastward. French reached the eastern shore of Wilge River, 7 miles south of Balmoral Station (5 miles east of Wilge River Station), on the afternoon of the 24th; the leading brigade (Stephenson's) of Pole-Carew's division arrived at the Elands River station (30 miles east of Pretoria); while Hamilton remained about S miles in rear, as a left flank guard. The Boers had offered no resistance at any point.

On the eastern shore of the Wilge River, however, French found a Boer commando of 2,000 Boers ready to resist his advance. Part of Hutton's mounted infantry attacked the right flank of the position, while French endeavored to pass around the left flank. The Boers retired, and French and Hutton pursued, but failed to get any material results.

On the 25th the center reached Balmoral Station, 10 miles east of Elands River. French and Hutton continued the pursuit over the Steenkoot River; where the condition of their horses compelled them to halt. A few detachments crossed the Olifant River, and reported strong columns of Boers in full retreat on Middelburg. The weather was very inclement, the rain falling in torrents, and a cold east wind blowing. This, together with the condition of the horses, prevented Roberts from taking advantage of the situation.

Roberts in person, and the troops of Hamilton and Mahon, returned to Pretoria, which they reached on the 30th. French and Pole-Carew (their forces amounting to about 15,000 men) continued the pursuit as far asMiddelburg, where they arrived on the 29th. Louis Botha withdrew into the hills of Wonderfontein with his main army, leaving a considerable force on the Bothas Berge, north of Middelburg, threatening the left flank of any further advance eastward on the part of the British.

Meanwhile Buller (who had previously moved from Standerton back to Paarde Kop, to be nearer Hildyard, who was constantly threatened by the forces under Christian Botha near Volksrust) sent Lyttleton and two cavalry brigades to threaten the Boer left flank east of Middelburg, these troops reaching Amersfoort (25 miles north of Volksrust) on the 5th of August. Clery was left to guard the railroad between Standerton and Heidelberg; Hildyard near Volksrust.

Botha at first retired before Buller, but finally made a stand on a ridge north of Amersfoort.

On August 6th the British attacked the position: Dun-donald on the west side, the infantry on the east; the latter, with the King's Royal Fusiliers on the right, and the Gordon Highlanders on the left, continued the attack, in spite of the heavy artillery fire, till 5 p.m., when the Boers retired. The roads were so bad that the train was so far to the rear; consequently Buller was compelled to remain in Amersfoort on the 7th.

On the 8th he continued his advance, reaching Rood (on the Vaal) on the 9th, and on the 12th Ermelo, in rear of the forces of Christian Botha, who were retiring on Carolina. On the 15th he reached Twyfelaar, near Carolina. Meanwhile French's reconnoitering parties from Middleburg over Wonderfontein had established communication with Buller.

The Boers made several attempts on Buller's line of communications. In the vicinity of Ingogo, south of Laings Nek, they brought a heavy gun into position with a view to destroy the iron railroad bridge there; near Ladysmith they made several efforts to break up the railroad; and finally, on August 21st, a Boer detachment destroyed the bridge 9 miles north of Newcastle, and broke up the railroad south of that point. West of Standerton also there were constant skirmishes with Boer detachments.

These interruptions caused Buller to delay his further advance.

The Chase After De Wet.

De Wet had intrenched himself in the vicinity of Vredefort, whither he had been pursued by Broadwood and Little. Methuen had been ordered down from Rustenburg over Potchefstroom, to take part in the pursuit of De Wet.

This Boer leader with his small column, with which was also President Steyn, was considered of such importance that Lord Kitchener was ordered to take the troops from Springs, reinforce Broadwood and Little, and conduct the operations, but Methuen was not placed under his orders, the latter retaining independent command of his own column from the northwest.

De Wet remained inactive from the 23d of July to the 7th of August, awaiting the approach of Methuen from Potchefstroom, and Kitchener, operating south of the Vaal. On that day, however, he marched his main column to Lindequees Drift, 20 miles up stream from Vredefort, and protected himself against Kitchener, sending a flank column over the Vaal at Venterskroon, 7 miles northwest of Vredefort, to cover his position against a flank attack by Methuen, which might impede his passage of the river. This flank column, on the morning of August 7th, had an action with Methuen's advanced troops, but retired in good order, reaching Buffelshoek, 7 miles northeast of Venterskroon, on August 9th (the day on which Lord Kitchener reached Lindequees Drift, and had a slight engagement with De Wet's rear guard), and was attacked again by Methuen. Neither British commander knew of the near presence of the other until the fighting at Lindequees Drift on the one hand, and Buffelshoek on the other, informed them; otherwise Methuen would have moved by his right, joined hands with Kitchener, and then rolled up De Wet's flank. De Wet drew his forces on the 9th from the two rear-guard actions, combined his forces, and retired on Welverdiend, 18 miles northeast of Potchefstroom, whereas Kitchener and Methuen did not join forces till the 10th, north of Buffelshoek.

At Welverdiend, however, De Wet found Smith-Dorrien, whom Lord Methuen had left behind to guard the railroad, and who now blocked his way northward. He had little difficulty, however, in slipping by these troops, following the Mooi River towards Rustenburg.

Kitchener and Methuen, moving in two separate columns, overtook De Wet again on the 13th of August east of Ventersdorp, Methuen succeeding in capturing one gun. On the-night of the 13th, De Wet liberated his 60 British prisoners, blew up three ammunition wagons and abandoned 30 Avorn-out horses, and escaped from his pursuers.

On August 17th De Wet reached Kommando Nek in the Magalies Hills, between Pretoria and Rustenburg, and came here upon Baden-Powell, who happened to have withdrawn to this point, for reasons which will be at once explained.

The British had posted three detachments to guard the line from Mafeking towards Pretoria, viz.: Carrington (who had come through Rhodesia and taken part in the first relief of Rustenburg) at Zeerust; Lieutenant-Colonel Hore, with 400 men at Elands River, 40 miles west of Rustenburg, and Baden-Powell, with 4,000 men, at the latter place, where he had been twice besieged and relieved, and was still constantly threatened by Delarey (who had recently been reinforced by Grobeler's commando).

As soon as Methuen left to operate against De Wet, Rustenburg was besieged for the third time, and this explains why Lord Roberts brought Hamilton's and Mahon's mounted infantry back from the campaign against Middelburg. Hamilton left Pretoria on his way to relieve Rustenburg on August 2d, and succeeded in joining Baden-Powell, Delarey retiring without resisting. Hamilton brought Baden-Powell to Kommando Nek, where the latter intrenched himself, and himself started southward to take part in the chase after De Wet, reaching Blaauwbank on August 13th.

No sooner was Rustenburg abandoned than Delarey turned on the weak garrison of Elands River and besieged it. Carrington, with 900 men and several guns, started out from Zeerust on August 3d to relieve Hore, but on the 5th, as he was approaching Here's camp, he found his way impeded by a strong Boer force with artillery. He was forced to retire, under heavy cross fire, and reached Zeerust, after considerable loss in men and material on the 7th; but at once decided to retire still farther. On his way to Mafeking he met another force of Boers at Ottoshoop and Malmain on the 16th of August, and had a skirmish with them, but drove them off.

Hore was thus entirely isolated after August 6th. On the 10th a messenger from Hore came through the Boer lines and reported the garrison still resisting. Roberts received this message on the 13th, and at once ordered Carrington and Hamilton to return to the relief of Hore. Meanwhile Kitchener, who saw the uselessness of further pursuit of De Wet, and hearing of Hore's dilemma, also started to his relief, reaching Elands River on August 16th, the Boers retiring northward. Methuen, giving up the pursuit of De Wet in the vicinity of Rustenburg, started westward to the region about Zeerust, Mafeking and Lichtenburg, to restore order at points threatened by the Boers.

When Hamilton on the 17th approached Rustenburg he learned of the relief of Elands River, and also of the near presence of De Wet, who, after calling upon Baden-Powell at Kommando Nek to surrender, had continued his march on the 18th towards the Sterk Stroom north of Rensburg. Hamilton had reached Olifants Nek, south of Rustenburg, on the 17th, and Mahon, his advance guard, came in touch with De Wet. Hamilton decided to continue the pursuit; meanwhile Baden-Powell, moving towards Rensburg on the Pretoria—Rustenburg road, attempted to strike De Wet's flank. On the 19th, while Baden-Powell continued his turning movement,

Mahon succeeded in engaging De Wet's rear guard in an action on the Crocodile River; but the latter escaped, and on the 20th camped near Hebron, 20 miles northwest of Pretoria.

It looked as if De Wet was aiming to cross the railroad north of Pretoria and join Louis Botha's forces.

Roberts meanwhile had sent Paget on the 18th of August along the Pretoria—Pietersburg road northward, and the latter, after forcing small Boer detachments out of the Homes Nek (10 miles northwest of Pretoria), had taken up a position near Hammans Kraal (27 miles from Pretoria). On the 20th, Roberts also sent Clements northward to take part in the pursuit of De Wet. Baden-Powell, turning out of the Pretoria—Rustenburg road, completed the line around De Wet.

On the 20th Paget allowed himself to be drawn into a fight by a detachment of De Wet's, and was held fast all day; and on the 21st Baden-Powell struggled all day against the rear guard of Grobeler (part of whose forces had joined De Wet). Meanwhile De Wet accomplished the main object of his long and dangerous march, viz.: to enable President Steyn (with a strong detachment) to escape eastward over the Pienaars River to join Krüger in Machadodorp through the unoccupied region over the Bothas Berge. De Wet himself, with a small force, turned back over the Magalies Berge to regain the Orange River Colony.

The force under Methuen remained in western Transvaal, while Paget and Baden-Powell took charge of the Pretoria—Pietersburg railroad.

Hamilton's division was taken by Lord Roberts on the new campaign against Botha.

THE SITUATION IN THE ORANGE RIVER COLONY.

The capitulation of Prinsloo at Fouriesburg, the escape of De Wet northward, and that of Olivier eastward, were the events that marked the end of July in this region. Macdonald, who was pursuing Olivier, reached Harrismith, which yielded without resistance; Hunter remained at Bethlehem, while Rundle also advanced to Harrismith, to secure the Ladysmith—Bethlehem railroad, which was now placed in operation.

Small Boer commandoes still infested the district, however, and as early as August 2d one attacked the line at Rhenoster Spruit, compelling Knox to move out against it from Kroonstad; while another derailed a train at Honing Spruit (south of Kroonstad). These disturbances were all the more difficult to control as the British forces had been greatly reduced by the removal of Broadwood, Little, Paget and Clements, who had gone in pursuit of De Wet.

Towards the middle of August, Olivier suddenly appeared south of Heilbron. Hunter moved out against him from Bethlehem and was joined by Macdonald. They attacked Olivier on August 15th, but failed to capture him, or, prevent his escape, and lost touch with him in the pursuit. Soon after, Olivier fell upon a British post at Ventersburg, inflicting a loss on the British of 2 killed and 5 officers and 24 men captured. On August 25th he attacked Winburg from three sides, but was defeated by Bruce Hamilton, and, with three of his sons, was made prisoner.

Soon after, a Boer commando appeared before Ladybrand and threatened the town.

These disturbances, evidently intended to keep the British forces divided, decided Roberts once more to institute a decisive stroke against the main Boer army east of Middelburg.

THE THIRD CAMPAIGN AGAINST LOUIS BOTHA.

Lord Roberts moved his headquarters to Wonderfontein Station (25 miles east of Middelburg) on the 26th of August, preparatory to resuming the offensive against Botha.

Buller had moved out from Twyfelaar (near Carolina) in a northerly direction on the 23d of August, French's cavalry clearing up his front and left flank. The latter met with considerable resistance, but the advance of Buller's division (especially the artillery) compelled the Boers to give way.

In this action (near Geluk) in consequence of a misunderstanding, two British companies advanced about 1,500 yards into a hollow, out of sight of the main firing-line, separated from the main body, and were surrounded by the Boers. They lost 1 officer and 12 men killed, 57 men wounded and 33 prisoners.

On the 24th and 25th of August, Buller and French met with increased resistance, and it became evident that the Boers were preparing to make a stand in the hills west of Machadodorp. Pole-Carew had occupied Belfast on the 25th, and came in contact with the main Boer army at Dalmanutha. The British line extended from near Belfast back along the railroad some 30 miles, and the Boer front facing-it was evidently strong and of considerable extent, and its artillery fire was well sustained. To form this line the Boer forces in the Bothas Berge, northeast of Middelburg, had to be considerably reduced, which explains the unopposed advance of Pole-Carew to Belfast, the Boer plan being to make an offensive advance with their left flank.

French, who had the duty of keeping up communication between Buller and Pole-Carew, by the concentric advance of the latter necessarily came up with his cavalry between these two divisions, thus bringing the cavalry in the center of the front of operations. Measures were therefore taken to concentrate the British troops and at the same time get the cavalry on the flank again.

On August 26th the battle raged all along the line. Buller, with Lyttleton's division and two cavalry brigades, attempted to force his way north from the southwest of Dalmanutha, working around the Boer left flank. French took his two cavalry brigades behind Pole-Carew's division to the left flank.

The reasons for putting the cavalry division on the left flank were: to keep the Boers out of the malarious and difficult country of the Lydenburg district, and to force them along the railroad into the Portuguese colony.

French forced a part of the Boers towards Lekenvley (on the Belfast—Lydenburg road, 5 miles north of Belfast), but the difficult country (hilly, broken and covered with dense brush) prevented his further advance and favored the Boer defence to such an extent that Pole-Carew had to move out in support. The advance met with stubborn resistance, the Boer positions being generally supported by guns of heavy caliber. But the Boer forces were not directed in such a way as to bring their tactics to bear with full effect, their resistance consisting in separate engagements, and was not based on any general plan. Consequently, in spite of the difficulties, the British made some headway, Buller forcing his way to Bergendal, while Pole-Carew broke the Boer resistance at Lekenvley.

On the 27th French, on the left flank, moved out over Lekenvley on the Lydenburg road as far as the Schwartz Kopjes (10 miles north of Machadodorp), and then cleared up the ground in front of Pole-Carew's division.

The Battle of Bergendal.

Buller, however, met with strong resistance at Bergendal (between Belfast and Dalmanutha), a town lying at the foot of two kopjes commanding the approach, which led over an open plain, about a mile broad. The attack was conducted with excellent skill and judgment. Buller opened with a heavy artillery fire which was remarkably effective, utterly demoralizing the supports of the Boer front, and then advanced the Inniskilling Fusiliers, who took the town without a halt, and also occupied one of the neighboring hills, thus forcing the Boers to retire precipitately.

Buller lost 1 officer and 13 men killed, 7 officers and 57 men wounded; the Boers left 20 killed and 19 prisoners on the field. The Boers, retiring on Dalmanutha, disputed the advance foot by foot till dark.

Buller's advance on the 28th, however, met with little resistance, and before noon his advance guard reached Machadodorp. The Boers retired northward, pursued by Dun-donald to Helvetia (7 miles north of Machadodorp), where the country became too difficult and dangerous for cavalry alone.

French advanced to Elandsfontein (9 miles west of Helvetia), establishing signal communication with Machadodorp. Pole-Carew followed French to the Schwartz Kopjes (10 miles north of Machadodorp).

Presidents Krüger and Steyn fled to Nel Spruit, near the Portuguese border.

Buller continued his advance on Lydenburg on August 31st, over Helvetia, crossing the Crocodile River on the 1st of September, meeting with little resistance from Botha's rear guard. On the 2d, however, he found the Boers (3,000) in a strong position in the hills commanding Lydenburg.

French and Pole-Carew, having received orders to make a demonstration eastward, did not join Buller's column. An inversion thus resulted, the original right flank now becoming the left, due to the fact that Buller had started on the pursuit of Botha from Machadodorp, while Pole-Carew was still far to the rear, and French found the country too difficult for a large force of cavalry.

Buller reconnoitered Botha's position, and tried to turn its right flank, but found it too strong, and his artillery was unable to silence that of the Boers.

On September 3d Roberts sent Hamilton from north of Belfast to reinforce Buller. Hamilton, whom Brocklehurst's cavalry brigade had joined, moved against the right flank of the Boer position, passing Dulstroom (27 miles southwest of Lydenburg) on the 4th, there coming in signal communication with Buller, who was at the time engaged in turning the Boer left flank.

This pressure on both flanks caused Botha to alter his position, withdrawing his right flank in a northeastern direction towards the Mauch Berg, while a strong detachment on his left flank occupied the Spitz Kop, 25 miles to the eastward of Lydenburg. By this change he avoided the outflanking movement against his left flank, and also withdrew his line out of reach of Hamilton's move against his right flank. Lydenburg was thus given up by the Boers, and was occupied on the 6th by Dundonald's cavalry (of Buller's division) and Brocklehurst's (of Hamilton's column).

Hamilton joined Buller on September 7th, and Buller prepared to attack the new position. A flank attack was impossible, consequently a frontal attack had to be resorted to; but as it was well supported by artillery fire, the British took the position with little loss.

The Boers had sent their artillery on to Krüger's Post (about 25 miles north of Lydenburg) and fought a delaying action only, finally retreating northward, pursued by Buller over the Mauch Berg.

Hamilton was sent back to Machadodorp to take part in Pole-Carew's advance, while Botha, with about 3,000 men, retired to Pietersburg, joining there Commandant Vorster.

Buller crossed the Mauch Berg 10 miles east of Lydenburg on September 18th, entering very difficult country, and, driving the Boers before him, arrived at the junction of roads from east and south near Spitz Kop on the 10th. He captured many wagons of food and ammunition, and divided the Boers, some retiring to Nel Spruit and others across the Sabie Drift. On the 12th he occupied Spitz Kop, and found there immense quantities of Boer supplies. He remained there till the 23d, replenishing his supplies, and then moved towards Sabie Drift against Viljoen's force north of the river. He met with little resistance and advanced to Macmac Eivor and Burghers Pass. On October 2d Buller returned to Lydenburg, after a circuitous march through the country from Spitz Kop via Pilgrim's Best and Krüger's Post.

Meanwhile, Roberts continued his offensive advance eastward, with Pole-Carew and French, the former moving along the railroad, the latter covering his right flank; and later with Hamilton on the left flank. French reached Carolina on September 7th, and moved on Barberton, but met with considerable resistance before he reached the upper Buffels Spruit. However, he forced the Boers out of a number of consecutive positions.

At the same time the advance of Pole-Carew and French compelled the Presidents to leave Nel Spruit and retire on Komatipoort.

Krüger, leaving Schalk Burgher in charge of the government, left for Lorenzo Marques, on his way to Europe, to ask for foreign intercession. Steyn, taking command of all the Boer forces which retired eastward from Machadodorp, organized his forces for further resistance.

French occupied Barberton on September 13th, and made large captures, among them the great park of railroad rolling stock, including 43 locomotives. At the same time Pole-Carew occupied Kaapsche Hoop, to the northwest of Barberton. The further advance of the British to the Portuguese frontier was practically unopposed. On the 18th of September 700 Boers crossed the border at Komatipoort and were disarmed; and a similar fate befell most of those who were forced over the Kaap Berge. But Viljoen, with a small force, succeeded in escaping northward, and marched over the hills of the Lydenburg district, to join Botha at Pietersburg.

Pole-Carew occupied the border station, Komatipoort, on September 24th, and made large captures of rolling material.

This ended the campaign, and practically ended all larger operations of the war.

GENERAL SITUATION.

On September 2d Lord Roberts announced the annexation of the Transvaal. It is to be called, it is stated, the Vaal River Colony.

Raids against the railroads still took place in all parts of the two colonies, bridges were destroyed, and (due to carelessness in outpost

Boer guerrilla fighters pose for the camera in the Second Boer War

duty) detachments were attacked and captured. Indeed, scarcely a day passed without some such incident.

A Boer commando under Erasmus, for example, made several energetic attacks on the British troops guarding the Pretoria—Pietersburg line, near Pretoria, in the month of September. South of Pretoria, portions of De Wet's and Theron's troops made attempts to destroy the waterworks of Johannesburg, and succeeded in liberating 500 prisoners from the jail at Klip River. Along the Ladysmith—

Johannesburg road, especially near Standerton and Utrecht, small Boer detachments threatened road and trains continually. On the Johannesburg—Klerksdorp road the Boers held Potchefstroom for a time. Even Methuen and Carrington, in the West, were kept constantly on the alert, and the little garrison town of Mamusa was surrounded by the Boers, and almost taken, before it could be relieved.

The most successful raids, however, were conducted in the Orange River Colony by Fouries, Grobeler and Lemmer, later also by De Wet. A Boer force of 3,000 suddenly appeared before Ladybrand and took it, but the approach of Hunter caused it to be evacuated again. At the beginning of September a Boer commando attacked Bruce Hamilton at Thaba 'Nchu, but was defeated.

The British were compelled to vacate Vrede, Bethlehem, Fouriesburg and Senekal, in order to concentrate their forces more effectually; Harrismith alone remained occupied.

In the vicinity of Kroonstad, and even just south of Bloemfontein, the railroad was occasionally destroyed.

On September 13th Macdonald at Winburg heard of a Boer raid on the railroad at Brandfort, and immediately set out in pursuit, crossing to the south bank of the Vet River, near Tafel Kop. He came upon them eight miles west of that place, drove them over the Vet River, and pursued them north of the Winburg—Smaldeel railway, utterly defeating them, and capturing a number of prisoners, wagons, oxen, ammunition and food supplies.

In spite of all these disturbances, however, the main military operations were ended.

Lord Roberts returned to Pretoria on September 22d, and was appointed commander-in-chief of the British Army, to succeed Lord Wolseley (retired), on October 1. On October 10th General Buller relinquished command of the Natal forces, to return home; Lyttleton was left in command of his troops.

The resistance of the Boers, headed by Botha, Steyn and De Wet, continued throughout the month of October and to near the end of November.

During these months Hildyard operated in the southeastern Transvaal, Clery in the vicinity of Standerton, Clements in central Transvaal near Rustenburg and Krügersdorp, Hart southwest of Krügersdorp, Methuen in western Transvaal, while Paget and

Plumer held the northern posts. Bundle was in the vicinity of Bethlehem, Knox at Kroonstad, Barton near Krügersdorp, Bradley near Heidelberg, Hunter near Mequathings Nek, Macdonald near Winburg and Senekal, Brabant at Heilbron and Lindley, Kelly-Kenny at Bloemfontein.

Guerrilla warfare continued at all these points, and detachments up to a strength of 1,500 or 2,000 occasionally assembled, although most of the raids were made by much smaller bodies.

One of the latest and most important of the combats with the Boer raiders was that of Bothaville (northwest of Kroonstad, south of Klerksdorp), where Colonel Le Gallais met a Boer force of 1,000 men (among them Steyn and De Wet) and completely defeated them. He captured six field guns, two machine guns, and 100 prisoners, the Boers leaving 25 dead and 30 wounded on the field. The British lost 3 officers and 8 men killed, 7 officers and 20 men wounded.

This guerrilla warfare gradually subsided towards the end of November, and the war virtually ended. Great Britain added two extensive colonies, rich in gold, diamonds and cattle, to her domains, and sustained a total loss in officers and men of about 12,S00.

COMMENTS.

At the opening of the fifth act in this war drama the, main Boer army in the west was at Middelburg and Hatherley, east of Pretoria, and the question for Lord Roberts to decide was, whether he should attack this army and disperse it, or send a strong detachment by rail to Volksrust, to assist Buller in his attempts to turn the Boer position at Laings Nek, and hasten the retreat of Christian Botha northward. After the performance of both these tasks he would be prepared to begin operations against the Boer troops waging a guerrilla war in the Lydenburg district, where the latter were strongly ensconced in the mountains, and well provided with supplies from Lorenzo Marques.

The effect of Roberts' advance to Pretoria undoubtedly made itself felt on the resistance of the Boers at Laings Nek, but Buller deserves great credit for the masterly way in which he maneuvered the latter out of their extremely strong position with little loss, and succeeded in cutting them in two.

Tactically, however, he failed to reap the full reward of his strategical measures, since the Boers escaped without loss in men or material.

This may have been due to the fact that, having learned the futility of purely frontal attacks, he went to the other extreme, and laid too much stress on outflanking movements, which are never very successful tactically; unless the frontal attack is pressed hard at the same time, in order to hold the enemy while the flanking columns roll them up.

Buller's movement had another great advantage in that it separated the Transvaal from the Orange Boers, occupying the Drakensberge and assembling to the southwest under President Steyn, and prevented the former from joining the latter. Had he turned their position by the east (his first plan), the strategic situation would have been far less advantageous.

It would appear at first sight that Buller's proper course after reaching Volksrust was to hasten northward to join Roberts in a combined attack on the Boers near Middelburg. But the reconnaissances from Roberts' army had determined the position of the latter, under Louis Botha, east of Pretoria, to be in a strong, although very extended line. Moreover, although Pretoria and Johannesburg were perfectly quiet, he feared the effect of such close proximity of a strong Boer army, and decided to attack it without awaiting the arrival either of Buller or Hunter.

Roberts' prompt decision to attack the center of Botha's position, as soon as he found it impracticable to turn the flanks according to his previous tactics, thus far uniformly successful, marks the general, ready at all times to suit his methods of warfare to the existing circumstances. His failure to pursue, however, after the battle, and determine definitely the whereabouts of the enemy, is open to criticism.

His comparatively small force, the danger threatening his line of communications, and the ravages of disease in the army (which were great in the months of May and June), no doubt determined him to risk no further engagement with Botha, but this does not excuse the neglect of reconnaissance of the enemy during the retreat of the latter.

The splendid strategic campaign of Lord Roberts ended, the weaknesses of the British army and their neglect of proper reconnaissance and the service of security and information once more come into prominence. To subdue the scattered forces of the Boers it became necessary to subdivide the army, thus throwing the responsibility for the minor tactical operations on the subordinate commanders; consequently surprises and captures of detachments became almost daily events. No doubt much of the neglect of outpost duty was due to the poor state of the cavalry horses, but most of the failure must be ascribed to the lack of proper training of the troops in such service.

Buller, after entering the Transvaal, had two courses open to him: on the one hand, he could have operated against the Boers retreating on Ermelo, and seized the Lorenzo Marques railway, cutting off Botha from his source of supply at the latter point, and thus ending the campaign in this region; on the other hand, he could move along the railway line to Johannesburg and complete the cordon around the Orange Boers, at the same time opening a new line of supply for Roberts' army.

The first plan would have compelled him to leave the railroad and organize a large train, which was well-nigh impracticable. Roberts, therefore, decided on the second plan, which would also bring Buller's force in contact with his own.

Turning now to the campaign against De Wet near Bethlehem, we find again one of the deficiencies of the British officer coming into prominence, viz.: the lack of proper service of security and information. The entire strategic plan of Roberts—the concentric advance on De Wet's position—was virtually defeated by the want of definite information of the exact position of the latter, and the slow advance of Hunter, the too dispersed order of march of Rundle, and finally the precipitate dash of Paget, who became involved in a position where he had to await reinforcements, and changed the proposed concentric advance into a mere forward movement of a single body.

Again, after Rundle discovered the Boers in strong force east of Rooikrans, which should have indicated to him that De Wet had selected this point for the breaking through, he made no special arrangements to resist his efforts, and allowed him to escape with ease, preserving his too extended order of advance even after the motives of De Wet were evident.

The capture of Prinsloo's force, on the other hand, was effected with skill and judgment.

It is a question, however, if De Wet would not have been wiser to have broken through to the eastward, over the Drakensberg passes, and joined the remains of the Boer army northeast of Laings Nek.

The surprise of the British garrison at Rustenburg by Lemmer must be ascribed once more to imperfect outpost service; and to this same weakness of the British troops the surprises at Uitvals Nek and Derdepoort must be attributed.

Campaign of Middelburg.

In the organization and execution of the advance, four points at once strike the military student, viz.: first, the placing of Hamilton's mounted infantry on the left, and French's much more mobile cavalry division on the right; secondly, the broad front of the advance, and the distance of the flanking columns from the main column; thirdly, the small force which Roberts selected for this service; fourthly, why Buller was allowed to remain practically inactive, when he might have brought fatal pressure to bear on the Boer left and rear.

In the first place, Hamilton's troops had to go a longer distance to reach the left flank than they would have had to take the right; and in the next place, both were familiar with the country (from their advance against Eerste Fabrieken) on the opposite flanks from those now assigned to them. Moreover, as Roberts' plan evidently involved preventing the Boers from retiring into the hills of the Lydenburg District, French's advance north of the railroad would have been far more in place. His flanking movements south of the railroad merely forced the Boers back on their line of retreat.

The broad front of Roberts' advance, and the far outflanking movements of French, prevented concerted action of the various parts on account of the distances to be covered. On this account, after French's scouts crossed Olifants River, and found the Boers in full retreat, it was impossible for Roberts to take advantage of the situation, because the center and left was still far in rear. A flanking movement can only be successful when the flank column reaches the enemy in good condition, and can count on the assistance of the rest of the army.

The force assigned to this service by Roberts had a strength of about 22,000 men, and was destined to attack a skillful enemy, well entrenched in positions of his own selection, about 12,000 strong. Decisive results could hardly be expected under such circumstances, and when Pole-Carew and French, with 15,000, were left alone to continue the pursuit, it is not surprising that they did not go beyond Middelburg.

Buller's advance against Middelburg would have protected the northern side of the railroad much better than quietly guarding it, and would have threatened the Boers in front of Roberts besides. Moreover, at that time there was little danger of Boer raids south of the railroad.

After it was found that Pole-Carew and French could not advance with safety beyond Middelburg, then at last was done what should have been done when the advance against Middelburg began—viz., Buller was directed against the Boer left flank and rear.

The Chase of De Wet.

One of the first points that strikes the military student in this pursuit of De Wet is the fact that the separate British columns acted perfectly independently, with no single controlling power to direct the movements on the field intelligently towards the common end. Kitchener and Methuen were independent, and when they struck De Wet neither knew the exact situation.

Smith-Dorrien, when he tried to block De Wet's way near Welverdiend, had only troops which had been worn out by constant marching to and fro, due to conflicting orders and the lack of a directing head, and so failed to stop the Boer leader.

And finally, Paget and Baden-Powell, by getting themselves involved in combats with small detachments at a critical moment, allowed De Wet to escape when he was practically surrounded: again, the independence of the individual leader caused the failure of the strategic measures.

Another point that strikes the military student is the fact that the British failed to distinguish between the important or essential and the unimportant or trivial. When Roberts had carried his campaign against the main Boer army, under Louis Botha, nearly to Middelburg, he returned with the mounted infantry of Hamilton and Mahon, giving up a serious campaign at a critical moment, to secure a subordinate (unessential) object—viz., the line to Mafeking, where he had 15,000 troops already posted in western Transvaal. Again, Methuen was taken away from this line to act against a paltry 1500 under De Wet. Finally, Hamilton, after being sent to the relief of Rustenburg, the object of which was evidently to secure the line to Mafeking, brought

Baden-Powell away from that point and left him at Kommando Nek, and himself joined in the pursuit of De Wet.

The last prominent characteristic of these movements is the fact that some of the British subordinate commanders did not prove equal to the tactical and strategical situation, and that they failed in intelligent, combined action. Carrington's decision, after having been ordered to relieve Hore, to retire not only to Zeerust, but even farther, does not seem warranted by the circumstances, and more concerted action by the other subordinate commanders should have brought better results.

The Third Campaign against Botha.

The third campaign against Botha, beyond Middelburg, was conducted in Roberts' true manner, and his measures substantiate our views on the second campaign in two leading particulars—viz., the fact that the place for the cavalry was on the left, and the necessity for Buller's advance in flank at the same time. Nevertheless, the transfer of the cavalry to the left flank at so late a stage failed to prevent Louis Botha from escaping into the Lydenburg district, as it would have done had it been on that flank originally; moreover, Buller's participation came too late for decisive effect in capturing the Boers, or in forcing them to fight a decisive action.:

The latter part of this campaign was a splendid achievement and illustrates the effect of properly applying a sufficient number of troops to a definite purpose, and pursuing this purpose with single-minded determination to the end.

The Boers, on the other hand, had split up their forces, scattered them over a wide area, had no concerted action under single leadership, and failed to concentrate for any definite purpose; consequently their resistance was rapidly destroyed.

TACTICAL DEDUCTIONS FROM THE WAR[5]

In drawing lessons from the war in South Africa the first point to be taken into consideration is the general character of the armies opposed to each other. On the one hand, there is a crude militia, insufficiently organized and trained in time of peace, but composed of excellent though undisciplined material, untrained in tactics, hence

---

5 The author is indebted for much of his information and many of his ideas to an anonymous article in Internationale Revue, Beiheft 14; and to the United Service Magazine.

incapable of the tactical offensive, so indispensable for decisive results. On the other hand, a European army, composed of a large nucleus of regular troops, disciplined and trained, but its greater part militia and volunteers of variable quality, generally only partially trained, with all the technical and scientific means of carrying on war at its disposal.

Fire effect serves as a basis for all tactical deductions. The Lee-Metford and the Mauser gun, in spite of certain advantages of the latter over the former, must be regarded as practically equal in the field. But the possession of a bayonet gave the British a decided advantage over the Boers (who were without one), not because hand-to-hand conflicts are liable to be very common in modern war, but because the moral effect of its possession confers tenacity on the defense and confidence and esprit on the attack.

As marksmen the Boers had the advantage, for they were all trained to this accomplishment from their youth,, and kept up their practice by their mode of life. They surpassed probably, in this respect, all European armies.

The Artillery Arm.

The field artillery material used by the two armies is an interesting study, but in judging of the relative degree of preparedness, the circumstances must be carefully considered. The Transvaal had been arming since 1896, purchasing the best material procurable, and it so happened that at this time the field artillery of Europe was in a transition stage, but on the Continent rearmament had commenced, consequently the Boers had their choice of the latest designs. England, however, had been slow to adopt the changes effected on the Continent, and had merely modified its existing carriages, while the guns remained the same. The result was that the Boers were possessed of the latest quick-firers, with fixed ammunition, and the ranges exceeded that of the British field gun by several thousand yards.

Small as these differences were, they soon proved great in effect, because it was this little difference that enabled the Boers with single guns to put a number of shell into a British battery before the latter could reply, and the only reason they failed to accomplish more than they did was because they had but a small number of guns and did not know the value of concentrating their fire; moreover, they were afraid to risk a stand-up fight.

It has been urged that field guns are not intended to engage siege guns; but the British guns frequently failed to reach even the Boer field guns when the latter could reach them. The 5-inch field howitzer had a range of only 4,900 yards, and frequently failed to be of use on that account. At Venters Spruit something might have been done to assist the British troops on top of Spion Kop if only their guns had had a little longer range: some forty British guns were forced to remain idle, while a few Boer guns shelled the crest of the hill. In the demonstration against Brakfontein heights, preceding the attack on the Vaal Kranz, six field batteries were so effectually outranged that they had to stand still, to be shot at; and a few days later the single Boer gun on the Doornkloof defied all the British guns in the plain or on the Schwartz Kop. In this last case a howitzer of sufficient range was all that was needed.

That it is possible to combine in the field gun increased range with mobility is proven by the fact that Boers accomplished it, and that Captain Scott constructed temporary carriages for the 12-pdr. guns of the Naval Brigade, which weighed (with gun, complete) approximately only two-thirds as much as the field equipment, while the guns were sighted up to 8,000 yards, and could be fired at even greater ranges.

The other advantages of long range in field pieces are that the enemy's advancing infantry can be brought under shell fire earlier, or a larger extent of front of his defensive position can be swept by the artillery without changing position; moreover, the artillery can be kept farther in rear and still be effective, a great advantage under modern infantry fire. On the contrary, short-range field guns can only come up behind infantry, and must be correspondingly slow in getting up.

In view of this great importance of range, it is evidently better to sacrifice some degree of mobility, if it be necessary to sacrifice anything, in order to secure a good heavy long-range field gun, provided only it can keep up with the infantry.

The effects of earthworks and their extensive use have merely substantiated what was predicted by the best authorities. They have demonstrated the necessity for a howitzer to search trenches, since ordinary field guns can only serve, by a constant storm of shell, to keep the enemy in them, but cannot reach him there.

The advantage of quick-firing guns was illustrated at Brakfontein, on February 5th, where three Boer guns easily maintained a rate of fire and a storm of shell on six British field batteries (unable to reply because outranged) such as a battery of six British guns could not have produced by using its most rapid rate of fire. Another advantage of quick-firing guns is that the number of guns to a battery can be reduced to four, and hence the target presented by a battery be made much smaller, and cover can be more easily secured. Quick-fire guns also offer the great advantage of quickly engaging a moving target and following it up readily: at Brakfontein the slow rate of fire of the British and their system of fire discipline allowed a Boer gun to retire and a pompom to be brought into action before a shot from a field gun could be fired.

The experiences in South Africa seem to point to the following as the proper equipment of an army as regards artillery:
- A quick-fire gun, perhaps a little more mobile than the present field gun, capable of accompanying mounted troops on the march.
- A heavier gun (including the howitzer) of long range, capable of moving with infantry.
- A light mountain gun in country where only pack-animal transportation is to be had.

The small actual effect of the pom-poms of the Boers, in spite of their great moral effect and their mobility (which enabled them to follow readily in pursuit), confirmed previous experience. Their high rate of fire (10 shots a minute) could not make up for the low weight of projectile, and the consequent limited action in depth of troops struck. The campaign shows that the use of guns of smaller caliber than 75 mm. is only permissible in mountain or barbarian warfare, or against torpedo boats.

The Physiological Effects of the Infantry Arm.

All authorities agree that the wounds from the small-arm bullets are more humane than those from the old large-caliber projectiles. According to the eminent English surgeon, Sir William MacCormac, the human body can in many cases be perforated by the bullets without fatal results. About 96 per cent of the wounded at the base of operations in South Africa recovered, and a large percentage returned to the front. Most of the wounds leave a very small opening at the points of entrance and of exit. Most of them stop bleeding themselves, and heal very rapidly. Prens, in the British Medical Journal, asserts that at ranges of from 1,500 to 2,000 yards the Mauser bullet goes through bones like a needle, and only at close ranges (up to 500 yards) does it shatter the larger bones, while breast wounds heal readily. Amputations are rarely necessary.

Losses in Battle.

One of the most interesting features connected with improvements in fire-arms is the fact that the losses in battle constantly grow smaller. The following table will illustrate this:

	Percentage of killed and wounded.	Percentage of the killed in the total losses.	
		Offensive	Defensive
Wars of Frederick the Great	15	19	25
Wars of Napoleon	13	10	21
Crimean War	12	17	29
Campaign of 1859	8	9	19
Campaign of 1866	8	9	24
Campaign of 1870-1	9	9	24
Battle of Ladysmith (10,000 British)	3		
Battle of Ladysmith (10,000 British)	3		
Battle of Stormberg (2,500 British)	3.6		
Battle of Magersfontein (10,000 British)	9		
Battle of Colenso (17,000 British)	5.3		
Battle of Spion Kop (20,000 British)	7		

The percentage of losses in officers is remarkably high. At Magersfontein, for example, it reached 25 per cent, or 1 officer for every 14 men killed, wounded and missing.

Relation between Losses in Battle and Losses by Disease.

As a general rule, losses by disease in long-continued wars far exceed losses in battle: the only known exception is the Franco-Prussian War of 1870-1. Another fact worth noticing is that the losses in battle grow smaller as war progresses, while those from disease grow greater, and the latter in a higher ratio for the men than for the officers.

The British losses at short intervals are given in the Appendix, but the number of sick is not clearly stated in the official reports.

The table opposite gives some idea of the relative numbers of those who were killed (or mortally wounded) in battle and those who died of disease (or accidents) at various intervals.

Transportation of Horses by Sea.

Between the 30th of September and the 24th of March about 24,333 horses were transported on some 70 vessels, with a loss of 5.5 per cent, not considering the Ismore, which stranded with 315

	Killed.		Died of Disease.	
	Officers	**Men**	**Officers**	**Men.**
Up to February 24	198	1748	20	722
Up to May 26	285	2672	95	3127
Up to July 30	324	3013	126	4270
Up to September 8	368	3462	152	5573
Up to October 21	391	3795	162	6350

horses on board, and the Rapidan, which did not proceed farther than the Irish Sea. In some cases the percentage was very low: in 9 ships, for example, it ranged between 1 and 2 per cent. In others, on the contrary, it ran very high: on the America, for example, as high as 24.3 per cent.

Lessons for the Defense.

The operations of the Boers illustrate fully whatever advantages attach to the strategical defensive. The reasons for their adopting this form were probably three: the peculiar characteristics and nature of the Boer, his lack of military obedience and discipline, and the difficulty of replacing losses in battle by new levies.

In Natal they combined the strategical offensive with the tactical defensive, and, as ever, they were defeated in the end.

Their positions were always well selected, and intrenchments in two tiers (one over the other) were very common. Fire was first opened from the upper tier, that of the lower being reserved for close quarters. The Boers also constructed dummy intrenchments, from which they fired with smoky powder. Perfect use of the configuration of the ground was generally made, and at Paardeberg a special form of trench widened at bottom (as shown elsewhere in the text) was made use of in the firm ground found there.

Wire entanglements were placed in front of positions, which not only delayed the attack, but also enabled the Boers to guard the ground in front with weak detachments, the noise of passing through the obstacle giving sufficient warning. Such was the case at Magersfontein, for example.

The occupation of advanced positions (in front of the general line) by the Boers is contrary to the accepted ideas of tacticians. But their success in the war was due to the fact that the British generally resorted to purely frontal attacks, and thus enabled the Boers to make the very best use of them. Moreover, the Boers were usually mounted, and their horses (owing to the terrain) could be kept close at hand, so that, when it came to the short ranges, they could quickly retire.

The question of when to open infantry fire is comparatively simple for the attack, as it is determined by the fire-action of the enemy's arm, the object being to get as near as possible to the inner limit of the medium battle ranges before opening fire. But for the defense the problem is more difficult, because the opening of fire at once discovers to the enemy our positions, and offers targets for their artillery. Most European nations would now open fire at about 1,000 yards, to prevent the enemy from ever reaching the close range (600 yards) at which the defenders' heads begin to be visible targets.

But the Boers wisely did otherwise, and allowed the enemy to come to close range before opening on him. This action is entirely justified because of the great superiority of the British in artillery, because at close ranges the latter can no longer take part. Moreover, the moral effect of a sudden, overwhelming infantry fire is enormous even on the best of troops, and in South Africa the withholding of the fire was particularly justified because the British often approached close to the Boer positions in closed masses, and in utter ignorance of the exact position of the enemy. Examples of these points will be found in the battles of Modder River, Magersfontein and Stormberg. In the first the losses of the subdivisions in front were considerable; in the second the actual losses were slight, but the demoralized battalions could not be assembled again until the following day; and in the last the losses in killed and wounded were only 34 per cent, but in prisoners it amounted to 25.3 per cent.

These examples illustrate the necessity of accurately locating the enemy's subdivisions in his position, and determining that position from a distance.

Whenever the Boers did open fire at longer ranges the British advance was generally stopped at 900 yards.

Lessons for the Attack.

The British mode of attack is characterized, at the opening of campaign, by its purely frontal form,, and by the insufficient numbers placed on the line; by taking up the formation for attack at too late an hour; and by laying too little stress on gaining superiority of fire.

At Magersfontein, for example, the artillery opened fire on the Boer position, while the infantry remained in rear and gave no assistance.

The result was that the Boers lay quietly in their trenches. The infantry of the attack must move up and support the artillery fire by its fire action, in order to compel the enemy to occupy his positions and thus offer targets for the artillery. The two arms must work together: artillery and infantry preparation for attack are not two successive phases of a battle, but must be simultaneous.

Night marches and night battles found considerable application in this war. On the Tugela, at Spion Kop, at Stormberg and at Magersfontein examples are found. In several of these cases the great objection to night marches—-namely, the danger of a panic, is decidedly in evidence. The only remedy, acknowledging the necessity for such operations, is for the officers to use all their power to prevent a panic, or to keep it in bounds. The great trouble with the British in these night attacks was the fact that they advanced without outposts; this may be risked by a singe company, but never by a column of all arms, 2,000 strong.

The examples prove that night battles on a large scale are impossible. The taking of the Spion Kop at night was a proper measure, as also would be an approach by night over open ground to an enemy's position, but all these require careful previous reconnaissance of the ground to be passed over. Moreover, the men should be fully impressed with the idea that night fire is not dangerous, and as soon as the enemy opens it all the troops must charge with all their energy.

These are a few of the lessons to be learned from the Boer War, but perhaps the most impressive lesson of all is the high significance, true for all time to come, of the tactical and strategical offensive.

APPENDIX

Distances Between Important Points.

BY SEA.
- Southampton to Cape Town: 5,978 Nautical Miles
- Cape Town to Port Elizabeth: 428 Nautical Miles
- Port Elizabeth to East London: 131 Nautical Miles
- East London to Durban: 253 Nautical Miles
- Durban to Lorenzo Marques: 300 Nautical Miles
- Lorenzo Marques to Beira: 488 Nautical Miles

BY RAILROAD.
- Cape Town to De Aar: 500 miles (27 hours)
- De Aar to Naauwpoort: 69 miles (3 hours)
- De Aar to Orange River: 70 miles (4 hours)
- Orange River to Modder River: 52½ miles
- Modder River to Spytfontein: 11 miles
- Spytfontein to Kimberley: 14 miles
- Kimberley to Warrenton: 44½ miles
- Kimberley to Fourteen Streams: 47½ miles
- Kimberley to Taungs: 84 miles
- Taungs to Vryburg: 43 miles
- Vryburg to Mafeking: 96½ miles
- Fourteen Streams to Mafeking: 176½ miles
- Mafeking to Ramathlabama: 15½ miles
- Mafeking to Lobatsi: 47 miles
- Mafeking to Crocodile Pools: 83½ miles
- Mafeking to Gaberones: 92½ miles
- Mafeking to Buluwayo: 389½ miles
- Port Elizabeth to Rosmead Junction (Route 1): 243 miles (14½ hours)
- Port Elizabeth to Rosmead Junction (Route 2): 283 miles (18½ hours)
- Rosmead Junction to Naauwpoort: 26½ miles (1½ hours)
- Rosmead Junction to Stormberg Junction: 83½ miles (7 hours)
- Rosmead Junction to Thebus: 37 miles
- Naauwpoort to Arundel: 18½ miles
- Arundel to Rensburg: 8½ miles

- Rensburg to Colesberg Junction: 9 miles
- Colesberg Junction to Norvals Pont: 24½ miles
- Norvals Pont to Springfontein: 32½ miles
- Rosmead Junction to Springfontein: 93 miles (5 hours)
- Bast London to Queenstown: 154½ miles
- Queenstown to Sterkstroom Junction: 35 miles
- Queenstown to Stormberg Junction: 67 miles
- Sterkstroom to Dordrecht: 41 miles
- Dordrecht to Indwe: 25 miles
- Sterkstroom to Indwe: 66 miles
- Stormberg Junction to Thebus: 46½ miles
- Stormberg Junction to Burghersdorp: 22 miles
- Burghersdorp to Bethulie Bridge: 42½ miles
- Bethulie Bridge to Springfontein: 28 miles
- Stormberg Junction to Springfontein: 92½ miles
- Stormberg Junction to Albert Junction: 25½ miles
- Albert Junction to Aliwal North: 29 miles
- Springfontein to Bethany: 50½ miles
- Bethany to Bloemfontein: 36½ miles
- Springfontein to Bloemfontein: 88 miles
- Bloemfontein to Karree: 21 miles
- Bloemfontein to Brandfort: 35 miles
- Bloemfontein to Vet River: 56 miles
- Vet River to Smaldeel (Winburg railroad station): 6½ miles
- Smaldeel (Winburg railroad station) to Kroonstad: 70 miles
- Kroonstad to Pretoria: 160 miles
- Springfontein to Viljoens Drift: 317 miles (13 hours)
- Bloemfontein to Viljoens Drift: 230 miles (9 hours)
- Viljoens Drift to Klip River: 22 miles
- Klip River to Blandsfontein: 20 miles
- Elandsfontein to Pretoria: 36 miles
- Viljoens Drift to Pretoria: 78 miles
- Elandsfontein to Johannesburg: 10 miles
- Johannesburg to Krugersdorp: 19 miles
- Krugersdorp to Potchefstroom: 67 miles
- Potchefstroom to Klerksdorp: 30
- Blandsfontein to Charlestown (Natal): 170 miles
- Pretoria to Waterval: 15 miles

- Pretoria to Nylstroom: 81 miles
- Pretoria to Belfast: 136 miles
- Belfast to Komatipoort: 155 miles
- Komatipoort to Lorenzo Marques: 51 miles
- Durban to Mooi River: 54½ miles
- Mooi River to Bstcourt: 21 miles
- Estcourt to Colenso: 27 miles
- Colenso to Ladysmith: 16½ miles
- Ladysmith to Glencoe: 41½ miles
- Glencoe to Newcastle: 37 miles
- Newcastle to Charlestown: 36 miles
- Ladysmith to Besters: 15½ miles
- Besters to Van Reenan: 21½ miles
- Van Reenan to Harrismith: 23½ miles
- Durban to Ladysmith: 188½ miles (12 hours)
- Ladysmith to Harrismith: 60½ miles (5 hours)
- Ladysmith to Charlestown: 114½ miles (6 hours)
- Beira to Umtali: 203 miles
- Umtali to Marandellas: 130 miles
- Marandellas to Salisbury: 40 miles

BY ROAD.
- De Aar to Prieska: 110 miles
- Belmont to Douglas: 52 miles
- Modder River Bridge to Jacobsdal: 10 miles
- Kimberley to Barkly West: 22 miles
- Kimberley to Boshof: 36 miles
- Colesberg to Norvals Pont: 25 miles
- Norvals Pont to Bethulie: 30 miles
- Norvals Pont to Springfontein: 31 miles
- Bethulie to Springtontein: 23 miles
- Bethulie to Smithfield: 40 miles
- Dordrecht to Jamestown: 24 miles
- Jamestown to Aliwal North: 33 miles
- Aliwal North to Rouxville: 20 miles
- Aliwal North to Bushmans Kop: 60 miles
- Aliwal North to Wepener: 77 miles
- Smithfield to Dewetsdorp: 52 miles
- Wepener to Dewetsdorp: 23 miles

- Dewetsdorp to Bloemfontein: 40 miles
- Dewetsdorp to Reddersburg: 38 miles
- Dewetsdorp to Thaba 'Nchu: 27 miles
- Kimberley to Boshof: 36 miles
- Jacobsdal to Koffyfontein: 24 miles
- Klip Drift to Paardeberg: 11 miles
- Paardeberg Drift to Osfontein: 8 miles
- Osfontein to Poplar Grove: 10 miles
- Poplar Grove to Abrahams Kraal: 17 miles
- Poplar Grove to Driefontein: 1 miles
- Poplar Grove to Aasvogel Kop: 10 miles
- Aasvogel Kop to Venters Vlei: 18 miles
- Venters Vlei to Bloemfontein: 18 miles
- Oolesberg to Fauresmith: 85 miles
- Pauresmith to Jacobsdal: 60 miles
- Boshof to Bulfontein: 60 miles
- Boshof to Hoopstad: 70 miles
- Bloemfontein to Sanna's Post: 18 miles
- Bloemfontein to Thaba 'Nchu: 38 miles
- Bloemfontein to Ladybrand: 72 miles
- Bloemfontein to Winburg: 68 miles
- Bloemfontein to Dewetsdorp: 40 miles
- Thaba 'Nchu to Dewetsdorp: 27 miles
- Pietermaritzburg to Dundee (over Greytown): 126 miles
- Frere to Potgieters Drift: 23 miles
- Ladysmith to Acton Homes: 26 miles
- Ladysmith to Bezuidenhouts Pass: 46 miles
- Ladysmith to Colenso: 16 miles
- Ladysmith to Pietermaritzburg: 100 miles
- Ladysmith to Dundee: 48 miles
- Ladysmith to Helpmakaar: 45 miles
- Mafeking to Johannesburg: 160 miles
- Pretoria to Tuli: 360 miles

***

The strength and composition of the British forces in South Africa at the outbreak of the war was as follows:

THE NATAL FORCE.

The Natal force was part of the Cape Colony force up to the middle of October, and Major-General Symons was in command of it. Afterwards General White, who had been in command of the Cape Colony forces, was sent to take command of the Natal force.

Infantry.
- 1st battalion Liverpool Regiment (originally in Cape Colony, sent to Ladysmith September 25): 750
- 1st battalion Leicestershire Regiment (originally in Ladysmith, sent to Glencoe September 25): 800
- 2d battalion Royal Dublin Fusiliers (originally in Ladysmith, sent to Glencoe September 25): 750
- 1st battalion King's Royal Rifles (at Glencoe): 750
- 2d battalion King's Royal Rifles (at Ladysmith, embarked at Calcutta and Bombay September 29): 750
- 1st battalion Devonshire Regiment (at Ladysmith, embarked at Calcutta and Bombay September 29): 800
- 1st battalion Manchester Regiment (at Ladysmith, arrived at Durban September 15): 750
- 2d battalion Gordon Highlanders (at Ladysmith, embarked at Calcutta and Bombay September 29): 800
- 1st battalion Gloucestershire Regiment (at Ladysmith, embarked at Calcutta and Bombay September 29): 800
- 1st battalion Royal Irish Fusiliers (at Glencoe, sent from Cairo) 700

Total: 7,650

Cavalry.
- 5th Lancers (originally in Pietermaritzburg, sent to Ladysmith September 25): 400
- 5th Dragoon Guards (at Ladysmith): 400
- 18th Hussars (originally in Ladysmith, sent to Glencoe September 25) : 450
- 19th Hussars: 400

Total: 1,650

Artillery.
- Field Batteries Nos. 13, 21, 42, 53, 67 and 69 and the 10th

Mountain Battery (42 guns in all): 1,218
- Field Batteries Nos. 18, 62 and 75 (18 guns in all) expected shortly from Aldershot: 530

Total: 1,748

Three of the batteries were originally in Ladysmith, sent to Glencoe September 25; 3 batteries (21, 42, 53) came from India.

Engineers (Pioneers).
- Field Companies Nos. 7, 8 and 23 and the 29th Garrison Company: 600

Train.
- Companies 9, 15, 31 and 41: 300

Volunteers.
- Natal Volunteers: 760
- Natal Carabiniers: 120
- Imperial Light Horse: 500
- Durban Volunteers: 750
- Mounted Police of Natal (with 9 guns): 550

Total: 2,680

Total: 69 guns and 14,628 men.

THE CAPE FORCE.
Infantry.
- 1st battalion Northumberland Fusiliers (sent from Aldershot): 770
- 1st battalion Royal Munster Fusiliers (arrived at Cape Town September 15): 750
- 1st battalion North Lancashire Regiment: 800
- 2d battalion Berkshire Regiment: 750
- ½ 2d battalion Yorkshire Light Infantry: 320
- 1st battalion Border Regiment (sent from Malta): 700

Total: 4,090

To arrive October 29th:
- 2d battalion Rifle Brigade (sent from Crete): 700
- 2 companies Garrison Artillery, Nos. 14 and 23: 200
- 5th and 22d Companies Train: 150

Total: 5,140

On the Western Border.
- Estimated (mostly volunteers): 4,000
- Naval Brigade, landed from the fleet at Cape Town (4 guns): 1,000

Total: 10,140

- Field Batteries Nos. 18, 62 and 75. 9th Lancers.

Grand total: 24,708 men and 69 guns.

The Mobilized Army Corps.

General Sir Redvers Buller.

First Division. Lieutenant-General Lord P. Methuen.

1st Brigade (Guards): Major-General Colville.

    3d battalion Grenadier Guards (from Gibraltar).

    1st battalion Coldstream Guards (from Gibraltar).

    2d battalion Coldstream Guards. 1st battalion Scots Guards.

    Supply column (Train Co. No. 19).

    Litter Bearer Co. No. 18.

    Field Ambulance No. 18.

2d Brigade (English Brigade): Major-General Hildyard.

    2d battalion Royal West Surrey Regiment.

    2d battalion Devonshire Regiment.

    2d battalion West Yorkshire Regiment.

    2d battalion East Surrey Regiment.

    Supply column (Train Co. No. 26).

    Litter Bearer Co. No. 2.

    Depot Field Ambulance.

    1 squadron 14th Hussars.

    Field Batteries Nos. 7, 14 and 66 (6 guns each).

    Ammunition column (1 reserve gun).

    Field Engineer Co. No. 17.

    Supply column (Train Co. No. 20).

    Field Ambulance No. 19.

Second Division. Major-General Sir C. F. Clery.

3d Brigade (Scotch Brigade): Major-General Wauchope.[6]

    2d battalion Royal Highlanders (Black Watch).

    1st battalion Highland Light Infantry.

    2d battalion Seaforth Highlanders.

    1st battalion Argyll and Sutherland Highlanders.

    Supply column (Train Co. No. 14).

    Litter Bearer Co. No. 1.

    Field Ambulance No. 14.

4th Brigade (Light Infantry): Major-General Lyttleton.

    2d battalion Scottish Rifles (Cameronians).

---

6 Killed at Magersfontein; succeeded by General Hector Macdonald

3d battalion King's Royal Rifle Corps.
1st battalion Durham Light Infantry.
1st battalion 1st Rifle Brigade.
Supply column (Train Co. No. 16).
Litter Bearer Co. No. 14.
Field Ambulance No. 14.
1 squadron 14th Hussars.
Field Batteries Nos. 63, 64 and 73 (6 guns each).
Ammunition column (1 reserve gun).
Field Engineer Co. No. 11.
Supply column (Train Co. No. 24).
Field Ambulance No. 3.

Third Division. Major-General Sir W. F. Gatacre.
5th Brigade (Irish Brigade): Major-General Hart.
    1st battalion Royal Inniskilling Fusiliers.
    2d battalion Royal Irish Rifles.
    1st battalion Connaught Rangers.
    1st battalion Royal Dublin Fusiliers.
    Supply column (Train Co. No. 30).
    Litter Bearer Co. No. 16.
    Field Ambulance No. 10.

6th Brigade (Fusilier Brigade): Major-General Barton.
    2d battalion Royal Fusiliers.
    2d battalion Royal Scots Fusiliers.
    1st battalion Royal Welsh Fusiliers.
    2d battalion Royal Irish Fusiliers.
    Supply column (Train Co. No. 36). Litter Bearer Co. No. 17.
    Field Ambulance No. 11.
    1 squadron 14th Hussars.
    Field Batteries Nos. 74, 77 and 79 (6 guns each).
    Ammunition column (1 reserve gun).
    Field Engineer Co. No. 12.
    Supply column (Train Co. No. 33).
    Field Ambulance No. 7.

Cavalry Division. Lieutenant-General J. D. P. French.
1st Brigade: Major-General Babington.
    6th Dragoon Guards.
    10th Hussars.

12th Lancers.
Horse Battery R (6 guns).
Ammunition column (1 reserve gun).
Field Engineer Troop.
1st battalion Mounted Infantry.
Supply column (Train Co. No. 13).
Litter Bearer Co. No. 9. Field Ambulance No. 9.

2d Brigade: Major-General Brabazon.
1st Dragoons.
2d Dragoons. 6th Dragoons.
Horse Battery O (6 guns).
Ammunition column (1 reserve gun).
2d battalion Mounted Infantry.
Supply column (Train Co. No. 11).
Litter Bearer Co. No. 12.
Field Ambulance No. 6.

Corps Headquarters and Reserve.

1st battalion Royal Scots.
Staff of the 14th Hussars.
13th Hussars.
Field Artillery Regimental Staff.
Field Artillery Battalion Staff.
Horse Artillery Battalion Staff.
Horse Batteries G and P.
Field Batteries Nos. 4, 38 and 78 (6 guns each).
Howitzer Battalion Staff.
Howitzer Batteries Nos. 37, 61 and 65 (6 guns each).
Engineer Regimental Staff.
Pontoneers Section.
1st Section Telegraphists.
Field Engineer Co. No. 26.
1st Engineer Field Park.
1st and 2d Balloon Section.
10th Railroad Co.
Ammunition Park.
Supply column (Train Co. No. 21).
Field Bakery No. 40 (Train).
Field Ambulance No. 5.

Supply Park (Train Cos. No. 4, 29 and 42).

Troops for Lines of Communication: Lieutenant-General Sir Forestier-Walker.

    2d battalion Northumberland Fusiliers.
    2d battalion Somersetshire Light Infantry.
    2d battalion Duke of Cornwall's Light Infantry.
    1st battalion Welsh Regiment.
    2d battalion Northamptonshire Regiment.
    2d battalion Shropshire Light Infantry.
    1st battalion Gordon Highlanders.
    1 Balloon Field Equipage.
    4 Train Companies (6, 8, 28 and 35).
    4 Stationary Field Hospitals.
    4 General Field Hospitals.
    Principal Depots for Medical Supplies.
    Advance Depots for Medical Supplies.
    Hospital Sections.
    2 Hospital Ships.
    4 Companies Army Ordnance Corps (1, 2, 3 and 4).
    1 Corps Pay Station.
    1 Infantry Depot.
    General Depot.
    Remount Depots.

DISTRIBUTION OF THE BRITISH FORCES AT THE END OF NOVEMBER, 1899.

- Ladysmith. General White: 10,000 men, 44 (36 field, 8 navy) guns, 12 machine guns.
- Natal. General Clery: 15,500 men, 24 field guns, 16 machine guns.
- Madder River. General Lord Methuen: 9,400 men, 22 field guns, 12 machine guns.
- Kimberley. Colonel Kekewich: 2,400 men, 12 field guns, 4 machine guns.
- Mafeking. Colonel Baden-Powell: 1,000 men, 6 field guns, 4 machine guns.
- Naauwpoort and De Aar. General French: 4,900 men, 6 field guns, 6 machine guns.
- Queenstown. General Gatacre: 4,300 men, 5 machine guns.

- Rhodesia. 1,000 men, 6 field guns, 4 machine guns.
- Cape Town. 3,500 men, 35 field guns, 2 machine guns.

The strength of the forces in South Africa after the arrival of the mobile army corps was as follows:

	Officers and Men	Horses.	Mules.
6 Infantry Brigades	25,674	408	5,244
3 Divisional Troops	3,579	2,289	1,119
2 Cavalry Brigades	5,370	4,884	2,282
Corps Troops	5,124	2,584	1,938
Cavalry Division Staff	42	38	33
Field Engineer Troops with the Cavalry	122	88	51
Total of Mobile Army Corps	**39,911**	**10,301**	**10,667**
Troops for Lines of Communication	9,387	885	2,683
Natal Force	14,628		
Cape Force	5,140		
Naval Brigade	1,000		
Total	**70,066**	**11,186**	**13,350**

The actual strength of the mobile army corps in line troops, exclusive of the Staffs, was:
- Infantry: 25,475
- Mounted Infantry: 1,172
- Cavalry: 4,252
- Artillery: 3,435

Total: 34,334 and 114 guns.

The Infantry arm is the Lee-Metford rifle of 0.3-inch caliber, the Cavalry arm is the Lee-Metford carbine of the same caliber, the field batteries have 15-pounder guns, the horse batteries 12-pounders, the mountain batteries 7-pounder guns and the howitzer batteries 5-inch guns.

The transports landed their first troops on November 12 at Cape Town, part being sent on to Durban. The following were sent on to Natal:

1st Brigade.
  2d Coldstream Guards.

2d Brigade: Major-General Hildyard.
  2d West Surrey Regiment.
  2d West Yorkshire Regiment.
  2d East Surrey Regiment.

6th Brigade.
  1st Royal Welsh Fusiliers.

2d Irish Fusiliers.

Also parts of the 2d Division and 3 field batteries. Major-General Clery (commanding 2d Division) was sent as commander-in-chief in Natal.

Lord Methuen (commanding 1st Division) was sent to Orange River Station with the following:

- 3d Grenadier Guards.
- 1st Coldstream Guards.
- 1st Scots Guards.
- 1st Northumberland Fusiliers.
- 1st Royal Munster Fusiliers. ½ 1st Royal North Lancashire Regiment.
- 9th Lancers (embarked at Calcutta and Bombay, September 29).
- Field Artillery.

The rest of the mobilized army corps (1st, 2d and 3d Divisions) embarked in the first and second weeks of November, and arrived early in December. White's troops at Ladysmith constitute the 4th Division.

New Organizations.

The 5th Division was ordered mobilized on November 8th and has the following composition:

Fifth Division. General Sir C. Warren.

10th Brigade: Major-General Coke.
 2d battalion Royal Warwickshire Regiment.
 1st battalion Yorkshire Regiment.
 2d battalion Dorsetshire Regiment.
 2d battalion Middlesex Regiment.
 Army Service Corps (Co. No. 32).
 Litter Bearer Co. No. 10.
 Field Ambulance No. 11.

11th Brigade: Colonel Woodgate.
 2d battalion Royal Lancaster Regiment.
 2d battalion Lancashire Fusiliers.
 1st battalion South Lancashire Regiment.
 1st battalion York and Lancaster Regiment.
 Army Service Corps (Co. No. 25).
 Litter Bearer Co. No. 6.
 1 Field Ambulance.

1 squadron 14th Hussars.
19th, 20th and 28th Field Battery.
Ammunition column.
Field Engineer Co. No. 37.
Army Service Corps (Co. No. 12).
Field Ambulance No. 15.

Total strength 11,000 men, 1,263 horses, 18 field guns, 9 machine guns. Embarkation the end of November on fast steamers.

Not Yet Brigaded:
1st King's (Liverpool).
2d King's Royal Rifle Corps.
2d Rifle Brigade.
1st Border Regiment.

In addition to the 5th Division the following troops were ordered to proceed to South Africa:

Three infantry battalions, the 1st Suffolk (from Dover), 1st Essex (from Warley), 1st Sherwood Foresters (from Malta) and 1st Derbyshire battalions were ordered to replace the Gloucester and Irish Fusilier battalions captured at Ladysmith.

The 4th mountain battery to replace the captured 10th. A regiment of Household Cavalry.

A siege train of 30 howitzers (14 six-inch and 8 five-inch and 8 four-inch) and 1,000 men.

On December 3d the mobilization of the 6th Division was ordered, beginning on the 4th and ending on the 11th of December. On the 16th the transportation to South Africa was begun, and the first troops would reach Cape Town about January 8th, or Durban about January 12th.

Sixth Division. Major-General T. Kelly-Kenny.

12th Brigade: Colonel Clements.
2d battalion Bedfordshire Regiment.
1st battalion Royal Irish Regiment.
2d battalion Worcestershire Regiment.
2d battalion Wiltshire Regiment.
Army Service Corps (Co. No. 7).
Litter Bearer Co. No. 8.
Field Ambulance No. 4.

13th Brigade: Colonel Knox.

2d battalion East Kent Regiment (Buffs).
2d battalion Gloucestershire Regiment.
1st battalion West Riding Regiment.
1st battalion Oxfordshire Light Infantry Regiment.
Army Service Corps (Co. No. 10).
Litter Bearer Co. No. 7.
Field Ambulance No. 18.
76th, 81st and 82d Field Battery.
Ammunition column (1 reserve gun).
Field Engineer Co. No. 38.
Army Service Corps (Co. No. 23).
Field Ambulance No. 6.

Total strength: 9,601 men, 744 horses and 2,405 mules.

On December 14th the mobilization of the 7th Division was ordered. Its embarkation took place between the 4th and 10th of January, and it reached the Cape about the end of January.

Seventh Division. Major-General C. Tucker.

14th Brigade: Major-General Chermside.
2d battalion Norfolk Regiment.
2d battalion Lincolnshire Regiment.
1st battalion King's Own Scottish Borderers.
2d battalion Hampshire Regiment.
Army Service Corps (Co. No. 31).
Litter Bearer Co. No. 19.
Field Hospital No. 13.

15th Brigade: Major-General Wavell.[7]
2d battalion Cheshire Regiment.
1st battalion East Lancashire Regiment.
2d battalion South Wales Borderers.
2d battalion North Staffordshire Regiment.
Army Service Corps (Co. No. 12).
Field Ambulance No. 13.
83d, 84th and 85th Field Batteries.
Ammunition column (1 reserve gun).
Field Engineer Co. No. 9.
Army Service Corps Co. No. 17.
Field Hospital No. 13.

---

7 General Prior first assigned, died at Aldershot.

No cavalry is assigned to this division; hereafter volunteer mounted infantry is to be attached—about 880 men to a division.

On December 17th Field Marshal Lord Roberts was appointed commander-in-chief in South Africa, with Lord Kitchener of Khartoum as his chief of staff.

The Government, about the middle of December, ordered the organization of the following for service in South Africa:

1. Imperial Yeomanry, 3,000 men (selected Yeomanry as mounted infantry); the companies to have a strength of 5 officers and 110 men.

2. Volunteer Mounted Infantry, 76 selected companies, one for each battalion to be sent out in future, 8,664 in all. A second selected company to be made up in the regimental district of each regiment.

3. A battalion of volunteers from the metropolis:
- City of London Imperial Volunteers, 1,400 men.
- 8 companies Infantry.
- 2 companies Mounted Infantry.
- 1 battery Field Artillery (4 Q. F. guns).

4. The 16th Lancers and 2,000 reserve horses from India.

5. 700 men of the Naval Brigade landed.

6. A field howitzer battalion of 3 batteries of 6 guns each: 43d, 86th and 87th Batteries.

The 8th Division was ordered mobilized towards the end of December.

Eighth Division. Major-General Sir H. Rundle.

16th Brigade: Major-General B. B. D. Campbell.

    2d battalion Grenadier Guards.
    2d battalion Scots Guards.
    2d battalion East Yorkshire.
    1st battalion Leinster (Royal Canadians), from Halifax.
    Army Service Corps.
    Litter Bearer Co. No. 21.
    Field Hospital No. 21.

17th Brigade: Major-General J. E. Boyes.

    1st battalion Worcester.
    1st battalion Royal West Kent, from Cairo.
    1st battalion South Stafford, from Gibraltar.
    2d battalion Manchester.
    Army Service Corps (Co. No. 37).

Litter Bearer Co. No. 22.
Field Hospital No. 22.
89th, 90th and 91st Field Batteries.
Ammunition column (1 reserve gun).
Field Engineer Co. No. 5.
Army Service Corps (Co. No. 38).
Field Hospital No. 23.

Each battalion has a strength of 1,019, in which is included for each a mounted company.

A cavalry brigade was ordered mobilized at the same time with the 8th Division.

Cavalry Brigade. Major-General J. B. B. Dickson.
7th Dragoon Guards.
8th Hussars.
17th Lancers.
Horse Battery M.
Ammunition column (1 reserve gun).
2 companies Mounted Infantry.
Army Service Corps (Co. No. 3).
1 Company Bearers.
1 Field Hospital.

Total strength: 2,518 men, 2,160 horses, 7 field guns and 2 machine guns.

An artillery corps was ordered to mobilize at the same time as the 8th Division.

Artillery Corps.
12th howitzer battalion: 43d, 86th and 87th Batteries.
13th battalion: 2d, 8th and 44th Field Batteries.
14th battalion: 39th, 68th and 88th Field Batteries.
15th battalion: 5th, 9th and 17th Field Batteries.

Total strength 2,630 men, 2,134 horses.

Each howitzer battery has 199 men, 162 horses; each field battery 175 men, 137 horses.

The following separate organizations have been ordered to South Africa:
1st battalion Cameron Highlanders (from Cairo).
1st battalion Sussex (from Malta).
2 battalions from Gibraltar.
16th Lancers from India (sailed January 8).

Horse Batteries A and J from India.

Ninth Brigade.

    1st Northumberland Fusiliers (Originally in Cape Colony Force)

    1st Loyal North Lancashire (Originally in Cape Colony Force) (part).

    2d Yorkshire Light Infantry (Originally in Cape Colony Force)

    2d Northamptonshire (Originally on Line of Communications.)

COLONIAL FORCES.

Rhodesia.

    Rhodesia Horse (one squadron in Natal).

    Protectorate Regiment (under Colonel Baden-Powell).

    Mounted Infantry (under Colonel Plumer).

Kimberley.

    Diamond Fields Artillery.

    Kimberley Light Horse.

    Kimberley Rifles.

Cape Colony.

    South African Light Horse (under Col. Byng and Capt. Villiers).

    Imperial Corps of Guides.

    Brabant's Horse.

    Warren's Horse.

    De Montmorency's Scouts.

    Railway Engineer Corps.

    Mounted Volunteers (Colonel Cole).

    Prince Albert Capo Artillery.

    Cape Garrison Artillery.

    Victoria Rifles.

    Cape Town Highlanders.

    Prince Albert Guard of Port Elizabeth.

    Kaffrarian Rifles of East London.

    Grahamstown Volunteers.

    Queenstown Rifle Volunteers.

    British South African Police (Colonel Walford).

    Cape Mounted Rifles Police (Colonel Dalgetty).

Natal.

    Imperial Light Horse.

    Uitlander Regiment.

    Imperial Infantry.

Vickers 12.5 Pounder Field Gun

Bethune's Horse.
Natal Carabineers.
Natal Field Artillery.
Natal Mounted Rifles.
Border Mounted Rifles.
Umvoti Mounted Rifles.
Corps of Colonial Scouts.
Corps of Guides.
Natal Mounted Police.

Amounted to 4,500 men in November, 1899.

Canada.
Royal Canadian Regiment of Infantry.
Canadian Mounted Rifles (2 battalions).
Royal Canadian Artillery: Batteries C, D, E (12-pounder B. L.).

Australia.
New South Wales Lancers Squadron: 80
New South Wales Infantry: 120
New South Wales Mounted Rifles: 75
Queensland Mounted Infantry.-: 264
Victoria Mounted Infantry: 250
South Australia Mounted Infantry: 125
West Australia Mounted Infantry: 125
Tasmania Mounted Infantry: 80

Total: 1,119

New Zealand.
Mounted Infantry: 213

GENERAL BULLER'S COMMAND. December 14, 1899.

2d Brigade: General Hildyard.
    2d battalion Royal West Surrey Regiment.
    2d battalion Devonshire Regiment.
    2d battalion West Yorkshire Regiment.
    2d battalion East Surrey Regiment.

4th Brigade: General Lyttleton.
    1st battalion Rifle Brigade.
    3d battalion Kind's Royal Rifles.

6th Brigade: General Barton.
    2d battalion Royal Fusiliers.
    2d battalion Royal Scots Fusiliers.
    1st battalion Royal Welsh Fusiliers.
    2d battalion Royal Irish Fusiliers.

Mixed Brigade: General Hart.
    2d battalion Cameronians (Scottish Rifles).
    1st battalion Durham Light Infantry.
    1st battalion Highland Light infantry.
    2d battalion Somerset Light Infantry.
    2 field batteries and 6 naval guns.

Mafeking: Colonel Baden-Powell.

Cavalry.
    Cape Mounted Police.

Infantry.
    Protectorate Regiment.
    Volunteers.
    B. S. A. Companies, Mounted Police.

Tuli. Colonel Plumer.

Kimberley.

Cavalry.
    Cape Police.
    Diamond Field Horse (part).
    Kimberley Light Horse (part).

Infantry.
    2d Royal Highlanders (detachment).
    1st Loyal North Lancashire (4 companies).
    Local Volunteer Corps.
    Townsmen.

BRITISH FIELD GUN WITH CLARKE RECOIL BRAKE.

Artillery.
  Field Batteries.
  Garrison Artillery.
  Diamond Fields Artillery.
Engineers.
  1 Detachment.
  R. A. M. C.
  Hospital.

British Artillery.

At the end of the year 1899 the British had in South Africa (omitting those lost in battle) the following artillery material:
- 4 batteries (G, O, P, R) Royal Horse Artillery, 6 guns each, 12-pounder, 3-inch, breech-loaders: 24
- 24 batteries (Nos. 4, 7, 13, 14, 18, 19, 20, 21, 36, 42, 49, 53, 62, 64, 66, 67, 69, 73, 74, 75, 76, 77, 79, 92) Royal Field Artillery, 6 guns each, 15-pounder, 3-inch, breech-loaders: 144
- 3 batteries (Nos. 37, 61, 65) Royal Field Artillery, 6 guns each, 5-inch field howitzers, firing shrapnel, canister and lyddite shell: 18
- 1 mountain battery (No. 4), 6 guns, 2.5-inch, muzzle-loaders: 6

Total: 192

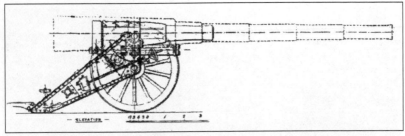

4.7-IN. Q. F. NAVY GUN, ON 6-IN. HOWITZER CARRIAGE.

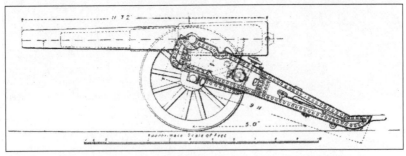

BRITISH 4.7-IN. NAVY GUN ON 10-PDR. CARRIAGE.

The Artillery of the Transvaal Boers.
Old Guns.
- 8 cm. field guns, Krupp, old: 40
- 6 cm. mountain guns, Krupp, old: 40

Total: 80

- 7-pounder R. F. Maxim-Nordenfeldt (captured in Jameson Raid): 1
- 3-inch R. F. Maxim-Nordenfeldt (captured in Jameson Raid): 1

New Guns.
- 7.5 cm. R. F. Krupp field guns, new: 8
- 7.5 cm. R. F. Schneider-Canet field guns, new: 16
- S cm. R. F. Maxim-Nordenfeldt field guns, new.: 5
- 3.7 cm. Automatic Maxim-Nordenfeldt guns, new: 24
- 12 cm. field howitzers, Krupp, new: 4
- 12 cm. field howitzers, Schrieider-Canet, new: 4
- 3.7 cm. R. F. mountain guns, Krupp, new: 4
- Dynamite gun (like Simms-Dudley), new: 1
- 15.5 cm. long siege guns, Schneider-Canet, new: 4

Total: 72

Machine Guns.
- 0.45-inch Maxim guns: 30
- 0.30-inch Maxim guns: 20

Total: 50

The Artillery of the Orange Boers.
- 7.5 cm. field guns, Krupp: 12
- 3.7 cm. field guns: 1

Total: 13
- Maxim machine guns: 6
- Guns captured by the Boers: 26

Small-Arms in the War.
- British: Lee-Metford gun.
- Boers: Mauser gun, M. 93, 95 and 98. Henry-Martini gun.

The small-arms used in the Boer War are of especial interest to the military world because in this war small-caliber magazine rifles are used on a large scale for the first time in history.

The arms of the two opposed nations are contrasted in the following table:

	British.		Boer.	
	Lee-Metford, 89, MII.	Henry-Martini, 95	Mauser, 93-95	Henry-Martini (old)
Wt. of rifle alone (mag. empty)	9.2 lbs.		8.4 lbs.	
Wt. of rifle and bayonet (mag. fall)	10.9 lbs.		9.6 lbs.	
Length of rifle alone	4 ft. 1½ in.		4 ft. ½ in.	
Number of cartridges in magazine.	5		5	
Caliber of bore	0.303 in.	0.303 in.	0.276 in.	0.45 in.
Number of grooves	5	5	4	
Mechanism	Bolt.		Bolt.	
Weight of bullet	14 grams.	14 grams.	11.2 grams	31.2 grams.
Charge	2.2 grams cordite.	2.2 grams cordite.	2.2 grams.	5.5 grams.
Total weight of round	28.3 grams.	28.3 grams.	24.8 grams	bl'k powder.
Velocity (muzzle)	21.49 f. s.		2389 f. s.	
Extreme range			4380 yds.	
Sight graduated to	1900 yds.			
Penetration in deal at 12 m.	38 in.		55 in.	
Rounds carried by soldier	115			

The British Army is armed principally with the Lee-Metford rifle 89 M. II., but in 1895 the old Henry-Martini guns wore altered at Enfield and furnished with a bore of the same dimensions as the Lee-Metford, and firing the same projectile. These guns were issued to the volunteers at that time, and it is probable that some of them are now in use in South Africa.

The Boer Army has mostly the Mauser gun; the Transvaal Boers the model 93-95, the Orange Boers the latest model (98); but the latter use in part the old 0.45-inch Henry-Martini, a number of which they purchased from England in 1894.

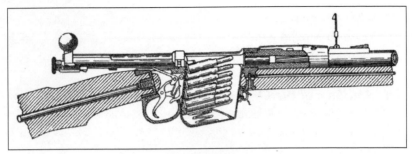

LEE-METFORD GUN

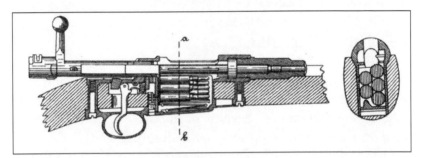

MAUSER RIFLE

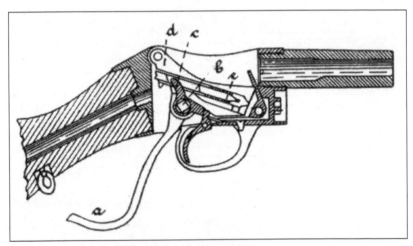

HENRY-MARTINI

Results of Firing of Mauser Rifle.
- Height of trajectory at 500 m: 3 feet 5 inches.
- Height of trajectory at 550 m: 4 feet 3 inches.
- Height of trajectory at 600 m: 5 feet 4 inches.
- Deviation (mean) at 200 m. vertical: 6 inches.

- Deviation (mean) at 200 m. horizontal: 5 inches.
- Deviation (mean) at 1200 m vertical: 4 feet 5½ inches.
- Deviation (mean) at 1200 m horizontal: 3 feet ½ inch.
- Deviation (mean) at 1500 m vertical: 10 feet 11 inches
- Deviation (mean) at 1500 m horizontal: 5 feet 10 inches.
- Deviation (mean) at 2000 m vertical: 20 feet 7 inches.
- Deviation (mean) at 2000 m horizontal: 5 feet.
- Space completely swept for Infantry: 1969 feet.
- Space completely swept for Cavalry: 2297 feet.

ADDITIONAL COLONIAL CONTINGENTS.

Canada.

1,247 men.
- 4 squadrons Mounted Infantry.
- 3 Field Batteries.

Australia.

Infantry. 1,250 men.
- 1 Field Battery.

New Zealand.

200 men, 4 Hotchkiss guns.

India.

250 mounted men.

Ceylon.

125 mounted men.

ADDITIONAL TROOPS ORDERED.

The 8th Division sailed from England in the latter part of March and arrived at Port Elizabeth and East London about the middle of April.

The 1st battalion Leinster Regiment came from Halifax, Nova Scotia, to England to be mobilized and did not embark there for South Africa till April 18th. The three batteries first assigned to the division were left behind, but after the loss of 7 guns at Koorn Spruit (March 31, 1900), two other batteries for this division were ordered mobilized at Aldershot.

Of the Militia 29 battalions have been (up to the end of April) sent to South Africa, 4 to Malta, 1 to Cairo and 1 to St. Helena (to replace other troops and, at the last mentioned place, to guard prisoners).

Of the Imperial Yeomanry 79 companies were organized into 20 battalions, besides a battalion of Sharpshooters, one of Rough Riders, and one called Paget's Corps. They began to arrive in South Africa on the 9th of February, and on the 21st of April there were 58 companies in South Africa, 12 at sea, and 9 still at home.

TROOPS IN SOUTH AFRICA.

At the opening of Lord Roberts' campaign, about the middle of February, England had the following troops in South Africa:

- Army of operations at the front: 110,000 men, 216 guns.
- In Ladysmith: 8,000 men, 46 guns.
- In Kimberley: 2,600 men, 76 guns.
- In Mafeking: 1,000 men, 16 guns.
- Reserves, and on Line of Communications:
    In Natal: 4,000 men, 32 guns.
    In the Center and West: 8,500 men, 32 guns.
    In Cape Town: 5,500 men, 32 guns.
    In Rhodesia: 2,000 men, 6 guns.
- Non-combatants: 22,400 men.
- Losses in killed, wounded and prisoners: 10,000 men.
- Sick: 5,000 men.

Total in South Africa: 179,000 men, 392 guns
    On the way to Cape Town: 17,150 men, 172 guns.
    Embarked: 4th Cavalry Brigade.
    Mobilizing: 17,150 men, 24 guns.
    Ordered mobilized: 9th Division.

The Boers had about 65,000 men, 110 guns.

Up to the end of February the total number of troops sent from England amounted to 141,165 men, 24,103 horses and 379 guns.

TOTAL BRITISH FORCES IN SOUTH AFRICA, INCLUDING COLONIALS.

February 15, not including 8th Division or 4th Cavalry Brigade.
- Unmounted (including artillery.): 15,142,800
- Mounted: 37,800

Total: 180,600

BOER LOSSES

Up to the middle of January.
- Mafeking: 500
- Belmont: 400
- Graspan: 250

- Modder River: 400
- Magersfontein: 700
- Kuruman: 100
- Douglas: 75
- Against Gen. French: 300
- Against Gen. Gatacre: 100
- Glencoe: 300
- Elandslaagte: 600
- Ladysmith: 2,000
- Sundry: 400

Total: 6,125

TOTAL BRITISH CASUALTIES (OFFICIAL)
Up to February 24th.
- 161 officers and 1,490 men killed.
- 194 officers and 5,795 men wounded.
- 133 officers and 2,669 men prisoners and missing.

Total, 488 officers and 9,954 men.

CHANGES IN COMMAND.
- Feb. 10, General Colville to command 9th Division, newly formed.
- Feb. 10, Colonel Douglas to command 9th Brigade, vice Colville, promoted.
- Feb. 27, General Hart to 2d Division, vice Clery, injured.
- Feb. 27, Colonel Norcott to 5th Brigade, vice Hart, promoted.
- Feb. 27, Colonel Kitchener to 11th Brigade, vice Wynne, wounded.

THE NAVAL BRIGADE.

The Terrible arrived at Simons Bay on October 14th, and while getting ready to land the small-arms and field guns, the captain (Percy Scott) concluded that heavier guns would be needed at the front, and therefore commenced to mount the navy guns on carriages for field use and on platforms, carrying on the work first on board and then in the dockyard. The Powerful arrived on the same day and took up the same work. On the 26th the latter was ordered to Durban, and on the day of arrival Captain Lambton took to Ladysmith two 4.7-in. guns, three long 12-pounders and one short 12-pounder, some Maxims, 300 rounds per gun, and 286 officers and men. On November 2d the Terrible received orders for Durban, arriving November 6th, and at

once landed the heavy guns:
- One 4.7-inch Q.F., on wheeled mounting.
- Sixteen long 12-pounders, on special mountings.
- Two short 12-pounders, on field mountings.
- Two Maxims, on field mountings.
- 300 rounds for each piece.

21 officers and 250 men were also landed, all for the defense of Durban.

Four 12-pounders were soon taken to Pietermaritzburg, to replace two long 12-pounders which had been landed by the Powerful, these having been ordered forward to the Mooi River.

On November 23d two more were sent from Durban, the four previously sent having also been sent forward to Mooi River and Estcourt. The guns sent forward were manned by men of the Tartar, Philomel and Forte. On November 26th two 4.7-inch guns and four more 12-pounders were ordered forward manned by the Terrible.

On December 1st Capt. Scott (Terrible) mounted a search-light on a railway car. On December 8th eight more guns were ordered to the front. The two 4.7-inch and six of the 12-pounders were in action at Chievely on December 12.

THE NATIVE VOLUNTEER BODIES.
- Bethune's Mounted Infantry.
- Border Horse.
- Brabant's Horse.
- British South Africa Police.
- Cape Garrison Artillery.
- Cape Medical Staff Corps.
- Cape Mounted Rifles.
- Cape Town Highlanders.
- Cape Town City Volunteers.
- Duke of Edinburgh's Own Rifle Volunteers.
- French's Scouts.
- Frontier Mounted Rifles.
- Imperial Light Horse.
- Imperial Light Infantry.
- Kaffrarian Rifles.
- Kaffrarian Mounted Infantry.
- Kitchener's Horse.

- Montmorency's Scouts.
- Prince Alfred's Own Cape Artillery.
- Prince Alfred's Volunteer Guard.
- Protectorate Regiment.
- Queenstown Rifle Volunteers.
- Rhodesia Regiment.
- Rimington Imperial Guides.
- Roberts' Horse.
- South African Light Horse.
- Thornycroft's Mounted Infantry.

COLONIAL CONTINGENTS.
Australia.
- New South Wales Lancers.
- 1st Australian Horse.
- Mounted Rifles.
- A Battery.
- Queensland Mounted Infantry.
- South Australian Infantry.
- Tasmanian Contingent.
- Victorian Contingent.
- Mounted Infantry.
- West Australian Contingent.
- New Zealand Mounted Rifles.

Canada.
- 1st and 2d battalions Canadian Mounted Rifles.
- 2d battalion Royal Canadian Regiment of Infantry.
- C, D and E batteries Royal Canadian Artillery.

Ceylon.
- Ceylon Contingent.

THE ARTILLERY MATERIAL.
BRITISH ARTILLERY: Strength and Distribution, February 15, 1900.

Field Guns.
- Roberts' Army: 156
- Buller's Army: 60
- Gatacre's Army: 18
- At Arundel and Naauwpoort: 26
- Cities and lines of communication: 100

Total: 360

Field Howitzers.
- Methuen's Corps: 12
- Buller's Army: 6

Total: 18

Navy Churns.
- Buller's Army: 12
- In Ladysmith: 8
- Roberts' Army: 12
- Elsewhere: 26

Total: 58

Additional: March 15, 1900.
- Field guns: 72
- Field howitzers: 18
- 4.7-inch Armstrong guns: 6
- Mobilizing: Field guns: 24

The Field Gun

The field gun is called a 15-pounder, M. 95; it is of 3-inch caliber, firing only shrapnel (besides canister), initial velocity 1,574 feet, weight 14 pounds; maximum range (15° elevation) 5,468 yards, but can fire 2,000 yards farther. Its mean dispersion (double the mean deviation) in range at 5,468 yards (for percussion shell) is 155 yards, while that of the German gun is only 54 yards. It is sighted up to 5,500 yards, but the shrapnel is timed only to 4,000 yards. It was not originally a quick-firer, but with the Clarke brake it is now practically such.

The City of London Volunteers were supplied with a battery of 3-inch Vickers guns. These guns are wire guns, firing a 12.5 pound shrapnel with a muzzle velocity of 1,575 feet. It is sighted up to 5,000 yards, and carries shrapnel and shell. It is mounted on an improved Darmancier carriage.

The City of Elswick Volunteers were supplied with a battery of 3-inch quick-firing Armstrong guns.

The Horse Artillery Gun.

The horse artillery gun is a wire gun of 3-inch caliber, 12-pounder.

The Mountain Gun.

A 7-pounder muzzle-loader.

The Field Howitzer.

The field howitzer is 5-inch caliber, firing lyddite shrapnel weighing 50 pounds, with time fuse graduated to 3,390 yards, maximum range

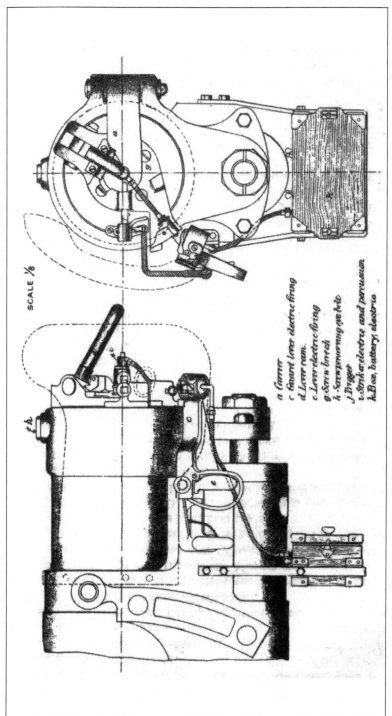

Ordnance. Quick firing, 4.7 inch, Mark I, II & III. Breech closing mechanism

4,900 yards. The guns of the siege train sent over from England on December 9th comprised mainly 6-inch, but partly also 4.7-inch and 4-inch howitzers, firing lyddite and other shell.

Navy Guns.

These are 6-inch, 4.7-inch and 3-inch.

The 4.7-inch navy guns with Methuen's column were mounted on 40-pounder carriages.

Those at Ladysmith on 6-inch howitzer carriages, the recoil gear for fixed platform removed.

This gun fires a 50-pound shell, with a muzzle velocity of 1,750 foot-seconds, and great range.

The Machine Gun.

Maxim gun firing small-arm ammunition.

BOER ARTILLERY.

44 quick-fire modern field guns, 7.5 cm. or 3-inch (Krupp Schneider-Creusot and Maxim-Nordenfeldt).

These guns fire (besides canister) shell and shrapnel, with from 1,475 to 1,510 feet muzzle velocity.

- 6 older 7.85 cm. (3.1-inch) guns.
- 4 old 6 cm. (2.4-inch) guns
- 4 new 3.7 cm. (1.46-inch) Krupp mountain guns.
- 24 3.7 cm. (1.46-inch) Maxim-Nordenfeldt.
- 50 Maxim machine guns firing either the ammunition of the old Henry-Martini gun, or that of the Mauser gun.

8 12 cm. (4.7-inch) field howitzers (Krupp or Schneider-Creusot). These fire shell, shrapnel and torpedo shell, and are much more mobile than the British howitzers.

- 6 long Creusot or Krupp 15.5 cm. (6-inch) siege guns (including the Long Tom at Ladysmith), firing an 88-pound projectile with a muzzle velocity of 1,574 feet.

The British cannot utilize the maximum range of their field guns (about 7,500 yards), because their sight is not graduated beyond 5,500 yards, and their tables are not worked out beyond this range; whereas the Boers, by burying the trail and by firing as they generally do from above downward, can attain the extreme range of 7,500 yards.

Moreover, the Boer (Krupp) fuse is graduated to 4,200 meters (or 550 meters farther than the British), so that they can fire with shrapnel farther than the British. The British have, however, fired their shrapnel (on account of the great range of the Mauser rifle) at too great ranges—ranges over 3,600 meters—where the shrapnel bullets have too low a velocity to be effective. Hence, the great advantage of the Boers in possessing also shell, in addition to shrapnel, by means of which they can fire effectively at ranges beyond the maximum effective range of the British shrapnel. The British have nothing in the way of a field piece to oppose to the Boer shell fire of over 5,000 meters, or even over 4,000 yards (the limit of the British time fuse).

The Boers have no real idea of tactics in their use of artillery, for we never hear of batteries in the various engagements that have taken place, but always of single guns, and after the second Upper Tugela fight a single gun only pursued the British.

The British, having only shrapnel, were practically without any effect on the Boer infantry in its S-shaped trenches, even when they had a flank fire on them. Such trenches could only be reached by high angle fire, but the maximum range of the British field howitzer is only 4,900 yards, and good ranging with this piece requires well-trained cannoneers, specially when the enemy is as expert in masking its trenches as the Boers were. Moreover, the British artillery lacked tactical handling, in that the superior artillery officers were generally detached, and the work was left mainly to the battery commanders: there was no concentration of groups of batteries, no fire control of the entire artillery; indeed, the great lesson of the war of 1870-71, the use of masses of artillery, seems to have been forgotten. In an attack the artillery preceded the infantry, but did not always accompany it in its advance, so that the latter really met unshaken infantry in the assault. There is no question of the excellent and fearless handling of the separate batteries in advance or in covering a retreat, but no great tactical result has been accomplished by a large mass of artillery on any of the fields, although the two groups in the battles of the 5th to the 8th of February seem to have worked in unison, and in surrounding Cronje, Roberts undoubtedly attained an artillery mass fire.

CHANGES IN COMMAND.

General Joubert died in Pretoria March 27th.

General Louis Botha succeeded to the command of the Transvaal Boers, while President Kruger assumed the command-in-chief of the Boer troops.

BRITISH CASUALTIES OF THE WAR TO MARCH 9.		
	Officers.	Men.
Killed	132	1,583
Died of wounds	38	309
Missing and prisoners	138	3,191
Died of disease	32	793
Died of accidents	2	20
Sent home as invalids	83*	2,428*
Total	8,739	

Includes some of the wounded.

General Clery returned to the 2d Division March 30th.

General White left Ladysmith on March 9th, to return to England for rest and recuperation. General Lyttleton took command of the Ladysmith garrison, with Howard and Knox in command of the brigades.

The 10th Division was placed under General Hunter. It comprised the 5th and 6th Brigades.

April 15th Gatacre was recalled to England, and Pole-Carew succeeded him. Colonel Inigo Jones received the Guards Brigade.

ORGANIZATION OF LORD ROBERTS' ARMY.
Before the Advance on Bloemfontein.
1st Division: Methuen
   1st Brigade: Pole-Carew.
   9th Brigade: Douglas.
6th Division: Kelly-Kenny
   13th Brigade: Knox.
   18th Brigade: Stephenson.
7th Division: Tucker.
   14th Brigade: Chermside.
   15th Brigade: Wavell.
9th Division: Colville.
   3d Brigade: Colville.
   19th Brigade: Macdonald.
Artillery.
   11 field batteries, 2 howitzer batteries, 4 navy 4.7" guns, 4 navy 12-pounders, 3 Vickers-Maxim automatic guns (37 mm.).
Mounted Troops.
Mounted Infantry Division.

    1st Brigade: Hannah.
    2d Brigade: Ridley.
Cavalry Division: French.
    1st Brigade: Porter.
    2d Brigade: Broadwood.
    3d Brigade: Gordon.
    7 horse batteries.
    1 balloon section.
    6 companies Engineers.

The 8th Division (Rundle) landed at East London March 30th, and was sent to the front at once, reaching Springfontein April 12th.

Before the Advance from Bloemfontein.
    1st Division: Methuen.
        1st Brigade: Douglas.
        2d Brigade: Paget.
    6th Division: Kelly-Kenny.
        12th Brigade: Clements.
        13th Brigade: Wavell.
    8th Division: Sir Leslie Rundle.
        16th Brigade: Campbell.
        17th Brigade: Boyes.
    11th Division. (Vacancy.)
        Guards Brigade. I. R. Jones.
        18th Brigade. Stephenson.
    3d Division: Pole-Carew.[8]
        22d Brigade: R. E. Allen.
        23d Brigade: W. G. Knox.
    7th Division: Tucker.
        14th Brigade: J. G. Maxwell.
        15th Brigade: C. E. Knox.
    9th Division: Colville.
        3d Brigade: MacDonald. (Highlanders.)
        19th Brigade: Smith-Dorrien.
        21st Brigade (Newly formed): Bruce-Hamilton.
    Cavalry Division: French.
        1st Brigade: Porter.
        2d Brigade: Broadwood.

---

8 Pole-Carew was later transferred to the new 11th Division, Chermside receiving the 3d.

3d Brigade: Gordon.
Independent.
4th Brigade.
Mounted Infantry: Hamilton.
1st Brigade: Hutton.
2d Brigade: Ridley.
THE NATAL ARMY.
April 15th.
2d Division: Clery.
2d Brigade: Hildyard.
4th Brigade: Cooper.
4th Division: Lyttleton.
7th Brigade: W. F. Kitchener
8th Brigade: Howard.
5th Division: Warren.[9]
10th Brigade: Coke.
11th Brigade: Wynne.
10th Division:[10] Sir A. Hunter.
5th Brigade: Hart.
6th Brigade: Barton.
Cavalry Division.
1st Brigade: Burn-Murdock.
2d Brigade: Brocklehurst.
3d Brigade: Dundonald.

BRITISH CASUALTIES OF THE WAR TO APRIL 7.		
	Officers.	Men.
Killed	211	1,960
Died of wounds	48	465
Died of disease	47	1,485
Died of accidents	3	34
Sent home as invalids*	29	1,828
Missing and prisoners	168	3,722
Wounded	627	9,883
Total	20,510	

Not including the wounded.

---

9 Relieved on account of his failure at Spion Kop, and sent to the western theatre on duty other than that at the front. Hildyard placed in command May 1st.

10 Early in April Hart's Brigade was transferred to the western theatre to join Brabant. Barton's followed and was sent to Kimberley.

TOTAL BRITISH CASUALTIES TO APRIL 28		
	Officers.	Men.
Killed	218	2,062
Died of wounds	53	492
Died of disease	64	2,028
Died of accidents		48
Sent home as invalids (not wounded)	29	3,101
Wounded	764	9,225
Missing and prisoners	171	3,925
Total (not including invalids)	22,180	

CHANGES IN COMMAND.

May 1st Hildyard received command of the 5th division, vice Sir Charles Warren.

BRITISH CASUALTIES TO MAY 19.		
	Officers.	Men.
Killed	224	2,131
Died of wounds	58	517
Died of disease	84	2,719
Died of accidents		54
Died in captivity	1	49
Sent home as invalids*	525	9,893
Wounded	697	9,522
Missing and prisoners	171	4,304
Total (not including invalids)	20,680	

Including some of the wounded.

CHANGES IN COMMAND.

June. Colonel Carew, 7th Hussars, appointed brigadier general commanding 1st Brigade Rhodesia Field Force, comprising 1st and 2d Bushmen's regiments. Colonel Grey commanding 2d Brigade.

TOTAL BRITISH CASUALTIES TO JUNE 16.		
	Officers.	Men.
Killed	243	2,353
Died of wounds	64	558
Died of disease	123	3,782
Died of accidents		60
Sent home as invalids	724	15,039
Missing and prisoners*	41	1,469
Total†	24,456	

Excluding those who have been recovered.
†*Excluding sick and wounded now in British hospitals in South Africa.*

OFFICIAL TABLE OF CASUALTIES. June 19, 1900.										
Casualties in Action.	Killed		Wounded		Died of wounds in S. Africa (included in wounded)		Missing and prisoners		Total killed, wounded, missing, and prisoners.	
	Officers	NCO's & Men	Officers	NCO's & Men	Officers	NCO's & Men	Officers	NCO's & Men	Officers	NCO's & Men
Belmont, Nov. 23	3	50	25	220	1	21			28	270
Colenso, Dec. 15	7	128	43	719	2	20	21	207	71	1054
Driefontein, March 10	5	58	19	342	1	18		2	24	402
Dundee, October 20	8	40	11	84	3		25	306	44	430
Elandslaagte, October 21	5	50	30	169		6		4	35	223
Enslin (Graspan) Nov. 25	3	13	6	163	1	3		9	9	185
Farquhar's Farm and Nicholsons Nek, Oct. 30	6	57	9	244		10	43	925	58	1226
Johannesburg & Pretoria	3	20	34	129	1	6	5	38	42	187
Karee, near Brandfort, March 29	1	20	9	152	1	11			10	172
Klip Kraal, Feb. 16		11	6	101		1		7	6	119
Ladysmith, Relief of, Feb. 19-27	22	241	90	1530	3	75	1	11	113	1782
Magersfontein, Dec. 11	23	148	45	646	3	35		108	68	902
Monte Christo (Colenso) etc. Feb. 15-18	1	13	8	180		3		4	9	197
Modder Kiver, Nov. 28	4	66	20	393		31		2	24	461
Paardeberg, Feb. 16-27	17	238	74	1135	6	65	7	63	98	1436
Potgeiters Drift, Feb. 5-7	2	23	18	326		8		5	20	354
Reddersburg, April 3-4	2	10	2	33	1	1	8	397	12	440
Reitfontein, Oct. 24	1	11	6	98		4		2	7	111
Sannas Post, March 31	3	16	16	118	2	7	18	407	37	541
Spion Kop, etc., Jan. 17-24	27	245	53	1050	6	39	7	351	87	1646
Stormberg, Dec. 10		32	7	51		1	13	619	20	702
Willow Grange, Nov. 23		11	1	66		2	1	8	2	83
At Ladysmith during investment - Battle of Jan 6	14	167	33	284	4	25		2	47	453
Other casualties	6	63	36	280	3	29		12	42	355
At Kimberley during investment	2	36	15	118		4	1	3	18	157
At Mafeking	5	63	10	147		6	1	40	16	250
Other casualties	65	453	215	1786	25	120	49	1026	329	3265
Total casualties in action reported up to June 9	235	2283	841	10564	63	551	200	4558	1276	17405

CHANGES IN COMMAND.

July 1. The 9th division broke up, General Colville relieved, Macdonald's (Highlander) brigade assigned to Hunter's (10th) division, Smith-Dorrien's to Methuen's 1st division.

TOTAL BRITISH CASUALTIES TO JUNE 23.		
	Officers.	Men.
Killed	250	2,384
Died of wounds	68	589
Died of disease	125	3,985
Died of accidents		66
Sent home as invalids	784	16,358
Missing and prisoners*	37	1,650
Total†	26,296	

*Excluding those who have been recovered.
†Excluding sick and wounded now in British hospitals in South Africa.

| TOTAL BRITISH CASUALTIES TO JUNE 30. ||
	Officers.	Men.
Killed	254	2.403
Died of wounds	70	610
Died of disease	133	4,204
Died of accidents		66
Sent home as invalids	844	18,433
Missing and prisoners*	65	2,624
Total†	29,706	

*Excluding those who have been recovered.
†Excluding sick and wounded now in British hospitals in South Africa.

| TOTAL BRITISH CASUALTIES TO JULY 13. ||
	Officers.	Men.
Killed	255	2,411
Died of wounds	70	625
Died of disease	137	4,398
Died of accidents		68
Died in captivity	1	84
Sent home as Invalids	916	19,742
Missing and prisoners*	59	1,927
Total†	30,963	

*Excluding those who have been recovered.
†Excluding sick and wounded now in British hospitals in South Africa.

| TOTAL BRITISH CASUALTIES TO JULY 27 ||
	Officers.	Men.
Killed	271	2,502
Died of wounds	73	681
Died of disease	141	4,836
Died of accidents	1	72
Died in captivity	1	85
Sent home as invalids	1,044	24,058
Missing and prisoners*	76	2,718
Total†	36,559	

*Excluding those who have been recovered.
†Excluding sick and wounded now in British hospitals in South Africa.

| TOTAL BRITISH CASUALTIES TO AUGUST 4. ||
	Officers.	Men.
Killed.	272	2,534
Died of wounds	74	696
Died of disease	145	4,937
Died of accidents	1	77
Died in captivity	1	85
Sent home as invalids	1,105	25,049
Missing and prisoners*	59	2,740
Total†	37,775	

*Excluding those who have been recovered.
†Excluding sick and wounded now in British hospitals in South Africa.

| TOTAL BRITISH CASUALTIES TO AUGUST 11. ||
	Officers.	Men.
Killed	272	2,549
Died of wounds	77	712
Died of disease	146	5,036
Died of accidents	1	81
Died in captivity	1	85
Sent home as invalids	1,151	26,123
Missing and prisoners*	55	2,768
Total†	39,057	

*Excluding those who have been recovered.
†Excluding sick and wounded now in British hospitals in South Africa.

| TOTAL BRITISH CASUALTIES TO AUGUST 18. ||
	Officers.	Men.
Killed	275	2,560
Died of wounds	78	724
Died of disease	147	5,130
Died of accidents	1	86
Died in captivity	1	85
Sent home as invalids	1,151	26,123
Missing and prisoners*	54	2,751
Total†	39,166	

*Excluding those who have been recovered.
†Excluding sick and wounded now in British hospitals in South Africa.

| TOTAL BRITISH CASUALTIES TO AUGUST 25. ||
	Officers.	Men.
Killed	281	2,599
Died of wounds	79	732
Died in captivity	1	85
Died of disease	148	5,215
Died of accidents	1	90
Sent home as invalids	1,188	27,309
Missing and prisoners*	55	2,778
Total†	40,561	

*Excluding those who have been recovered.
†Excluding sick and wounded now in British hospitals in South Africa.

| TOTAL BRITISH CASUALTIES TO SEPTEMBER 1. ||
	Officers.	Men.
Killed	283	2,655
Died of wounds	83	758
Died in captivity	1	85
Died of disease	148	5,332
Died of accidents	3	95
Sent home as invalids	1,213	27,937
Missing and prisoners*	45	1,007
Total†	39,645	

*Excluding those who have been recovered.
†Excluding sick and wounded now in British hospitals in South Africa.

TOTAL BRITISH CASUALTIES TO SEPTEMBER 8.		
	Officers.	Men.
Killed	283	2,683
Died of wounds	85	791
Died in captivity	3	86
Died of disease	149	5,472
Died of accidents	3	101
Sent home as invalids	1,219	27,937
Missing and prisoners*	40	945
Total†	39,785	

*Excluding those who have been recovered.
†Excluding sick and wounded now in British hospitals in South Africa.

TOTAL BRITISH CASUALTIES TO SEPTEMBER 17.		
	Officers.	Men.
Killed	285	2,718
Died of wounds	r	86
Died in captivity	3	86
Died of disease	149	5,582
Died of accidents	3	107
Sent home as invalids	1,239	28,199
Missing and prisoners*	12	809
Total†	40,075	

*Excluding those who have been recovered.
†Excluding sick and wounded now in British hospitals in South Africa.

TOTAL BRITISH CASUALTIES TO SEPTEMBER 22.		
	Officers.	Men.
Killed	287	2,738
Died of wounds	86	813
Died of disease	149	5,653
Died of accidents	3	108
Died in captivity	3	88
Sent home as invalids	1,279	29,957
Missing and prisoners*	9	793
Total†	41972‡	

*Excluding those who have been recovered.
†Excluding sick and wounded now in British hospitals in South Africa.
‡ The great majority of those invalided home had recovered and rejoined.

TOTAL REDUCTION OF BRITISH FORCES THROUGH THE WAR.		
	Officers.	Men.
Deaths in South Africa	528	9,400
Missing and prisoners	9	799
Invalids who died in England	4	183
Invalids discharged for disability		814
Total	11,737‡	

‡ The great majority of those invalided home had recovered and rejoined.

TOTAL BRITISH CASUALTIES TO SEPTEMBER 29		
	Officers.	Men,.
Killed	287	2,750
Died of wounds	86	825
Died of disease	150	5,753
Died of accidents	3	114
Died in captivity	3	89
Sent home as invalids	1,326	30,300
Missing and prisoners*	7	812
Total†	42,505‡	

*Excluding those who have recovered.
†Excluding those in South African hospitals.
‡ The great majority of those invalided home had recovered and rejoined.

TOTAL REDUCTION OF BRITISH FORCES THROUGH THE WAR.		
	Officers.	Men.
Deaths in South Africa	529	9,531
Missing and prisoners	7	812
Invalids who died in England	4	193
Invalids discharged for disability		873
Total	11,9491‡	

‡ The great majority of those invalided home had recovered and rejoined.

TOTAL BRITISH CASUALTIES TO OCTOBER 31		
	Officers.	Men.
Killed	302	2,902
Died of wounds	89	893
Died of disease	155	6,115
Died of accidents	4	145
Died in captivity	3	90
Sent home as invalids	1,422	33,077
Missing and prisoners*	7	822
Total†	46,026‡	

*Excluding those who have recovered.
†Excluding those in South African hospitals.
‡ The great majority of those invalided home had recovered and rejoined.

TOTAL REDUCTION OF BRITISH FORCES THROUGH THE WAR.		
	Officers.	Men.
Deaths in South Africa	553	10,145
Missing and prisoners	7	822
Invalids who died in England	4	208
Invalids discharged for disability		1,030
Total†	12,769‡	

†Excluding those in South African hospitals.
‡ The great majority of those invalided home had recovered and rejoined.

OFFICIAL TABLE OF CASUALTIES
(Principle actions only)

	Killed		Wounded		Missing	
	Officers	Men	Officers	Men	Officers	Men
Sunday River. April 10		1		13		1
Wepener. April 9-18	6	17	17	105		
Zwartkopjesfontein. April 19-20		3		16		26
Dewetsdorp. April 20			1	9		
Wepener. April 17-24		8		36		
Wakkerstroom. April 21, 25			3	19		
Karrefontein. April 22		3	2	26		3
Grootefontein. April 24		3		35		
Thaba 'Nchu. April 28-30		3	3	46		13
Gen. Ian Hamilton's force. April 30	1	3	10	6	1	9
Jacobsrust. April 30-May 3		5	2	35		10
Brandfort. May 2-5		3		48		8
Wellow. May 4	2		1	6		
Boordam. May 4		8	2	35		1
Kroonstad. May 10-11		3	1	37		3
Wepener. May 10	3	27	14	109		1
Zand River. May 10	1	15	5	31		1
Maritsani. May 13		5	1	22		3
Vryheid (ambuscade). May 20	3		3			1
Winburg. May 25-26.		3		16	1	1
Kheis. May 28	1	4	5	17		
Roodepoort. May 28		1	2	31		
Hammonia. May 28-29		3	1	4	2	38
Senekal. May 29	1	41	11	129		11
Florida. May 26	1	19	11	112		
Douglas. May 30		18	2	36		
Lindley. June 1	1	18	9	43		13
Bothas Pass. June 6-8		8	2	34		
Swalkranz. June 4					1	53
Roodeval. June 7		6	1	21		4
Heilbron. June 7		2	1	2	1	6
Vredefort. June 7					1	17
Roodeval. June 11		1	1	17		
Diamond Hill. June 11	6	6	10	119	1	3
Almonds Nek. June 11		17		116		
Diamond Hill. June 13	1	21	1	81	2	
Leuwspruit. June 14		1	4	4		60
Vredefort. June 17			1	18		11
Rhenoster. June 17		1		3	2	51
Honingspruit. June 22	1	4	2	18		
Amersfoot. June 29		2		7		
Machadodorp. July 3						25
Lindley. July 3	1	2	3	10		8
Reitzfontein. July 7	2	4	1	28		
Bethlehem. July 6-8		10	6	111		
Rustenburg. July 7		2	1	4		

OFFICIAL TABLE OF CASUALTIES (continued)
(Principle actions only)

	Killed		Wounded		Missing	
	Officers	Men	Officers	Men	Officers	Men
Derdepoort. July 11	1	2	2	5		18
Uitvals Nek. July 11	1	16	3	50		183
Krugersdorp. July 11	1		2	33		
Potchefstroom. July 19-22				3		23
Bank (captured in derailed train). July 19						31
Palmeitfontein. July 19		4	4	18		3
Oliphants Nek. July 20		2	1	5		
Koster River. July 21		5	6	20		6
Spitz Kop. July 21-22		4	2	20		
Stafferts Nek. July 23	1	8	3	28		
Retiefs Nek. July 23-24		9	6	77		
Rooi Koppies. July 24		2	1	21		
Stinkhoutboom. July 24		4	8	24		
Slaapkrans. July 28		3	3	27		
Stepannskraal. July 29	1		1	21		
Frederikstad R. R. accident. July 30		18	1	43		
Zelekats Nek. August 1		2	2	41		
Elands River. August 4-6	1	4	1	32	1	9
Elands River (Carrington's force). August 4-6.	1	2	1	10		1
Amersfoort. August 7				22		
Venterskroon. August 7		1	6	13		
Greylingstad. August 13-14		2		5		8
Wilport. August 14		4	1	41		
Buffels Hoek. August 19				6		9
Klipfontein. August 19					5	21
Hammans Kraal. August 20	1	1	1	11		
Van Wyks. August 21		7	2	22		5
Geluk. August 23-26		19	2	97	2	51
Belfast. August 24-26		3	2	45		3
Doomoek. August 26			1	10		6
Bergendal. August 29	1	12	9	95		
Jaehtfontein. August 29		1	1	6		1
Kwaggasfontein. August 31		5	6	11		2
Badfontein. September 1-4			1	17		7
Mauchberg. September 9			1	6		
Lydenburg. September 4-10		3		34		2
Rochfontein. September 11		2	1	14		
Ventersburg. October 10	1			11		
Jagersfontein. October 13-16		11	1	13		
Carolina. October 13-14		6		21		
Carolina to Bethel. October 15-19	1	5	3	21		3
Frederickstad. October 19-25	1	22	4	89		3
Jacobsdal. October 25		11		16		
Bethlehem. October 26		3	1	16		
12 miles south of Belfast. November 2	1	1	2	12		1
Bothaville. November 6	2	6	7	24		

MORE FROM PARCHMENT PUBLISHING

All books are available in paperback and ebook format.
Please visit **www.parchmentpublishing.co.uk**
for more information and new releases.

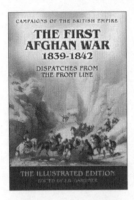
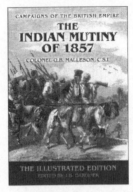
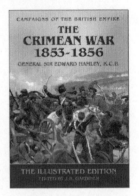
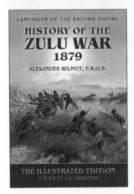
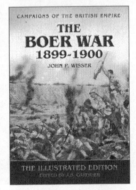
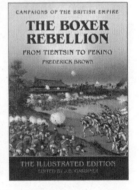

Printed in Great Britain
by Amazon.co.uk, Ltd.,
Marston Gate.